PRAISE FOR
The Place of Cold Water

"In this gripping account of life on three continents, world events shape the story of a family uprooted by political turmoil in India and by the emergence of independent African states. Written with unsparing honesty and an eye for vivid detail, The Place of Cold Water recounts a journey both global and spiritual, from war-torn Kenya to Bombay, from a village clinic in Punjab to the AIDS wards of America."
—Joan Delfattore Ph.D., M.S., Professor Emeriti, English and Legal Studies, University of Delaware, Author of several books and essays.

"A fascinating -and entertaining- voyage through the experience of the Indian diaspora, Anand Panwalker is a storyteller of the highest caliber, unflinching with himself, and generous with others. His observations on foreignness, medicine, and cross-cultural interactions places this as a must-read for fans of modern South Asian history, medical literature and the immigrant experience in the US".
—Omar Khan MD, Associate Professor of Family Medicine; Physician Leader; and Author of *The End of Polio?* and *Readings in Global Health.*

"In this beautifully told and moving family memoir, Anand Panwalker shares a compelling and enchanting tale. It is an Indian story, an African story, and a very American story, filled with memorable characters, magical and tragic moments of everyday life, momentous events, and instances of infuriating racism. Most importantly, it is a story of the triumph of resiliency, integrity, determination, decency, and love."

— Bennett Lorber, MD, D.Sc. (Hon), MACP, Distinguished Professor of Medicine, Temple University, Philadelphia.

"The Place of Cold Water is the story of a physician of Indian descent, born in British Kenya. The memoir reads like a novel, beautifully written with picturesque descriptions of daily events, relationships and emerging nationalism. Lingual differences, religious identity, ethnicity, race, and social evolution are interpreted with personal perspective and passion. It is a jewel."

— George G. Jackson, MD, Distinguished Professor (Emeritus) of Medicine, scientist, scholar and former editor of the *Journal of Infectious Diseases.* Salt Lake City, Utah.

"It is the story of a remarkable journey! I loved the intertwining of world and local history into the memoir - so enlightening especially for someone who loves reading history. Very well written!"

—Joseph DeSimone MD, F.A.C.P., Professor of Medicine, Sidney Kimmel College of Medicine at Jefferson University, Philadelphia.

To Sonal & Bharat,

THE PLACE OF
COLD WATER

A MEMOIR

*With a feeling that
our paths will cross
again. Best wishes*

ANAND PANWALKER

*Anand. Panwalker
October 22, 2017*

ISBN 13: 978-1548789084

ISBN 10: 1548789089

On the cover:

The cover photograph, taken in 1906, shows Dr. Rosendo Ayres Ribeiro making his rounds in Nairobi on a zebra he had tamed. He had arrived in 1900, from the Portuguese-ruled colony of Goa in India, and was the first private physician in Kenya. In addition to discovering a new malaria drug, he identified an outbreak of bubonic plague, which led a British public health officer to order that all the affected areas be burned to the ground. The fire accidentally consumed the doctor's clinic. He was compensated with 16 acres of land, and a road was named after him. A philanthropist and founder of the Ribeiro Goan School, he is buried in Nairobi, the Place of Cold Water.

Printed with permission from Dr. Olaf Ribeiro, a grandson of the famous doctor.

Interior and cover design by The Happy Self-Publisher.

In memory of:

Departed Elders, Revered Teachers, and Dear Friends

TABLE OF CONTENTS

PREFACE

There is no greater agony than bearing an untold story inside you.
~Maya Angelou

Nairobi, the "place of cold water," was just a snake-infested swamp in Kenya. A spot where thousands of laborers, who built the rail line from the coast to Lake Victoria, could rest. It became the home of a handful of immigrants from the western shores of India. Their energy and entrepreneurial spirit gave birth to a beautiful city, where they hoped to live in peace forever.

This is the story of the struggles and triumphs of two Indian families during an era when Britain ruled much of the world. Of the tumultuous historical events that shaped their lives, the deep racial divisions and separation based on skin color, caste, and religion that tore them apart. It is a tale of resilience, courage, and tragedy amid global upheavals; and of the quest for acceptance, human dignity, and freedom.

The author, born in Nairobi to such immigrants, is shunned by the country of his birth and tormented by dysfunction within the family, a stranger in the land of his ancestors and a foreigner wherever he goes. Great challenges await him in America, where—as a "foreign medical graduate"—the bar for him is set higher; the challenges steeper, and the opportunities fewer and further between. The discrimination, a form of medical apartheid, is deeply rooted within the establishment. The perpetrators sometimes were those persecuted elsewhere before they too found shelter in America.

The stories within are true. Several paraphrased dialogues reflect memories of an oral history communicated by elders. Some identities are concealed to avoid embarrassing people who are held in high regard. Some events are omitted because they may be too painful for others. The author asks readers to forgive any hurt caused by unintended words; they flow from the pen of an imperfect person. No malice is intended.

The author's love for and gratitude to Kenya and Kenyans, India and Indians, the United States and Americans, in spite of the ups and downs of life, is unconditional.

CAST OF CHARACTERS AND RELATIONSHIP TO AUTHOR

Panwalker Family (paternal side)

Grandfather:	Moreshwar (Azoba)
Grandmother:	Saraswati (Aji)
Father's Uncle:	Mahadev (Doctor Kaka) brother of Moreshwar
Father:	Prabhaker (Baba)
Mother:	Kusum (birth name Bhagwat)
Aunt:	Sunder (Atya); father's sister
Uncle:	Dinkar (Dinkar Kaka); father's brother
Cousins:	Prakash, Pratibha, Pramila and Pramod (Children of Dinkar Kaka)
Author's Wife:	Asha (birth name Asha Sathe)
Author's Son:	Sandeep

****

Bhagwat Family (maternal side)

Grandfather:	Gopalrao (Dada)
Grandmother:	Shanta (Mai)
Mother:	Kusum
Uncles:	Prabhaker (Bhau), Sharad, Anil, and Subhash
Aunts:	Sudha and Mira

****

Sathe Family (in-laws)

Father-in-law:	Vishwanath (Kaka)
Mother-in-law:	Indutai (Aai)
Brothers-in-law:	Suresh and Vijay
Sister-in-law:	Kumud (Kumutai)

PROLOGUE

Red roses bloomed in our tiny garden under an always beautiful, blue Nairobi sky. The sun basked in its orange glow as it dipped under the western horizon on that lovely August afternoon in 1949. The barefoot, dust-covered Indian children, hungry and tired of their street games, had clear instructions to be home before dusk.

I flung open the front door on entry, expecting to see the table laid out for dinner. Instead, the two-room apartment, normally bright and sunny, was quiet and dark. The thick curtains had been drawn closed. A neighbor, slouched in a chair in the living room, swiveled toward me urgently, placing a finger on his lips. His other hand gestured with some irritation toward another chair. I disregarded the instructions and walked on.

My father had been brought home by coworkers, who said he had a high fever and had been talking nonsense. He lay on a bed in the center of the room, his hands and feet tied down. A mosquito net hung from a hook in the ceiling, enclosing the bed. Sweat poured down his drawn face as he jabbed at non-existent objects with tremulous fingers. Intermittent shrieks shattered moments of eerie silence. The slightest sound startled him. His restless eyes wandered, looking but not seeing, searching but not finding, as if desperately seeking a familiar face or voice. Sporadic spasms shook his entire body. A white scarf, soaked in cool milk, had been placed on his forehead to bring down the fever, just as my grandma used to do.

My mother, standing quietly at the bedside, looked away as I entered. The tall, bespectacled, Indian doctor, summoned urgently, stood on the opposite side looking uncharacteristically worried. His normal boisterous voice had been reduced to a soft murmur.

Kindly squeezing my elbow, he stepped out to the other room. My mother followed. A short woman, not quite 4 feet 10 (although she claimed she was 4 feet 11), she craned her neck upward to see the doctor's mustachioed lips. They whispered. Promising to return the next day, the doctor left the home, closing the creaking door gently. As my father screamed again, the neighbor, sensing a need for privacy, left the room. I rushed to my father's bedside.

"What is wrong, Baba?"

I waited for a response, any response. He calmed down for a fleeting second. Then the bed shook and groaned as the agitation and thrashing resumed. The tight cloth restraints did not yield. Tense blue veins on the back of his hand bulged, threatening to burst any moment. Fresh bruises appeared on his strong wrists as he tried to break free from his shackles. A drop of purplish blood trickled down reluctantly to the white bedsheet, now stained by dirty, yellow sweat. He tried to raise his head. A loud gasp escaped his parched lips. Exhausted, he slumped back in the soggy bed, sighing, moaning, and gurgling.

Frightened, I ran to my mother for answers. Sobbing silently, she said nothing. A premonition of impending doom sent a shiver down my six-year-old spine. Many years would pass before I understood what had happened.

BOOK ONE:
The Beginning

BOMBAY: The State of Maharashtra, British India

My father, Prabhaker Moreshwar Panvalkar, boarded a ship in 1938 at age 24, without informing his widowed mother that he was going to British East Africa. After an exhausting eight-day and 2400-mile voyage, the ship dislodged most of its Indian passengers in the port city of Mombasa in Kenya. The rest sailed southward to Dar es Salam, Tanganyika, passing the islands of Zanzibar to the east. The 247-mile journey to Moshi, a small town at the foothills of Mount Kilimanjaro, was hot and dusty; the roads unpaved and full of potholes. His destination was the home of the only person he knew on the entire continent of Africa—his uncle, Mahadev G. Panvalkar, who had established one of the first medical practices in the country.

Why was he in such a rush to leave India? Was it necessity, boredom, scandal, unknown danger, or a quest for adventure? There were vague rumors of debt from a failed laundry business, angry creditors and threats to his life and limb. He was restless and tired of the monotony of life in the small apartment that he shared with his mother and sister.

His father, a postmaster, had died in that apartment during the deadly influenza pandemic of 1918, when he had been only 4 years old. My grandmother (we called her Aji), a poorly paid schoolteacher, had been left alone to raise a 6-year-old daughter named Sunder, my father, and a yet unborn boy to be named Dinkar. As expected by society, the widow withdrew from social discourse, donned a white sari, and removed the *kunku* (the red dot) from her forehead and the *mangalsutra*, a necklace that never leaves a married woman's neck. The children lived in this dreary home devoid of color or joy. None could afford an education beyond high school.

The cluster of ramshackle four-story buildings, called *chawls*, with a dusty central courtyard, housed numerous families; all Marathi speaking, and by convention, clustered by similar caste, in this case Hindu Brahmins. Wide, wooden stairs led to a shared walkway on each floor, which led to individual units consisting of two small rooms. The walkway circled around the apartments so one could enter each room from opposite ends. A rickety wooden railing along the outer edge grudgingly protected residents from falling to the ground below, where children played and farmers brought their bullock carts to sell fresh vegetables. Little children in cloth diapers, too young to play with the older boys, stuck their heads through the railings, unperturbed by the swaying and creaking of the rotting guardrails. The adults expressed little alarm.

The walkways, squeaking stairs, and rotting balconies groaned under the weight of so many residents, but had miraculously endured. The fixed monthly rent of 18 rupees (equivalent to around 20 US cents today) had remained unchanged for decades due to prevailing laws favoring poor tenants. The owners had no incentive to maintain the *chawls* and suffered no penalty for the poor maintenance. They dreamed of the day when all the tenants, and their descendants, would evacuate or be consumed by a major calamity. They could then build better buildings for higher profit in the expensive metropolis. Our family, oblivious to these schemes, had lived here for two decades and had no intention to leave.

The first room in Aji's fourth-floor apartment was the living room, which also served as a bedroom. The inner room functioned as a kitchen, an extra bedroom, and a place to bathe. Bare electric bulbs hung precariously from twisted wires that emerged from roughly cut holes in the ceiling. Dim lighting hid smears, scratches, and peeling paint.

Communal toilets, a short distance away, were essentially holes in the stone floor, deep enough to swallow a child. A pitcher of always-scarce water was used to flush the stuff down and to wash their bottoms. There were no phones. A few radios, turned on loud to share a medley of film songs with neighbors, competed with the scratchy sounds of students learning to play the *sitar* or drumbeats. A Primus stove, pumped by hand and fueled by kerosene, was the most modern contraption available.

All the families knew everything about each other. Secrets and scandals were never private.

The sound of rationed water spurting from parched taps into thirsty metal buckets at 4:00 AM each morning served as the communal alarm clock. Tenants anxiously awaited the *tip tip* of this elixir of life, the water used for cooking, cleaning, and bathing. At dawn, as the city woke up, school children crossed paths with vendors selling fruit and vegetables and traders trying to sell jewelry and saris. Black bears and mischievous monkeys sometimes entertained the children. Occasionally, a mesmerized cobra ascended gracefully from a wicker basket, seduced by the notes emanating from its master's flute.

In a remarkable feat of transportation, each working adult left for work around 9:00 AM each morning, came home for lunch around noon, had a siesta for two hours, then returned to the job from 3:00 to 6:00 PM. Women cooked fresh food all day. Poverty was not a sufficient reason to eat leftovers; it was considered unhygienic, unsafe, and contrary to Brahmin custom to ingest stale food. There were no refrigerators in which to store the stuff anyway. After dinner, happier families went for a walk to the nearby beach near Shivaji Park, the sea breeze providing gentle relief from the oppressive heat of the day. Tots squealed in delight as their tiny feet touched the cool, wet sand. Young girls, fragrant jasmine flowers weaved into their hair, watched the gentle waves of the Arabian Sea as they lapped the shores of India. Vendors sold *samosas, bhel, pani puri*, coconut water, ice cream, and bottled beverages.

The mood in my father's family, however, was somber and sad, with little laughter. A sense that things would always be difficult pervaded the entire household. Beaten down by circumstances, Aji, my grandmother, understood her karma in the curious way many Indians accept whatever happens. Her fate had been predestined, and she was being punished for her presumed misdeeds in a previous life. She had become a robot, robbed of her feelings, trapped by fate, and helpless to change her destiny.

That was the life my father had left behind. Essentially penniless, with little in his tin suitcase, he found his beloved uncle—his father's brother, Dr. Mahadev Panvalkar—in the shadows of Mt. Kilimanjaro. He was ready to start a new life abroad.

Figure 1: East African Community

Dr. Panvalkar, LCPS (Licentiate of the College of Physicians and Surgeons of Ireland), was shocked to see his nephew on his doorstep. The handsome and dashing young man had arrived unannounced, without the courtesy of a letter or a telegram before setting sail.

"Prabhaker, what are you doing here? Why didn't you write? This is so unexpected."

Figure 2: Doctor Kaka with my father (right)

No hug, no handshake. Simply stunned silence. This was not going well. My father was taken aback. Surely his transgression was not so severe that his uncle would treat him this way. After a few uncomfortable moments, the uncle moved aside, unsmiling and silent, and allowed his itinerant nephew to unload his small, banged up metal suitcase in the home they would now share. Arrangements were made for an uneasy and perhaps reluctant coexistence in the doctor's tiny apartment which had little furniture or food. They saw very little of each other, since the physician worked long hours.

Doctor Kaka (uncle), also born poor but determined and ambitious, had somehow managed to get into medical school, borrowing textbooks from friends each night. When the flame in the oil lamp flickered out and there was insufficient fuel to bring it back to life, he simply walked out and studied under streetlamps. He was not averse to doing menial jobs on the side to earn some money. Armed with a medical degree from Bombay and further training in Ireland, he set up a practice in Moshi. This was in the middle of nowhere. How and why he chose this remote corner of the world is unknown. Possibly he knew some of the Indians who had been hired as administrators by white South African diamond mine owners in nearby Shinyanga.

The only doctor in town caring for the local Asian and African population, he sent no bills and never tried to collect a fee. This was a one-man enterprise. Sometimes he was paid in cash, at other times in kind. Beneficiaries of his benevolence left food, flapping fowl, and fruit on his doorstep. He was content to accept any expression of gratitude in lieu of the fee. A humble man, he was embarrassed when Indians expressed their respect by touching his feet. African women were known to honor him by naming their babies *Mganga* (the Swahili word for doctor).

Immersed in his work, he had little time to reflect on his personal life and rarely wrote to his family in India. He was perpetually tired. His broad shoulders stooped and concealed a powerfully built man. His kind eyes, seated in a dark and symmetrical face, betrayed a profound, deep and lingering sadness. A graying moustache adorned his lip. People wondered why he chose to live without his family. He was likely delinquent with his taxes, because he did not have a clue how much he earned or owed. He became wealthy enough to buy a large apartment complex in Matunga, Bombay. His first wife died in this building, leaving behind one boy. His second wife — an extremely fair, obese, and sedentary woman — remained in India much of the time, unwilling to live permanently in this remote spot in Africa.

Once a year, the doctor packed his few belongings and traveled to Bombay for two weeks. That is how he sired five children, including one from his first marriage. Fatherless most of the year, the children never knew him. The three boys were destined to live miserable, dysfunctional lives. Lacking direction and ambition, they found an escape in alcohol, causing lasting harm to their own young families. The two daughters, despite the neglect, thrived and did well in sports, academics, and marriage.

****

Lest he be perceived as a lazy freeloader, and being restless by nature, my father immediately began an earnest search for a job. He went from door to door, willing to do anything to earn a living. He learned to type on a machine he bought secondhand, taught himself shorthand using the system invented by John Robert Gregg in 1888, and sent typed applications to British companies and Indian merchants. Prospective employers invariably asked him if he was related to the doctor. He accepted the first job offered, in a field that was totally alien to him. The verbal agreement with his English employer was sealed with a handshake.

He became a manager (at least that is what he told everyone) for one of the coffee plantations on the sloping, verdant highlands around Moshi. The Colonial Government, in a concerted effort to attract more white farmers, sold the most fertile land to the new owners for a pittance. They hired Africans for the hard labor and Indians for accounting and managerial functions. My dad knew nothing about coffee. Most Indians, at least those from Bombay, typically drank sweet and milky tea, sometimes spiked with ginger or spices. But he was hardworking with good math skills, spoke excellent English (unusual for someone who had attended school in India in those days), and was a man who could be trusted.

If he and his uncle ever quarreled, the arguments were likely quiet. Neither of them was prone to yelling, shouting or the use of foul language. Baba resented that Doctor Kaka had not helped his widowed mother and his siblings. Instead, he had let them suffer in that miserable *chawl* in Dadar, while his own family lived in comfort and style just a few miles away in Matunga.

The doctor's second wife, with a penchant for expensive gold jewelry (thus earning the nickname Fort Knox) and the finest saris, had little interest in helping others. She did not feel any moral, ethical, or legal obligation to do so. Tall and fair, her soft skin was marked by purple-blue veins. Her large watery eyes, their lashes lined with kohl, drooped languidly, like weeping willows over a lake. People had a variety of theories about the reasons the poor doctor had gone overseas. She probably had not approved of my father's travel to Moshi.

During this entire period, there is no evidence that the doctor was unkind to my father. On the contrary, he allowed my father the full run of the house. But there was an undercurrent of tension, which led to my father's decision to leave Tanganyika after three years. He had saved enough to move on. He packed a few things, made a meal for his uncle and, true to his habit, left the home without any fanfare, leaving just a forwarding address for the British Army headquarters in Nairobi.

****

The 147-mile journey to Nairobi, on a narrow dirt road, traversed the vast plains east of the Serengeti, where he might have observed the deadly interplay between predators and their prey, seen giraffes craning their necks to graze on acacia trees, or heard the hoof beats of huge wildebeest herds thundering along the plains in a spectacular annual migration. Possibly the vehicle yielded to fearless elephants, little ones in tow, taking their time to cross the road.

Traversing the prairie adjacent to Masai Mara in Kenya, he may have heard of boys, armed only with spears, killing lions as a rite of passage to manhood, to become worthy of marriage and to be respected as warriors. Or witnessed an arrow pierce the jugular vein of a surprised cow with deadly accuracy, the subsequent gush of blood quenching the thirst of a warrior. The Masai—tall, lean, and muscular—leaning on their spears, their bodies covered with red ochre and adorned with colorful beads, may have looked on curiously as the vehicle sped by in a swirl of red dust. The vast plain, with its tall, brown grass gently swaying in the evening breeze, would have risen gradually to the fringes of Kenya's thick forests. If they looked back, they would have seen the snowcapped dome of Mount Kilimanjaro in the south breaking through the cloud cover.

Nairobi, near the equator, stood a mile high. A swift river carrying rich silt from higher ground flowed through the center of the city. Numerous jacaranda trees with orange blooms graced its banks. The scent of fragrant flowers wafted through the cool, fresh air. The swampy land was also home to deadly insects, snakes, and other wild beasts.

To the best of my knowledge, Baba had known no one in Nairobi. How he had found Gopalrao and Shanta Bhagwat, teachers from India who also spoke his mother tongue, Marathi, is an unsolved mystery.

The hosts were impressed by his gentle manner, good looks, and a certain swagger. Rumors of his occasional drinking and smoking, vices in a conservative Hindu–Brahmin society, were dismissed as the temporary indulgences of an immigrant who had been suddenly freed from the shackles of societal pressures.

He met his future wife and my mother, Kusum Bhagwat, the eldest daughter of his hosts, during the 10 days he spent with this generous family. This event would alter the course of our lives in totally unpredictable ways. He was 27 and she was only 16.

NAIROBI: The Place of Cold Water

Jomo Kenyatta, the future president of an independent Kenya, in his anthropologic thesis titled "Facing Mount Kenya," wrote of a prophecy that would shake the very roots of his nation. He wrote that the sage and prophet Mogo wa Kebiro had dreamt that foreigners with the skin of light-colored *kiengere* (frogs) would arrive by sea. They would bring an iron snake with as many legs as *monyongoro* (a centipede). The snake would spit fires and would stretch from the big water on the east (the Indian Ocean) to the big water to the west of Gikuyuland (Lake Victoria). They would carry magical sticks that would produce fire.

Kebiro predicted that the foreigners would forcibly take over their ancestral land. That a famine would precede the takeover and children would become disrespectful of their elders. Tribes would fight each other. The social structure would disintegrate. Kenyatta wrote that the prophet had been so shaken by this that he was rendered speechless for many hours, until a goat was sacrificed and he was anointed by tribal elders with the oils and blood of the slaughtered animal.

The snake is, of course, considered a reference to the still-to-be-built railway line. The British did arrive with magical sticks, presumably rifles, took over the best land, and built the railway between the two large bodies of water.

Over 30,000 Indian laborers (known as "coolies") were brought in by the British to build this railway around 1895. It was labeled the Lunatic Express or Lunatic Line because of a perception that this was a dangerous and foolhardy project, of little consequence or importance. The rail line progressed slowly through the arid plains. Approximately 2,500 laborers died, four for every mile of construction. At least 38 were devoured by 2 lions, both 9 feet long and without manes. They were dubbed the "Man-eaters of Tsavo." The beasts were ultimately shot by Lt. Colonel Patterson, in December 1898, using "the magical stick which spit fire." He wrote "Bones, flesh, skin and blood. They devoured all and left not a trace behind them." The animals, with poor dentition, chose humans over other prey since they were easier to catch and kill. There was speculation that the lions had acquired the taste for human flesh after devouring carcasses of dead or dying slaves abandoned by Arab traders. The carcasses of the now embalmed animals were later sold to the Chicago Field Museum for $5000.

The railroad construction moved steadily westward from Mombasa, despite the hardships. They reached what would become Nairobi, the "place of cold water," from which on a clear day one could see the snowcapped peaks of Mount Kenya (17,057 feet) 93 miles to the north and Kilimanjaro (19,320 feet) 128 miles to the south. Mount Kenya's peaks were defiant and dangerous; Kilimanjaro, with its snow cap, was gentle, beguiling, and alluring. Years later, growing up in Nairobi, I was astonished to see the peaks of two of the highest mountains in Africa from a grassy hilltop.

The tracks reached Lake Victoria, the source of the Blue Nile, in 1901, and ultimately Kampala in Uganda. Living conditions for the laborers were harsh and many perished from malaria, typhoid, or dysentery. Some of the hardier survivors, perhaps no more than 2,000 men, settled down and opened small businesses and shops. They bartered trinkets, flour, salt, daily necessities, clothes, and matchsticks with incredulous natives for livestock, fruit, and vegetables. Other coolies, exhausted and homesick, returned to India to resume their miserable lives.

It was under such circumstances that a few adventurous men like Dr. Rosendo Ayers Ribeiro arrived in Nairobi in February 1900 from Goa, the Portuguese colony in India, to become the first private doctor in the area. Nairobi then was nothing but a barren swamp with hardly any buildings or infrastructure. He lived for a while in a tent with an assistant. Lacking transportation, he tamed a zebra — the first man in the world to do so — and rode it to work. The iconic photograph on the cover of this book was taken in 1906. The doctor made quite a mark on Kenya with his discovery of a malaria drug, the diagnosis of bubonic plague in the city, and his philanthropy. Indeed, he founded the Goan Institute and funded a well-known school named after him in Nairobi. Several years later, Dr. Ribeiro examined Sudha, my maternal aunt, for extensive burns from scalding hot water.

A second wave of Indian immigrants arrived in the 1930s. These were generally teachers, doctors, architects, engineers, shopkeepers, bankers, and businessmen. Among them were restless young adventurers like my father. Most settled down along the route of the new railway line, and many chose Nairobi for its natural beauty, opportunities, established Indian presence, and fine weather. They were enticed by new jobs, a great demand for special skills, an adventurous spirit, or an inability to make ends meet in India.

There were no bureaucratic barriers for the new immigrants looking for greener pastures. India and the colonies of Kenya, Uganda, and Tanganyika (collectively called the East African Protectorate) were ruled by Britain. Thus the Indians held, or were eligible for, British passports.

Indians provided the infrastructure and support for commerce and construction; they were the backbone of the civil service and staffed hospitals in Nairobi and remote parts of Kenya. They spread out along the rail line, across the Great Rift Valley, toward Lake Victoria, and into neighboring Uganda to the west. They settled in the little towns along and away from the rail line.

Schools catering to various religious denominations began to sprout up. More teachers arrived. Carpenters, cobblers, cooks, and clerks were followed by tailors, machinists, artisans, and priests. Men brought brides from India. Maternity homes were built to welcome a new generation of Indians to be born on African soil. The immigrants— Hindus, Sikhs, Muslims, Christians, Parsis, and an occasional Jew— worked hard. Their shops or businesses on the ground level were open for long hours and they often lived on the second floor or in the shop. They brought ingredients for Indian cuisine, including grains, *atta*, spices, and masalas, adorned statues of their gods with expensive silk saris, and bathed them with milk and honey. Law-abiding immigrants, they built temples, *masjids*, *gurdwaras*, and churches. Gymkhanas sprouted. Even the tiny Maharashtrian community built a *mandal* (club) for sports, theatrical productions, social events, and promotion of Marathi culture.

Settlers knew almost instinctively where they were allowed to build and live. The "European areas" were restricted to white expatriates (*Mzungus*), who lived in bungalows with beautiful lawns and trees. To avoid ambiguity, an occasional sign proclaimed: "Indians and dogs not allowed." British laws forbade the sale of land in the fertile highlands to Africans or Indians. There was no multiracial housing. Asians (*Muhindi*) lived in apartments or stone homes built by Indian masons, and the Africans in mud and thatch huts in the villages, in the reservations, or in slums within and around the city. The well-enforced policy of racial segregation was, for unknown reasons, not called apartheid. The term "color bar" was used instead.

Europeans, when accused of crimes, were tried by all-white juries. Africans and Asians faced one judge and three assessors. Sharad Rao, a family friend and a leading legal authority in Kenya, said during a lecture in Mombasa that only one white man was ever hanged. Peter Harold Poole's crime: He had killed an African house servant who threw a stone at his dog after the animal bit him.

While there were linguistic, cultural, and religious differences among the immigrants, the Indian diaspora was held together by ancestral bonds. The immigrants imported their Indian heritage, culture, social customs, religion, music, and unique clothing to create a distinct identity — a "Little India" — in Kenya. They were British by colonial occupation, but segregated from the white *sahibs* who ruled and the blacks who toiled doing menial jobs. They were further separated by disparities of culture, customs, culinary preferences, income, education, religion, and social norms.

There seemed to be no clamor for desegregation among the Indians. The majority — the owners of this land, the black Africans — suffered silently. They too had no voice. Africans were restricted further by a system requiring them to carry an identity card (*kipande*) and to obey curfew rules, especially after a Kikuyu insurgency called Mau Mau began. Even the animals in the game parks had more freedom to roam where they wished. The black African people remained fenced. High walls spiked with glass shards and barbed wire came later.

The prophet Kebiro had been correct. The African, the true owner of the land, had everything stolen from him by guns, deceit, and treachery. He could choose to live relatively "free" in the village, but would probably starve. Life on their little farms, or *shambhas*, was hard. One had to eke out a living growing a few rows of maize, potatoes, and yams in the relatively arid land allotted to Africans. The fertile, verdant farmland in the Aberdares Forest and the foothills of Mount Kenya was available only to whites. Pushed out of the best land and unable to feed their families, African men came to the big city to find menial domestic jobs and lived in slums without any amenities. Indians often paid low wages, provided few benefits, and made the servants work long hours, seven days a week.

Indians generally did well, since they were well educated and hardworking and had the requisite skills needed to develop the country. They did not concern themselves with the misery of others and were content to live segregated lives in their own communities. Nevertheless, the racial divisions, disparities, and injustice inflicted upon the Africans were to affect the destiny of an entire second generation of Indians in Africa.

It was in this setting that my father met his future bride in Nairobi.

****

Historians tell us that at least two million Indian soldiers served Britain and its monarch during the great wars of the 20th century. My father was one of those. He was hired as an administrative clerk, since he spoke English and had completed high school. He wore a military uniform, but was unlikely to ever engage in combat. The coffee plantation manager was now a dashing and handsome officer (for he did not like to be called a clerk) in a British military uniform. Before long, word got out, and young men from Bombay joined him. But this life was dull. An old photograph shows these British–Indian army officers, with no military background or training, lined up in His Majesty's service in khaki uniforms. They were young Hindus, often Marathi-speaking, and Brahmins who were going to fight Britain's enemies whenever asked to do so. There was no evidence that the soldiers had any qualms about siding with the British at a time when many Indians had joined Mahatma Gandhi's civil disobedience movement to demand Indian independence. In fact, I rarely heard my father speak about freedom, or his opinion about the British, Gandhi, or the concept of civil disobedience. He seemed quite happy, like the majority of Indians, doing what he was doing.

He and his friends supported war operations with their clerical work. World War II was raging across Europe, but its imprint had not yet been felt in East Africa. There was endless speculation about Hitler's ambitions and his nexus with Mussolini of Italy and emperor Hirohito of Japan. As German forces marched through Europe, Subhash Chandra

Bose, who had fallen out with Gandhi, formed the Indian National Army in Singapore and joined Japanese soldiers approaching Burma. Bose assumed that the Japanese would hand over India to Indians after defeating the British in Calcutta. America had not entered the war yet.

There was little for these new recruits to do. One pastime for these lonely young men was to drink beer and smoke cigarettes, knowing full well that these vices would have been frowned upon by their elders in India. They also expressed a longing for the "good old days" in India, a land that they had abandoned for greener pastures.

The British changed the spelling of my father's last name from Panvalkar to "Panwalker" to fit their idea of what it should sound like. My father either did not object or was overruled.

Mahatma Gandhi, the most famous son of this state, had returned to India from South Africa to lead the Indian National Congress and the independence movement. My maternal grandfather, Gopalrao Bhagwat (Dada), and grandmother, Shanta Bhagwat (Mai), joined the freedom movement, abandoning their educational aspirations, and donated their modest property to the cause.

Mai gave birth to Kusum, my mother, on December 11, 1925.

To be imprisoned by the British was considered a badge of honor. Violations of a curfew, shouting slogans, or marching peacefully were adequate reasons to get beaten up and be dragged into waiting trucks. Gandhi got the idea of nonviolent civil disobedience after reading an essay penned by Thoreau, of Walden Pond fame. It was often said that this tactic, to shame the oppressor and appeal to the conqueror's conscience, worked with the British, but would not have been effective with the murderous Nazis. Such generalizations were made as a matter of fact, with little debate.

Both Dada and Mai were sentenced to two years in prison in 1930.

Growing up, I asked Dada why he had allowed Indian policemen employed by the British to keep hitting him. He told me I would understand when I was older. Elders had this irritating habit of postponing answers to uncomfortable questions. They assumed that our curiosity would die with time. When pestered, he offered that it took greater courage and self-control not to retaliate. Violence would have been futile anyway. British weapons would quickly overwhelm any armed rebellion. The goal was to make them feel guilty for their oppression. As a young boy, I was not convinced that was such a good idea. I did not like someone beating unarmed citizens for trying to reclaim what was theirs in the first place. The bigger surprise was that

Dada, a man with a famously short temper, could maintain such self-control.

Mai told us, with evident pride and nostalgia, about a brief period when she was in the same jail cell as Kasturba Gandhi, the wife of the Mahatma. During a visit to the prison, my mother—then just 5 years old—had her hair combed by this revered woman.

A premature two-and-a-half-pound baby boy, also named Prabhaker, had been born 11 months before Mai's arrest. During their incarceration, my mother assumed her infant brother's care in addition to the numerous chores she was required to do in the homes of relatives who gave them shelter. These were not happy days for her.

Six months after her incarceration, an anonymous benefactor intervened, and Mai was released on compassionate grounds to take care of this baby. Always forgiving, she said the British had a heart after all.

Dada remained in jail for two years. He and Mai, both penniless and living on the charity of friends, realized that there was no hope for Indian independence in the foreseeable future. They still attended political rallies. Dada, a scholar and voracious reader, found assignments to translate books from Marathi into Gujarati. One was *Sushila Cha Dev* and the other *Majhi Janmathep*, a biography of Veer Savarkar, another freedom fighter, who disagreed with Gandhi's policies and had called him a "sissy." This kept Dada gainfully occupied for a while. Then they reached a point where food, clothing, shelter, and education required attention as well. A third child, Sharad, was born in 1935.

Desperation now drove their decisions. They had heard about the need for teachers in British East Africa and made a momentous decision to leave India. They had given up several years of their young lives fighting for something that seemed out of grasp. The decision to travel abroad with a young family was one of the most difficult ones they would ever make.

Citing a dearth of high schools in Zanzibar, they left their 11-year-old daughter (my mother) with relatives in India. The boys, Prabhaker and Sharad, would accompany their parents.

ZANZIBAR: Isle of Spices

Commercial sea lanes between India and Africa had existed for centuries before the Portuguese "discovered" them. In 1936, Dada and Mai made the voyage to Zanzibar, off the coast of East Africa, from a port in Gujarat on an old Arab *dhow*.

The *dhow* swayed precariously on the high seas, a frightening experience for those who had never sailed before. They were seasick and miserable. They docked in Mombasa for a day or so, teetering like drunken sailors, before sailing on to Zanzibar. They were exhausted, dehydrated, hungry, and oblivious to the beauty of this paradise island that was to be their new home. A family of Gujarati teachers greeted them.

Mai learned that she would be the principal and supervise Dada. That did not sit well with her sulking husband!

Sudha was born in Zanzibar in 1937. Her oldest sister, my mother, remained in India, ostensibly so she would not miss her education. Extremely unhappy doing household chores for relatives around the clock and too exhausted to go to school, she wrote to Dada repeatedly, begging to rejoin her siblings.

Zanzibar was a beautiful island with spectacular beaches and thousands of coconut palms, and was a major supplier of cloves. Indeed, one could get a whiff of the spice as one approached the island by sea. The dark history of this tranquil paradise was unknown to most immigrants.

Three ethnic groups lived here. Arabs, also called Shirazi, had high status, owned land, and were under the protection of sultans who had ruled for centuries from Muscat, Oman, until they moved the capital to Zanzibar. There were a few thousand Indians, and the rest were dark-skinned Africans.

The prosperity of the Arabs was in large part due to the slave trade in which Indians (and Africans) had been complicit to some degree or other. The African majority did menial tasks for the Shirazi people and Indians. The tensions of this racially unbalanced system, as well as the hierarchy of power, led to massive upheavals in later years.

Life in Zanzibar was uncomplicated. There was enough food on the table and the children went to nearby Indian schools run by Indians. Dada, the head of this family in a patriarchal society, continued to grumble about his wife being the head of the school. She, in turn, was very careful not to upset him. He spent much of his free time over the next two years trying to find another job. His persistence paid off. An Indian school in Nairobi invited him to be the principal. Mai would have a job too, but she would now report to him. The tables were turned!

They packed their few belongings, said farewell to friends, and arranged to travel to Mombasa by ship. A train took them westward on the very same rail line that had been built by an earlier generation of Indian coolies. They ascended from sea level to a cool elevation of 5,500 feet as they reached Nairobi. Someone took them from the tiny railway station to the second-story flat in an apartment complex. Six people needed to coexist within two small rooms, a kitchen, one balcony, and one toilet. Dada sent for my mother in 1938, after settling in Nairobi.

They bought bunk beds and an armchair for Dada. He was a rotund man who found it hard to get out of the chair once he sank into it. Sometimes a child would be summoned to give him a hand. A small balcony overlooked a dusty alley where nothing happened. Occasionally a stray, sickly dog with shaggy fur limped through the lane in an unending quest for scraps of food. There were Indian shops across the courtyard downstairs. The shopkeepers, or *dukawallahs*, knew each other. Tailors, grocers, *halwaiis* (sweet makers), and cobblers from all religions lived nearby in harmony. Children walked to school. There were no phones, few cars, and minimal public transportation.

The Nairobi River, carrying rich brown silt from the highlands, flowed through the city. On the other side of the river was the slum reserved for Africans.

This humble home hosted the famous Indian writer Kaka Kalelkar and the great exponent of Hindustani classical music, Hirabai Barodekar.

This was the home where my father was provided shelter for 10 days after he arrived from Moshi to join the British Army, where he met his future wife (my mother) for the first time.

No one could have foreseen what was to come.

****

Without seeking counsel from his own mother, my father asked Dada and Mai for their daughter's hand in marriage. This was a golden opportunity, they thought. Where in Africa would they find an employed, handsome, Hindu, Marathi-speaking Brahmin of the same sect as their own? It was a match made in Heaven, a gift from God. To find a match in India would be cumbersome and expensive. To top it all, my father had not demanded the customary dowry, which they could not afford anyway. "A bird in the hand...," they might have said to themselves. My mother might not have had a choice in the matter. It is unknown how they addressed her dream of a higher education.

I am quite convinced that Dada and Mai loved her, wanted to do the right thing, and felt that this marriage was the best option under the circumstances. Any concern about my father's occasional drinking and chain-smoking was relegated to the background. He was always careful not to indulge in their presence.

18th January 1942.

Figure 3: My parent's marriage

This was an odd couple. The age difference of 11 years was not uncommon in that era, but he was a foot taller, mature, bold, and adventurous, standing ramrod straight as befits a soldier. He had an honest and infectious smile, and an occasional stutter did not hinder his confidence. The words sometimes struggled to escape from his mouth. She was mischievous, childlike, and athletic, and had dreams far beyond the realm of reality.

The marriage on January 18, 1942, in Nairobi was a low-key affair.

Months passed. My father continued to work for the British Army. There was not much to do, since East Africa had remained relatively free of the conflict that had engulfed the rest of the world. Being restless, he opened a dry-cleaning business. Quick Cleaners was a huge success, especially with white expatriates who preferred smart, starched shirts and well-ironed trousers. Indians, known for their frugality, preferred to wash their clothes at home in buckets and dry them in the sun. The Africans rarely had the means or opportunity to wear nice, laundered clothes.

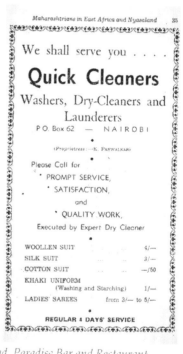

Figure 4: Quick Cleaners employees and ad, Paradise Bar and Restaurant

The business thrived. Two Indian partners joined in, and they opened a second laundry and purchased the Paradise Bar and

Restaurant, serving western and eastern dishes. Smack in the center of the city, it boasted the finest china, cutlery, and cuisine. My father said that Jomo Kenyatta, the future president of Kenya, occasionally dined there. The money flowed in.

****

He bought a simple stone house in Pangani, a suburb of Nairobi. The name "Kusumaker," a blend of Kusum and Prabhaker, was etched into the concrete just above the entrance. An American car was parked in the large, barren lot, which needed the touch of a gardener. It was said that this was one of the wealthiest Indian homes in Nairobi. Indian professionals became friends and neighbors. Word got out that Prabhaker Panvalkar from Bombay had become a rich man. New immigrants from Bombay congregated to this generous home, using it as a stepping stone to careers in Africa. My father helped secure jobs for some of the newcomers. The hospitality was genuine and unconditional. Nothing was expected in return. Homesick men from Maharashtra found food and friendship in this home.

A cigarette case, carefully carved by Italian prisoners of war while they languished in Ethiopian camps waiting for repatriation to Italy via Nairobi, held cigarettes of the highest quality from Britain. The beautiful wooden case was polished to perfection. The lid opened on soundless hinges and displayed 3 rows of 10 cigarettes each. It closed neatly, like a concertina, without a single cigarette getting crushed. Intricate carvings on the outside were symbols of the proud workmanship. It seemed so unlikely that these gentle and expressive Italians had fought a vicious war on behalf of Mussolini.

Working for the British Army while growing his own businesses suited my father well even though he fretted about racism. He hated that he and his friends were once asked to leave a posh "whites only" hotel where they had hoped to enjoy a cool beer. They were dressed in British Army uniforms but, being colored, were unwelcome. I am not sure how he responded. What he told others about the incident was possibly embellished a bit, to protect his own pride and self-respect and to impress the listeners. In general, most Indians did almost nothing to protest the color bar.

The boy whose father had died in that *chawl* in Bombay when he was just four years old, who had no more than a high-school education, and who had shocked his mother with his unannounced departure to

Africa had beaten the odds. He had married the woman he loved, built an empire others could only dream of, and had good friends and trusted business partners. All this was achieved in less than four years. He shared his good fortune with others, with unparalleled generosity.

He felt free for the first time in his life. He was grateful for the good life. Not one to rest on his laurels, he had big dreams of expanding his business ventures further.

****

I was born in the early hours of March 3, 1943, in a hospital in Ngara, Nairobi. I was named Anand, meaning joy. According to custom, I acquired my father's anglicized last name, Panwalker. Sweets were distributed. Gifts were lavished upon Ganesha, the elephant-headed god who removes all obstacles and Laxmi to ensure prosperity. Priests were fed meals fit for kings.

Mai and Dada celebrated their first grandchild, who was a boy, to boot!

By all accounts, Baba doted over me and spoiled me with toys and treats. High-quality toys were imported from Sweden, red wagons and train engines carved out of wood with colorful wheels. He relished the idea of fatherhood, although he had not known his own father. There is one faded picture, from a few months later, of my father carrying this infant on his shoulder. Later pictures, all black-and-white, show me wearing a gray-striped wool blazer and shorts made from the cloth left over from my father's custom-made suits. He always suspected that the tailor sold us far more wool than needed to make the baggy suits people wore in that era. Wising up to that sleight of hand, he routinely asked the tailor to use the remaining cloth to make me a suit. My well-polished, custom-made, black leather shoes were exact miniature copies of the shoes my father wore. My mother, a slim, short, and slight woman, wore a sari and an almost sleeveless blouse, as was the custom in those days.

Fond of English movies, we often drove to a theater downtown. One time, I chose to remain in the car while they watched a thriller. Somehow I had managed to pull some wires, which caused a short. Smoke emerged from under the hood. Seeing a message on the theater screen, my father rushed out to douse the small fire with his brand-new wool jacket.

Figure 5: With my parents

Another time, I opened the car door while we were driving home at night and fell out onto the road. My drowsy parents did not notice my absence until they got home several minutes later. Retracing their steps, they found me sitting nonchalantly on a nearby bench. Dr. Neurgaokar was summoned and declared that I was fine, but my mother needed treatment for anxiety.

Baba read the *East African Standard* every morning and *Time* magazine each week. He was the center of attention during gatherings and told stories about the war as though he had actually been in combat. These young men also spent hours speculating about what would happen now that the Americans had entered the war. Strangely, there was no discussion about Gandhi and the Indian struggle for freedom. And the idea of freedom for Kenya had not yet entered the political conscience.

World War II ended after Japan capitulated. Mussolini was hanged, and Hitler committed suicide. The process of mobilizing thousands of Italian prisoners began in earnest. My father had some administrative role in that process and made many friends among the Italians. He saw them as victims rather than enemies. Some of these

Italians settled in Nairobi and opened bakeries and pastry shops or became artisans and mechanics.

In later years, my teenage friends and I saw a beautiful young Italian woman with olive skin and blue eyes behind the counter of a bakery near the Shan Cinema, which showed Indian movies. The aroma of the delicious western breads was foreign to us. We often stopped outside the bakeries to steal a whiff and peek in the windows. The woman smiled shyly. She knew that it was not the bread we were staring at. Every Indian schoolboy passing that shop fell in love with her, even before any of us knew anything about love or sex. This visit to the bakery became a daily occurrence—sometimes up to four times a day!

We never saw anyone buy the bread and assumed their sales occurred when we were in school. One day she was gone, and only the aroma of fresh bread remained. The new person behind the counter, a swarthy white man with pockmarks and unruly hair, shooed us away, knowing we had no interest in his bread and could not afford it.

Life was good. Friends, family, fame, fortune, and foreign cars. Servants, successful businesses, and a thriving social life were the rewards for hard work, endless ambition, and courage exhibited by my dad, a Maharashtrian—a man from a tribe of people typically content to work as salaried government servants, clerks, or teachers. He took great pride in this self-sufficiency and success.

Dada and Mai rejoiced at their good fortune and the decision to allow their daughter to marry this fine young man.

Two high-school graduates had succeeded in a foreign country, despite great odds.

My father resigned from the British army in 1946. His discharge papers mentioned his "exemplary character."

****

The same year, expressing regret that he had abandoned his mother eight years earlier, my father informed Aji that my mother and I, now three years old, would visit Bombay to pay respects to her. He could not come, since he had businesses to look after.

If he had accompanied us, he would have noticed that nothing had changed except everyone was eight years older. The stairs still creaked and the railing around the balconies had deteriorated further, but the new babies were just as nonchalant about the dangers as their elder siblings had been. The concrete walls had the same unattended blemishes. The electric bulbs remained bare but high enough not to singe someone's hair. (I have no recollection of this trip except what my mother told me later.)

Aji doted over me. She expressed no opinion about her daughter-in-law, Kusum. Curious neighbors, having heard rumors of my father's wealth, peered intently at these "African" visitors. Seeing regular people who looked and dressed just like them, they lost interest and receded into their daily lives.

There was a cacophony of noises. Songs from movies, the hourly news on All India Radio, the *chun chun* of tiny bells on the ankles of little girls in a dance class, the sounds of a sitar, the *dha dhin dhin dha* of a novice *tabla* (drum) player, the high-pitched shouts of vendors, the heart-rending pleas of limbless beggars, crying babies, and screams of angry parents. And always- in the background- the distant hum of city traffic and the rumble of receding carts pulled by weary oxen. No place for silence or solitude here.

Aji cut one ripe and fragrant Alphonso mango, procured at great expense, and gave me the thickest slice.

Not used to sharing anything, I said belligerently in Swahili, "Mimi apana maskini." (I am not a beggar.)

Aji looked at my mom and asked in Marathi what I was saying. My mother likely lied to avoid embarrassment.

When it came time to return to Nairobi, Aji cut an entire mango for me. A rare, knowing smile appeared on her tired and weathered countenance.

I imagine her warm touch and knew that she loved me, her first grandson, as much as she did her errant son who she had not seen in eight years. In my mind's eye, I see Aji and my aunt Sunder and uncle Dinkar waving to us, tears in their eyes, as they say goodbye.

No one knew when we might meet again.

****

The good times ended abruptly. We became paupers overnight.

There are several versions of what happened, but there is no official written record of these cataclysmic events. What I put together is garnered from overheard, hushed conversations, rumors, and stolen glances at forbidden correspondence received and sent by my parents.

Details will always remain sketchy. My parents never addressed the topic in my presence.

Baba, the senior partner, had placed all the property and money in my mother's name, even though she was very young and not financially savvy. Indeed, advertisements for Quick Cleaners showed that the proprietress was K. Panwalker. The other partners and shareowners, both Indians, shared the paperwork. Occasionally, my mother was asked to sign documents for the laundries, hotel, or bar. She never checked the details, because honesty and trust were pillars of how we lived and expected others to live.

My mother's signature on an ordinary-looking document, which was in fact a promissory note to one partner, led to the overnight loss of all our property rights, shares, and income. We had suddenly become destitute. This fraud, committed by a family "friend," destroyed our lives. Trust, the foundation of all dealings my father ever had with others, was shattered by my mother's naiveté. There was no legal redress possible. We were bankrupt.

My father, now with no assets of his own, was unable to repay the debts. Astonishingly, we were also required to pay back "loans" that had never been made. For a variety of reasons, my mother became responsible for these obligations. Once she found a job, she made monthly payments to the creditors for over 10 years. Even though we had been cheated, once we signed the receivership papers, it was my family's intention to pay back whatever they said we owed them.

For unknown reasons, the Paradise Hotel and bar business fared poorly after this deceit and declared bankruptcy on August 13, 1949. The Quick Cleaners laundries were sold to two Indian investors on October 3, 1950. We received none of the profits.

Most of our "friends," frequent recipients of our unending generosity, suddenly disappeared. We had to vacate Kusumaker, the monument to my parents' love for each other, their personal Taj Mahal. The name remained carved in the concrete façade in front of the property for years, a cruel reminder as I walked by daily on my way to school. At age six, I was quite oblivious to the turmoil engulfing their lives.

There was no overt sign of despair. We needed to find a new place to live. A small two-room rental flat was found in Eastleigh, a suburb of Nairobi. The Sikh owner, Chanan Singh Bharij, and his wife,

Surjeet Kaur, welcomed us with genuine warmth. They were aware of the treachery that had impoverished us. They did not want any deposit or any rent in advance. They said to pay them when we could, if we could. No papers were signed. Chanan Singh said my father's word was good enough for him.

Perhaps my affection for Sikhs began around this time. Harinder Singh, their son, became my best friend. Their home became my second home. And some years later, the bond became stronger, when Surjeet Kaur heard screams and saved my mother's honor and life by fighting off a trusted servant who had turned rogue and attacked her. The servant, stronger and bigger, ran out of the house all the way to his village.

My father and Chanan Singh followed him and whipped him until he begged for his life.

****

It did not take very long for my father to bounce back. He decided to chalk it up to experience. For him, it was simple. He had come to Kenya with nothing, but he was sure he could rebuild what he had lost. He would just start all over again. It was not a big deal. He had forgiven the man who had deceived him.

Confident, upbeat, and optimistic, he dreamt new dreams. He often said, "All I need is a pack of cigarettes, a pen, and a writing pad, and I will create a new business." His deep voice and clear diction impressed those who spoke little English. The occasional words of contempt I heard from him were that "the man cannot speak a proper sentence in English." That terrible flaw, according to him, guaranteed failure. The other criticism he had of Indians was that they were generally unhealthy with "high blood pressure or diabetes." Implicit in that comment was his belief that they were lazy and sedentary. Certainly, athleticism had never been a forte of these immigrants. He often proved his point by winning badminton games handily in the club.

Despite his lofty goals, as time passed and our need for cash grew, he settled for a job with Patel Brothers, a bookstore that also sold stationery and school supplies. He kept inventory, ordered needed items, and generally kept an eye on the store. He continued to wear suits and starched shirts at work, while his bosses wore shabby clothes and sandals. He was critical of these "sloppy shopkeepers wearing pajamas," for not combing their hair and for blowing their noses on the sidewalks. How could they grow a business looking like that?

When he got home, he would remove the tie—his *galfasa*, a Marathi word for noose—and heave a huge sigh of relief. Most Indians in Kenya did not wear a tie or a suit, and no one had told him he needed to. My father's hair had a "dry look," unlike most Indian men and women, who smothered their hair with fragrant sticky coconut oil, which came in green and red bottles. He wore his shiny leather dress shoes until bedtime. He was impeccably dressed anytime he was awake.

Unlike my mother's side of the family, my father spoke little Gujarati. The Patel brothers, savvy traders and entrepreneurs, spoke broken English and no Marathi. They managed to communicate efficiently nonetheless through a clumsy admixture of gestures and mangled phrases from all three languages with a sprinkling of Swahili words.

He sang songs of recovery. On his most exuberant days he sang, "Awara hun mein" (I am a vagabond), with absolutely no sense of rhythm or melody. His voice cracked at crucial moments. With a twinkle and mischief in his eyes, he sang this one line repeatedly until we begged him to stop. It was a well-known song from the 1950 Hindi movie *Awara* about a down-on-his-luck Indian who was nonetheless quite content and happy. It made the actor Raj Kapoor very famous in other countries too. The theme especially resonated with Russians, who apparently felt the same way as the loafer. My dad was sure this song had been written for him.

There was another favorite song, "Mera joota hai Japani, patloon Englistani, saar pay laal topi Roosi, phir bhi dil hai Hindustani." (My shoes are Japanese, trousers are English, my hat is Russian…but my friends, my heart is Indian.) Lacking musical genes, no amount of practice was going to improve his performance. He did not care. Unlike the scenes in Hindi movies where the stars burst into song with a full orchestra at the most tragic or happy moment in their lives, Baba sang whenever he felt like it. He got a kick out of the invariable reaction his singing provoked.

My mother had been an aide at the Government Indian Girls' School since 1943, but was urged to attend a teacher training course by Mrs. Lincoln (the school principal) and two other British expatriates, Mrs. Blundell and Mr. Clement, who saw some promise in her. They took her under their wings. Their names were spoken of fondly in the home. We guessed they were English. For us, every white person was from England. We did not know how to identify someone from Scotland, Wales, Ireland, or Germany. The Hindi word *Angrez* in India and the word *Mzungu* in Swahili (both meaning English) were used as generic labels for all white people. On the other hand, it was easy to identify a white American. All one had to do was watch a war movie. In the movie *Stalag 17*, for example, a German officer suspected William Holden of being a spy based on the way he ate with a fork in his right hand. A European would never do something so improper and uncouth!

Schools were segregated based on race and gender and often named for British dignitaries. Thus, the Government Indian Girls' School was renamed the Duchess of Gloucester School. No one knew who the Duchess was or where Gloucester (pronounced incorrectly as "gloss-ester") was located. It remained a school for Indian girls. So that the Duke would not feel left out, the Government Indian Boys' School in another part of town was renamed the Duke of Gloucester School. This separation by gender significantly delayed our hormonal development.

My mother became a teacher at "the Duchess." The job promised a pension if she served long enough. Mom maintained a cheerful disposition, worked very hard, and never spoke of hardships. She made friends easily with the mostly Indian teachers at the school. Her mastery of multiple languages made it easy for her to mingle with those from other states in India. She did not have a mean bone in her body and never spoke ill of others. Her smile, full of mischief, was infectious, and at heart, she was still a child. Athletic despite her short stature, she routinely outran other women in races arranged by local clubs. She would tie her sari in a way so it would not flutter like a sail, and she would be off like a bolt of lightning. Other less competitive Indian women would lumber along, stopping prematurely, and huffing and puffing for dear life. Her integrity and playfulness endeared her to others. Her demeanor and actions did not betray any trace of the turmoil in her life. She was happy around people and volunteered for all activities that were available. Our home once again attracted people because of its open-door philosophy.

There was no self-pity about the disaster that had struck us and no overt pleas to God for help. My father never prayed. We did not go to a temple and, contrary to custom, my mother did not have a corner of the home set aside as such, though she did place little idols and images of Ganesha in her cupboard.

I recall being a happy child. I inherited my father's love for reading and organization and my parents' resilience under adverse conditions. We were content.

****

Ours was one of four apartments. Harinder and I used to hang out together, even though he was a year older. Honesty, doing our duty, and doing the right thing came naturally to all children growing up in that conservative environment. Respect for elders and our teachers was a necessary virtue. Touching their feet was considered a sign of respect, just as it might when one bows to God in a place of worship. I was unaware then that bowing to another human being is considered inappropriate in some religions, since they reserve such deference only for God.

Violation of rules was rare; when it happened, there was swift retribution. A telltale stare was the first major expression of disapproval. We knew that look. It was not okay to be out late after sundown, to be late for meals, to go anywhere without asking for permission, or to receive notes from school about bad behavior or incomplete homework. It was definitely not okay to get a B grade in anything or to speak out of turn, and we were never to brag about anything. Teachers were allowed to mete out corporal punishment on behalf of the parents, and I got my share of the cane in school.

Indians of all castes and religions mingled with a total disregard for our differences. Whereas others went to their place of worship every week, the Hindu community did so only on special occasions such as Diwali or Holi. This was quite consistent with the concept that God was in our homes and hearts, and one did not have to go searching for Him. Little mini temples were often set up to "house" the omnipresent and omnipotent God who was already there and always would be.

We walked to school and occasionally jumped onto a bullock cart passing by. The owners let us ride for a while, but mostly shooed us away. At times, we gathered loquats, mangoes, and guavas from trees that did not belong to us. We did not consider that stealing. Our rationale was that the branches were hanging outside the yard and the fruit would be wasted on the pavement below. How could we permit that, knowing that people were starving all over the planet? However, one time we entered a fenced yard, climbed up a guava tree, and grabbed bags full of the ripe, yellow, delicious fruit. The Indian owner and his servant ran after us, waving their *pangas* (machetes) and screaming obscenities. Harinder could barely hold on to his turban as we ran for our lives.

We built catapults. Target shooting of cans and bottles was the goal. One time, I aimed at a bird perched on an electric wire. The stone flew off the catapult on a curved trajectory and hit the bird with a sickening thud. A bright, greenish-yellow lump and beautiful feathers fluttered limply to the ground. Surprised and dismayed by my accuracy — for I had not intended to hurt a living thing — I ran out to see how badly the bird was injured. In the few seconds it took me to round the corner, I saw a feral cat grab the obviously incapacitated flapping creature and heard the deadly crunch of sharp teeth. The cat turned toward me, quite annoyed at the intrusion, and ran off into a nearby cluster of bushes, carrying the carcass in its mouth. This is the first time I noticed that cats have vertical pupils in their eyes. I felt a profound sadness, threw the catapult in a nearby ditch, and never built another one again.

I asked myself why I did not feel the same sadness when I ate chicken curry on a fairly routine basis.

Another time, a few of us went to a nearby muddy pool of water perhaps 8–10 feet wide. We thought we might find gold nuggets in this muddy water, just like we had seen in American movies. Stripped down to our underwear, we entered cautiously, in foolish defiance of a forbidden act. One friend chickened out and ran home to tell his parents.

Now, knee-deep in the mud and still curious and foolish, we continued down the muddy bank. The bottom of the pit was much deeper than anticipated. Waist-high, we realized we were sinking, pulled down by our own weight. We tried to crawl out, but kept slipping back in. Frantically, we tried to pull ourselves to the brink, clawing at the wet soil and the bare and slimy roots of little bushes. The roots and twigs broke and we slid down again. We grabbed each other, but that made it worse. Finally, we managed to extricate ourselves from this hellhole. My heart was thumping so hard, I thought it would fly out of my chest. I knew that there was going to be more trouble when I got home. I had never done anything so rash and stupid before.

We tried to clean and dry our muddy clothes and bodies in a nearby stream, but telltale signs remained, particularly the brown mud on our black hair, in our ears, and on our eyelashes. It was also past mealtime, and my parents had been searching for me. My father gave me the first and only thrashing of my life. My mother simply gave me "the look." I believe all my friends, except for the snitch, received a similar reception when they got home. We unanimously agreed that we deserved it. We reverted to more benign adventures, improvised games with nothing more than a worn-out tennis ball, sticks, and stones.

The teachers and students at the Desai Road Primary School were all Indian. I learned science, mathematics, history, and geography in Gujarati, since they did not teach Marathi in this school. In grade 5, we were suddenly switched to an English medium of instruction, and were fined 10 cents if we spoke any other language. In this setting, I spoke English in class, did arithmetic in Gujarati in my head, spoke Gujarati or Hindi on the playing field, Marathi at home with my parents, and Swahili with the servants. In later years when we lived in a joint family, we recited prayers nightly in Sanskrit, a language none of the children understood.

****

There were signs that things were changing. For one, no one ventured out after dark. I was afraid to walk alone past the thick bushes near our home. Could someone be watching? Even slight sounds startled me.

The governor imposed a rigid curfew on Africans. We noticed increased British troop movements, especially in and out of the military airport in Eastleigh. For the first time in our young lives, we saw troops patrolling the streets. The young white soldiers, no older than teenagers, arrested Africans for curfew violations but also for trivial reasons. Those without the *kipande* were placed in the back of a truck and taken away to an unknown destination. White and brown people could roam free at any time, but we were now urged to be careful, to be home before dusk, and to always walk in groups.

Our routines and lifestyles did not change much, but doors were now locked and bolted from inside. Steel bars were inserted on first floor windows. More families felt the need to own a dog. Signs warning trespassers to stay out began to sprout up. Homes were built with ever taller walls with sharp glass shards on top to keep intruders away. Businesses hired *askaris* to guard their premises.

There were whispers that servants had developed an "attitude." They were now occasionally questioning the tasks given to them. Car windows were raised so that thieves would not snatch items from unwary passengers at stop signs. The words *Mau Mau* reverberated throughout the British colony and indeed throughout Britain.

DISCORD

Outwardly, Baba did not linger over our financial mess. He had found the job with Patel Brothers rather quickly. A bus ride had replaced the car drive. He started coming home a little later than usual. We smelled alcohol on his breath. Now he preferred to go straight to bed after just a few pleasantries, which were not reciprocated.

Mom was anxious about the drinking and its effect on the family. We worried that he might fall and hurt himself or get into an altercation at a bar. Chanan Singh, a teetotaler, pleaded with Baba to drink at home if he must. So it transpired that he drank on his way back from work and then again at home, pretending he'd had nothing all day. This state of affairs persisted for months, but we somehow managed. I was shielded from the ugliness when things got tense. My parents were careful to avoid arguments in my presence. There was no shouting or yelling in our home.

One evening, Baba entered the apartment, stumbled, and almost fell. Somehow, he managed to become perpendicular again. He wobbled unsteadily, pretending he was in full control. His demeanor—a guilty face begging for forgiveness—was that of a schoolboy caught stealing cookies.

We sat down to dinner, and I noticed he was playing with his food rather than eating it. The meal had required a lot of work, and we were celebrating a special religious day—Diwali, or the Festival of Lights. Several minutes passed. My mother was irritable and angry. She had the "look." They exchanged some words about *daru* (alcohol) without any shouting. She glared at him. He avoided her gaze, looking down instead. After listening quietly for a while, he got up without touching his food and almost fell again. As he retreated to the other room, my mother screamed at him, while still at the table- an unusual combination of anger, frustration, and indescribable agony. I was still seated as well, transfixed.

My father turned slowly to see why she was yelling. A thin stainless steel dinner plate, the type often used in Indian homes, flew like a Frisbee across the room. It hit my father, who was standing perhaps 10 feet away, on the left side of his forehead, causing a gash and bleeding. The plate fell noisily to the concrete floor, its bloody edge wavering and uncertain. It bounced up slightly and rolled a few feet clumsily, leaving a thin, bloody track on the floor. The clatter and din reverberated through the room. The agitated steel finally quivered and fell upside down on the floor, one edge permanently bent as a reminder of this fateful evening. Mixed in with spattered blood was the food that had been lovingly prepared for a religious feast, now inedible, unwanted, and lying unceremoniously on the floor.

Surprised by this unexpected assault, Baba held a hand to his forehead, noticed the blood, and stared with his mouth open at my mother. Then, instead of getting angry, he broke into a silly smile.

I watched intently. The gushing blood unnerved my tearful mother, who rushed to his side, apologized profusely, and placed a handkerchief on his forehead. She then went into the other room and burst out crying.

My father slumped in a chair by the dining table. I remained quiet. This was the first time I had seen an expression of anger and violence in our home. I was also impressed that, despite his unsteadiness, he had not fallen.

He turned toward me, noticed my expression, and stood up again to make sure I was okay. A sickly whiff of stale alcohol hit my nostrils. I was numb. Not sure how to react, I ran out to inspect the roses.

It was still sunny. The air was fresh, the sky was blue, and the birds continued to tweet. Large colorful butterflies hopped onto the rose petals then fluttered away. I caught one gently and examined it on my palm. It stared back at me and then angrily flew off, in its haste depositing a little of the golden powdery pigment.

The neighbors heard the commotion and rushed in. Someone summoned my mother's brothers. Prabhaker (Bhau), the eldest of the men, was the calm one. He assessed the scene and tried to figure out a solution. Sharad and Anil, the more volatile of the brothers, were upset that Baba had caused distress to their sister and were in a fighting mood. The imagery of the "cavalry" arriving to rescue a distressed woman and her child remains vivid in my mind today.

After a short discourse, it was decided that my mother and I should leave the home until the family could make some long-term plans. Soon we had packed a suitcase. I looked back from a neighbor's car –since we no longer owned a vehicle- and saw my father's lonely figure staring from the doorway.

The neighbor took us to my grandfather's apartment. This is how we ended up in the home where my parents had first met, a place with two rooms, eight people, and one toilet; where authors and musicians came to visit and where my grandfather had the armchair that no one else could use. And where the small balcony faced an alley frequented by a stray dog searching for scraps of food.

We began living with my grandparents and my maternal uncles and aunts. I touched my grandparents' feet as a mark of respect and greeted my uncles and aunts (some older, some younger) with an embrace. I felt genuinely welcomed and was happy to have company. The younger uncles and aunts immediately took me on a tour of the neighborhood. The elders needed some privacy to engage in weighty discussions.

My mother protested, rather limply, that the two rooms would be inadequate for the family, which had grown to eight relatives (grandparents, four uncles, and two aunts) and a servant, Wambua, who slept in the kitchen. She was assured that no one minded, and we were one family after all. Now 11 people would live here.

My father was left alone to nurse his physical and emotional wounds with the servant Thyomo, who had cared for me as I was growing up.

After several months, I was surprised to learn we were returning to Eastleigh. Apparently Bhau had arranged a truce and extracted promises from my father as the Sikh owners waited patiently. They were rooting for a reunion and welcomed us warmly with a Punjabi meal.

The gash on my father's forehead had healed quickly, but became a permanent scar, and was a daily reminder of what had happened. The body's ability to heal such physical wounds amazed me.

My parents pretended nothing had happened. No one, at any time, asked me what I wanted. If asked, I would have said I was pleased about the reconciliation.

****

Thyomo, an elderly Kikuyu who had worked for us many years, had remained with Baba during the separation. He had looked after me since I was a baby, had cooked, cleaned, and been a reassuring presence in an otherwise unstable household. He and another servant were fortunate. The kind owner had built a shack in the backyard where the two could live and bathe from a spout nearby. Here they were spared from the rigors of the curfew, travel to the slum, violence from Mau Mau, and the impatience of British soldiers.

Rarely, when upset with my parents, I retreated to Thyomo's hut, where I shared a meal of *ugari* (a cornmeal dish) and *posho* beans with him and his roommate. Away from their loved ones, with little to look forward to in life, these generous and noble men shared their meager meals with the brown son of their employer.

It took me a long time to understand how detached we had been from the aspirations and needs of fellow human beings, simply based on their color and social status. There was sadness in his aging eyes.

Feeling old and lonesome, he eventually decided to return to his village, where his wife grew maize and cassava on a small plot of land. He received no pension or social security and had minimal savings. But he was back with his family.

We moved on with our lives without much fanfare or fancy farewells. No gold watch for him. We did not have the resources to reward him well for his years of faithful service to his onetime rich and brown employer. I wonder if he even had a decent burial.

****

Months passed. There was peace. Baba resumed singing his favorite songs, but without some of the mischief and gusto. The twinkle in his eyes was gone. Busy with our routine of school, work, and play, we rarely had much conversation in the home. Occasionally, my parents asked me about school, my favorite subjects, or teachers. Baba did not know what fatherhood entailed, but remained generous with gifts and stories about politics, and intermittently tortured us with his uniquely awful rendition of songs about a loafer with his Japanese shoes, English trousers, Russian cap and yet an Indian heart. I knew he loved me, but outward displays of affection were not too common in those days.

He made a valiant effort to remain sober by changing his work route, habits, and friends. He avoided situations where he would be tempted to take a drink or two. His success was a matter of pride for him and a matter of joy for us. He had abstained for several months, and I had seen a new person — more confident, more interactive, and steadier on his feet. His employers had been pleased. We saw a rejuvenated man. He gained weight and remained a wonderful host to visitors. He had substituted his drinking with chain-smoking. A cigarette always dangled from his lips as he admired the exhaled rings of smoke in concentric circles. His fingers were stained. His clothes smelled of nicotine and so did the curtains and sheets.

But like a curse that never leaves, he succumbed to temptation, and booze became his ally once more, a source of comfort from whatever was ailing him. It was initially just a sip or two, but over time he got bolder. The memory of the first separation and how he had to beg us to return had faded. The drinking and unsteadiness became obvious to everyone except him.

My mother warned him to stop immediately and threatened to leave again. He listened. He was not going to risk losing his family again. He continued working. Several days after my mother's warning, we noticed that he was irritable, and he said he felt unwell and tired. He was not sleeping well. His appetite slacked off and a tremor developed.

The high fever, agitation, hallucinations, and delirium were noticed by the employer who brought him home. This man who had always been in control was now incontinent and incoherent, babbling things no one understood. I now know what my mother had not told me before. Baba had had the DTs (delirium tremens), a sign of withdrawal from alcohol, potentially fatal if managed improperly. Plying him with alcohol would have speeded his recovery, but it seemed intuitively absurd to do so. Dr. Neurgaokar chose instead to treat him with concoctions of vitamin shots, milkshakes, and injections of unknown substances. He said he was prescribing the tincture of time and urging prayers for his recovery.

The fever broke after a few anxious days; he was more lucid and the pins and needles in his feet hurt less. The fiends, the snakes, and the beasts left our home. It took many months for him to heal. Frightened by the experience, he vowed once more never to drink again.

He lost his confidence. I never heard him sing again. The spark had gone out of him.

Patel Brothers held the job for him while he was on unpaid leave. When he did return to work, he appeared restless and agitated. Being a bookkeeper in a stationery store was not challenging enough, and he was not paid much. Many months passed uneventfully.

He began to look up his old contacts to find new leads. That led to social drinking, which once again caused scenes at home. He was unable to keep his promise to abstain from alcohol. It became common knowledge that he had a drinking problem and was bankrupt, and there was discord in the family. He continued to work regularly, but headed to a bar on his way home. He could not understand why a single shot or a beer would cause problems when others imbibed much more.

He was not supposed to drive. That did not stop him from buying a used, black Ford Pilot. He drove to my school one afternoon to give me a ride home. I usually walked home, so I was surprised to see him. He wanted me to be the first passenger in his new car. He drove rashly, out of control. Frightened children dodged, and chickens lifted their heavy bodies for short desperate flights to get out of the way. I had never seen chickens fly. Feathers flew off the squawking birds. Once safe, the children dropped their bags and cursed in whatever language they spoke at home. The bad English words we knew in those days included "bloody fool," "bugger," and "idiot." As our vocabulary grew, we called our enemy a "bastard," a terrible insult reserved for the most dastardly of all. None of these words were ever used at home. The four-letter curse word starting with the letter F was unknown to us.

Miraculously, no one was hurt. When we got home, he asked me—with the same silly grin from when he had been hit by the flying steel plate—whether I had enjoyed the ride. I turned away and walked angrily into the home. I chose not to share the story with my mother, but she found out anyway.

A few days later, we received a telegram from Bombay. Apparently, his younger brother Dinkar's wife, Chandu Kaki, had committed suicide. My father, slightly tipsy and grief-stricken, started crying. His tears fell onto the dinner table, into his plate, and onto the floor. I did not know that human tears could be so large.

He cried for what seemed like hours. Finally, he fell asleep on the sofa. He was late to work the next day, somewhat disheveled and unshaven. When he returned in the evening, unsteady on his feet—

reeking of alcohol and fearing a rebuke—he refused dinner and went to sleep. We were now concerned that he would lose his job.

By now, I had learned to read my mother's facial expressions. Her forehead lost its creases when she was angry. We also knew she was annoyed if she stopped making eye contact. This evening she had that look.

Two days later, Bhau was at our doorstep again. I had come to associate this beloved maternal uncle's visits with crisis. He gently informed my father that the promise of abstinence had been broken and that the current living situation was unacceptable.

Once again, we were whisked away to my grandfather's rented flat. The packing had been done already. Harinder, my Sikh friend, his sister and parents waved goodbye to us.

My father said nothing and remained on the sofa. He did not ask for another chance. He did not stand in the doorway as he had done another time to watch the car recede. He cut a pathetic figure, unrecognizable from the strapping man in a military uniform who had told stories of war and courage to spellbound listeners.

Just six years old, I would not see him again for five years.

THE JOINT FAMILY

We resumed our stay with the extended family and were welcomed with open arms. Dada's armchair, now a bit frayed, still sat majestically in the middle of the larger room, restricted from use by others.

In this joint family, we inevitably fought over trivial things. The house was small and we were stepping over each other all the time. Anil, Mira, Subhash, and I, all about the same age, were the main combatants whose allegiances changed daily. Solemn promises were commonly betrayed, coalitions were built and broken. Our fickle feuds were short-lived. Provocateurs laughed and spurred on the verbal combatants. But at the end of the day, we rarely remembered what we had quarreled about. Deep down, all of us knew that we could not manage without each other. Intricately woven into the fabric of this family, forgiveness and laughter came easily and quickly.

One method we used to really irritate each other was to place a thumbnail against our incisors and make a sound like *kitta,* a signal that we were no longer on speaking terms. Communication was now held via an intermediary who had remained neutral for this skirmish. The juvenile banter brought jeers, tears, or cheers depending on which side one was on.

I sensed that my grandparents felt sorry for my mother and me. Did they regret that they had married my mother off, perhaps against her wishes? Did they pity me? At times, I thought they favored me over their own children. After all, I was their first grandchild.

Months passed. Busy with school and sports, I did not miss my father. Sometimes, I came across a letter that had been left inadvertently on the tabletop. His handwriting was distinctive, with a prominent slant and without any punctuation or spelling errors. The theme was always similar. How much he missed us and how sorry he was. He wanted another chance. Promises he would try to keep. There were pleas to see me. Could he buy me some new clothes and take me to an ice cream place? Just a few minutes, please?

Over time the letters became infrequent and had a tone of resignation. There was no anger or bitterness and never any accusations or threats. He tried to camouflage the self-pity. Other than a mailbox address, we knew nothing about his life, how he managed his meals, whether he was sober, where he lived, or how he spent his free time. He apparently found jobs — one time with the Kenya Police, in the remote desert of Northern Kenya, where no Indian dared to go.

I was too busy to miss him. I wasn't angry. Instead, I felt betrayed and abandoned; with a deep sadness that alcoholism (considered a vice rather than an illness in those days) had affected our lives so profoundly. I also knew that this good man would not be able to change. I was resigned to this becoming a permanent state of affairs.

One time, the quarrels between the children crossed a threshold that the exasperated elders could not bear. We had been with the extended family for a year or so and I was just 7.

My mother called me aside and said, within earshot of others, "Perhaps you should go live with your father." She was under pressure, as were others, to end the incessant squabbles between the children.

Never willing to acknowledge that I was the main culprit in any quarrel, I felt my own mother had turned against me. Shouting, "I don't want to live here. No one cares for me except my father!" I stamped off as though to pack a bag that I did not own. My meager possessions, including clothes, would have fit neatly into one pillowcase, and the entire packing process would have taken about two minutes.

The room became eerily quiet.

Dada rose from the deep hammock that served as his armchair with some difficulty and placed his hand on my shoulder. "She did not mean it."

Then he proceeded to reprimand my mother in as gentle a manner as possible. She probably heard little of what was said between her sobs. Emboldened now that I knew they would not send me away, I insisted that they send me to my father immediately.

For extra effect, I added, "He will be kind to me, buy me ice cream and nice toys.

Pleased to see that they had beaten a hasty retreat, and having expressed my outrage eloquently, I left the room to go play. We decided to go down the street to harass the shopkeepers by riding our homemade planks on wheels.

One uncle was not as victorious after a fight. Finding no one to support his cause, he climbed up the inside ledge of the second-floor window, with the implicit threat that he was going to jump to the concrete courtyard one floor below. He did hold on to the edge of the window frame firmly. Family members walked in one after the other, saw him perched on the sill, asked him what he was doing, and walked away before he could answer. He had expected someone to beg him to get away from the window, to be told that he was loved, and so on. Not hearing any of that, he found himself in a quandary. It was a matter of self-respect or life. He chose life, stepped away from the window, and glanced around furtively to see if anyone was laughing. We pretended that nothing had happened, and he assumed we had forgotten about the episode. We still tease him about it.

Then there was an incident with my homemade bow and arrow. Missing its intended mark, a cardboard cutout, the tiny arrow lodged in one uncle's left temple. Luckily, the missile missed his eye and was only superficially embedded in his skin. If only I'd had a camera to capture his shocked expression.

A spat I had with another uncle was more serious. He reported to Dada, "Anand gives me no respect, even though I am his *Mama* (maternal uncle)."

My response was that "Lord Krishna, the great warrior in *Mahabharata*, killed Kauns, his maternal uncle, because the man was evil." I remembered reading that story somewhere.

Dada tried to restrain a smile, but eventually lost control, laughing so hard he could not stop. His ample paunch shook in spasms. Tears flowed from his eyes, his face flushed and contorted, as he tried to compose himself. He removed his glasses to wipe his eyes, paused, sighed…then burst into laughter again. Curious family members joined this contagion of mirth, even though most did not know what was so funny. The uncle was now tremulous and visibly angry. He looked pleadingly at others for support after this betrayal by his father. Then he stormed out of the room. He planned to sulk in private and contemplate who his real allies in life were. He did not head for the window ledge that his brother had chosen.

****

My mother gave half her small salary to my grandfather each month to help with the expenses. What remained was enough to sustain our simple needs. We did not crave unattainable things. Our vegetarian meals were affordable. We sat on wooden slats on the ground, called *paat* in Marathi, and took turns eating since there was not enough space for all. The children ate first, the elders later. We were always hungry, but there was plenty of food available. I do not know who did the dishes or washed the clothes. It was not the men or the boys.

The boys, looking like penguins, wore tailor-made white shirts, black trousers, and black shoes. Ready-made clothing had not entered the market yet.

The walks to school kept us fairly fit and active. Those more fortunate rode bikes, which were invariably stolen. We were generally happy and content. We did not need, and could not afford, refrigerators. Farmers brought their vegetables door-to-door. Life was uncomplicated.

There was not much to do except study and play sports. The strict rules in school and at home kept us well anchored, obedient, and out of trouble. We were poor but proud. One time, we found a shilling coin on the street and immediately went to a nearby shop and bought a bag of roasted peanuts. Since we had been taught to share, we took some home. The reprimand was immediate and swift. We were told we should have looked for the owner (impossible on such a busy street), left it on the ground, or donated it to the nearby temple as an offering. It was wrong to spend it since we had not earned it. It was someone else's labor. Begging, stealing, or picking up someone else's property were forbidden. We were glad we had learned this important lesson about coins on the street *after* consuming the snack.

I was sensitive to our financial status, so I did not ask for toys, gifts, an allowance, or the sporty blue bicycle with curved handles that I wanted so badly. Occasionally I craved something and, after much hesitation, asked my mother for it. Like the time I wanted a brown windbreaker. It was made of faux leather, had a metal zipper, and cost about 20 shillings (worth 19 US cents at today's exchange rate). Fortunately for my mother, it was always out of stock.

Instead, we made our own toys. A favorite was a plank with wheels, assembled using materials found in a nearby junkyard. We hurtled noisily down the concrete slope to the river, annoying every one of the shopkeepers and pedestrians who were placed at risk by reckless teenagers. We were too fast, and the shopkeepers too fat to catch us. Irate pedestrians, especially those who had been whacked by this contraption, stepped out of the way quickly as soon as they heard the clatter of metal wheels on the sidewalk. Accidents and injuries were common, and I am told I was never without a bandage somewhere on my body.

These were happy days. We felt there was no place on the planet like Nairobi, mostly because it was the only place we knew on the planet. The fresh, clean air, beautiful blue skies...the gentle drizzle at night...the vast expanses of green grass and abundant flowering trees. After the rains, the river turned red as the silt washed into it from denuded earthen banks far away.

In this joint family, there was love and togetherness. At night, we sat on the floor in a circle, closed our eyes, and prayed. Sanskrit *shlokas,* starting with "Mukam karoti vachalam..." were recited faithfully, but only the elders knew what the words meant. Dada kept one eye open to make sure we were not fooling around. One of our favorite activities was to pinch the person next to us, perhaps in an effort to make them giggle or shriek and thus incur the wrath of the elders.

I froze one day when he interrupted the prayer and asked me to focus on the prayer and "be sincere." Keeping one eye open implied a lack of devotion and disrespect to God. My soul was already at peace, and I found this nightly ritual very boring. I was sure the others were insincere too, but simply pretended they were pious. My instinct said *Apologize and go on with the prayer.*

But I threw caution to the winds instead and asked, "Dada, how did you know my eye was open?" And immediately wished I had not asked the question.

He said, "I saw you."

"That means your eyes were open too!" Silence. *Very bad idea*, I thought.

My uncles and aunts looked warily at each other, expecting fireworks. Then I saw a tiny hint of a smile around Dada's pursed lips.

But his stern mask took over quickly. He said nothing. The younger ones looked at me with some envy for getting away with prohibited speech. The prayers resumed.

I loved this family and the way they had cared for us in our times of need. It was an idyllic existence for the children, who were blissfully unaware of life's hard realities and financial strains. There was food on the table when we were hungry and books on the shelf when we felt like reading.

The undisputed king of the household was Dada, my grandfather, who ruled his little empire with love and discipline. He was the glue that held things together. Mai, my grandmother, a gentle woman with beautiful dimples, a generous spirit, and tremendous dignity, kept us from trouble by simply being there. Neither her voice nor her hand was ever raised in anger. I felt very lucky in spite of the misfortunes in my young life.

We were quite proud that Dada and Mai had been freedom fighters at a time when most Indians had succumbed to the temptation of a steady government job and rule by foreigners. My uncles and aunts had treated me as a sibling.

However, over the years, these bonds of affection, which had kept us together as a joint family, were torn apart by circumstance and upheavals all around us.

DELHI: A Tryst with Destiny

Momentous changes taking place in India impacted immigrants in Kenya. Indian calls for freedom would light a fire throughout Asia and Africa.

Britain, bankrupt and exhausted after the Second World War, had little appetite to hold on to India. A new viceroy, Earl Mountbatten, was dispatched to India in 1946, and immediately started negotiations with Indian leaders, including Mahatma Gandhi and Jawaharlal Nehru (both Hindus), who favored a single nation with equal rights for all religious minorities. Fearing oppression by the majority Hindus, Mohammed Ali Jinnah wanted a separate Muslim nation. Although the two communities had lived together in relative peace for centuries, there had been historical tensions.

The same year, mobs of Muslims attacked Hindu homes and shops in Calcutta, killing and maiming many. The riots spread to Bihar. Hindus retaliated. Gandhi, deeply saddened, traveled to villages and towns pleading for peace, but Muslim attendance at his meetings dropped dramatically. Bones and thorns were thrown on the path that the shoeless Gandhi would walk on.

Nehru, convinced there was no other option, reluctantly agreed to India's partition. It appeared that Gandhi was marginalized. Many Muslims were jubilant. The task of drawing new borders was left to Sir Cyril Radcliffe, a civil servant, who arrived from London just 36 days before the division was to occur. He had never been to India, knew little about it, and had a mandate to work within tight time frames. Part of Punjab, he decided, would now be in the new nation of Pakistan. Bengal would be bisected to create East Pakistan. Thus, the new and mostly Muslim territories of Pakistan flanked the predominantly Hindu India on each side like the wings of a bird, as described by Salman Rushdie in his book *Shame*.

The enormous haste resulted in one of the greatest tragedies humankind had ever witnessed.

The date for independence, initially planned for June 1948, was suddenly moved to August 1947, leaving just a few months for the transition. Mountbatten, strongly warned by some about possible bloodshed, did not budge. It is said that he was watching a Bob Hope movie with his wife on television on the eve of independence. The British began withdrawing their troops. Remaining soldiers watched from the sidelines as the massacres began.

On August 14, 1947, Pakistan "the land of the pure" hoisted its new green flag. Ironically, its founder did not follow many of the tenets of Islam. That same night, at the stroke of midnight, Jawaharlal Nehru, the first prime minister of independent India, spoke in Delhi.

Long years ago we made a tryst with destiny and now the time comes when we shall redeem our pledge. At the stroke of the midnight hour, when the world sleeps, India will awaken to life and freedom. A moment comes, which comes but rarely in history, when we step out from the old to the new, when an age ends, and when the soul of a nation, long suppressed, finds utterance...

It was considered one of the greatest speeches of the 20th century. The new tricolor was raised with much pomp as the British flag came down. Millions thronged to hear Nehru, a handsome man with his traditional red rose in the lapel of his *achkan*, as he spoke in English. There were great visions of restoring the lost glory of India.

Those dreams were shattered when millions of refugees fled. Hindus and Muslims began a long trek on foot, by train, and on bullock carts — in opposite directions — to find shelter with people of their own faith. People died drinking water from poisoned wells. Rations ran out; many dropped from sheer exhaustion. Orphans lay abandoned by the roadside. Trains with the corpses of slaughtered passengers arrived at railway stations in India and Pakistan. Strangers killed strangers. Neighbors killed neighbors. Countless millions were homeless, injured, or dead. Hindu mobs spared men with intact foreskin and killed the circumcised. Muslims did the opposite. Sikh soldiers, concerned about protecting their religion, families, and way of life, provided weapons and training to their neighbors in Punjab. Sikh mobs evicted Muslims from their homes in India. Some Sikhs fathers stranded in Rawalpindi, Pakistan, beheaded their daughters fearful of abductions, rape or forcible conversions. Hindu families in Lahore, a highly liberal cosmopolitan city, worried that the city would cede to the Muslims, packed up and left for safer havens in India.

Nisid Hajari, in his book Midnight Furies, wrote: "Gangs of killers set whole villages aflame, hacking to death men and children and the aged while carrying off young women to be raped. Some British Soldiers and journalists who had witnessed the Nazi death camps claimed Partition's brutalities were worse: pregnant women had their breasts cut off and babies hacked out of their bellies; infants were found literally roasted on spits."

There were far fewer stories about people protecting each other. Many who wished to migrate could not. Religious minorities became trapped in nations in which they did not feel safe.

Britain had abdicated its responsibility for a safe transition. Their ineptitude, and the thoughtless lines they drew on pieces of paper, dismembered an entire subcontinent. Perhaps nowhere in the annals of stupidity did one nation do more harm to another than during this partition. Winston Churchill's prediction that Indians would not be able to rule themselves became a reality due to the callous incompetence of his country's leaders. Gandhi, Nehru and Jinnah, all lawyers trained in Britain, watched helplessly as their followers killed each other.

The British had never truly cared for the people they had ruled. Their gilded castles and tall towers held the jewels stolen from India. When they had no further use for its colony, it was discarded like an old shoe — tattered, disfigured, and worn-out by centuries of abuse. They planted the seeds of religious hate within the population and postponed, for decades, the hopes and aspirations of a free India.

Many Hindus were enraged. Gandhi's pacifism was blamed for the division, destruction, and death and he was particularly reviled by the paramilitary Rashtriya Swayamsevak Sangh (RSS), a national self-service and unity movement, and the Hindu Mahasabha.

We did not know this at the time, but the RSS was to become a part of our lives in Nairobi.

****

It was a typical cold but sunny day in New Delhi on January 30, 1948. Gandhi, accompanied by an assistant on each side but no bodyguards, began his slow morning walk around the Birla Gardens. People bowed in reverence. Crowds parted to make way for the trio. A nervous man approached with folded hands. He bent down as though to touch the Mahatma's feet. Suddenly, shots rang out. Gandhi collapsed to the ground.

Nathuram Godse, a Maharashtrian, and a member of the Hindu Mahasabha and the RSS, had pumped three bullets into Mahatma Gandhi's chest. The great apostle of peace was no more. It was alleged that the assassin and his accomplices had met Veer Savarkar earlier that January to plot the murder.

Godse was hanged for the murder.

Most people refute rumors that the killer was an alcoholic, insane, or brainwashed. Many shared Godse's rage related to the division of India and the appeasement of Muslims. He never apologized, and some in India consider him a patriot and a hero. Every year, a small celebration is held in Pune to commemorate his "bravery" and sacrifice. Sweets are distributed. A small group of Hindus overtly proposes building a temple to honor him.

Savarkar—a former president of the Hindu Mahasabha, a fiery orator, and former inmate in a British prison in the Andaman Islands—was acquitted of conspiracy charges for a lack of evidence. The RSS was banned in India, but oddly it took root in Kenya.

Dada had translated Savarkar's autobiography, *Majhi Janmathep,* in 1932, from Marathi into Gujarati. He did not share any opinion about the assassination—or the assassin—with us. I believe (but cannot speak for the rest of the family) that he'd had second thoughts about civil disobedience and sympathized with the RSS. This transformation had a huge effect on our family.

He enrolled us in a branch of the RSS called the Shivaji Shakha. I found a deep contradiction in this decision. However, we were not in the habit of questioning decisions made by our elders, and dutifully attended the weekly sessions. We learned that the *lathi,* a wooden stave, was to be used for self-defense and to protect the integrity of the nation and our religion.

The walking stick used by Gandhi, by implication, was essentially an orthopedic device for the weak. Interestingly, many Gujarati members of the RSS revered Gandhi, a fellow Gujarati, and yet could embrace the militant movement with ease. I found that very odd.

We were told that joining the RSS was good for our health, would instill a sense of purpose and discipline, and was a service to India. Dada did not tell us that the organization had been banned for a while. We awoke at 4:00 AM on Sundays to march toward a playing field a mile away. Someone had arranged for us to wear khaki shorts, white shirts, and white caps. *Lathis* were also provided. In all the years I attended those meetings, I never knew who our enemies were. There was no anti-Muslim or anti-Gandhi rhetoric. Our job was to get there, exercise, and listen to brief speeches about Indian patriots, and to defend ourselves against an unknown enemy. Women were not permitted to join. After all, it was the men's job to protect our womenfolk.

Astoundingly, Nairobi had three branches of the RSS, each named after great Indian warriors, all of whom had fought Muslim invaders.

At the meetings, we saluted the Indian flag, sang its national anthem, and did the *surya namaskar* (a prayer to the sun), followed by other physical activities. One Sunday, there was a competition to see who could do the most sit-ups. We sweated, moaned, and groaned until agonizing cramps drove most to the sidelines. Then there were only two left. I remember the clapping, cheering, and chanting. Then a sudden blackout!

The panicked group had carried me a mile to our second-story apartment. I remained unconscious for several hours. The good Dr. Patwardhan, a staunch RSS man himself, was called to serve a fallen *sevak*. He advised rest and observation. There was not much else we could have done anyway. The family kept a silent vigil most of the night. A moratorium was placed on feuds at home.

Several hours later, when the sun had not quite risen and the rooster had not yet crowed, my sensorium cleared and I heard a hum of humanity rising from the concrete courtyard below. The entire Shivaji Shakha had come to pray for me. They had been there for hours, anticipating terrible news. The days of modern medicine and technology had not yet arrived, and the few good hospitals were unavailable to Indians and Africans. Expectant observation and prayer substituted for what would now be considered utterly inadequate care.

I tried to sit up, but flopped back into bed. Ecstatic family members helped me to stand. Groggy, I took a look through the window at the crowd below. The soft murmur of prayers erupted into a cheer.

"Anand-ji, Anand-ji, Anand-ji!" they yelled, waking up startled neighbors and frightening the curious mongrel dogs, who put their tails between their legs and ran as far as they could.

I had earned their respect through sheer grit that day by being the second best in the sit-up competition. Most people thought I was a Bhagwat. That never bothered me, but it felt good that the Panwalker name, tarnished by addiction and bankruptcy, now had a little luster returned to it.

MURDER AND MAU MAU

In 1952, we were stunned one morning to learn that a young Indian man and his wife had been killed, chopped up with sharp machetes, and stuffed into a large wooden barrel. Body parts hung out over the edges of the container. Nothing was stolen. It was presumed that Mau Mau committed the murder. The alternate theory was that it was a murder–suicide.

Mr. P, the man's father-in-law — our tailor, photographer, and supplier of miscellaneous things — was inconsolable. The fact that he was a scoundrel who fleeced people by selling them too much cloth did not diminish our sympathy for him. He used to plead that bell-bottoms, the latest craze, required more cloth. When Dada implied that he preferred simplicity, the tailor sulked. He would do whatever was asked of him, but he did not want the Bhagwat family to look like newly arrived peasants from India; his reputation was at stake. He invariably won.

Each year, Mr. P went to India for a few weeks to buy "high-quality cloth" and other supplies, but there was a year when his trip was considerably longer. Turned out he had been imprisoned for tax evasion, fraud, and circumvention of Indian laws. He insisted the Indian authorities had punished him for refusing to pay bribes. Almost no one believed that he was capable of such high principles.

He now cut a pathetic figure. His wife wept silently. It was surreal. The bodies in the barrel brought home the realization that life in Kenya had become dangerous.

Mau Mau wanted to drive white settlers out of Kenya. The uprising in Kenya had begun in August 1951, when reports emerged about secret meetings of predominantly Kikuyu tribesmen. Attacks on white settlers, previously unheard of, made headlines in the *East African Standard*. A curfew was imposed in Nairobi a year later, and the movement of Africans was severely restricted. The governor declared a state of emergency, which was not lifted until 1960.

Chief Waruhui, a Kikuyu who spoke out against the organization, was speared to death. This led to repressive measures by the British. Mau Mau retaliated. More troops landed at the Royal Air Force base at Eastleigh Airport. We saw large trucks carrying uniformed white men in red berets speeding toward an unknown destination. A friend said the guns with attached knives were called "buy-your-nets." (He of course meant bayonets.) Another sage, who claimed to know everything, said that the men were Royal Fusiliers from Lancashire.

Everyone was home before dusk.

The British suspected that Jomo "Burning Spear" Kenyatta, the 63-year-old Kikuyu school principal, was the brains behind Mau Mau. A colorful character, he had spent years in London, Birmingham, and Moscow. He was extremely critical of the occupation of Kenya's most fertile land by white settlers.

His admirers called him "*Mzee*," a word meaning respected elder. The British, wary of his growing influence, imprisoned him in October 1952. He was sent to a remote town called Kapenguria to isolate him from his people. However, this move backfired and instead galvanized the nation. He became the symbol of the freedom movement.

Black soldiers of the Kenya African Rifles, working with the Lancashire Fusiliers and under the command of white officers, engaged in torture, rape, dismemberment, and executions. One of those soldiers was Idi Amin, who would terrorize Uganda in later years. Thousands of Africans died during the Mau Mau insurgency. But they did not make the headlines in local newspapers. The front page was reserved for the far fewer white (or, to a lesser extent, brown) deaths.

I saw Kenyatta at close range at an RSS camp just before his incarceration. The Commissioner General Apasaheb Pant, representing the newly independent Republic of India, had brought Kenyatta to this camp. We, the brown-skinned Indians of British Kenya, gave Kenyatta a rousing welcome. The tall, fair, and handsome envoy walked hand in hand with the shorter, stocky, and black African revolutionary, both freedom fighters. We clapped until our palms hurt and screamed for freedom. They smiled and waved. It was unforgettable.

It is not widely known that Indians initiated and participated actively in the struggle for Kenyan freedom. I learned the details from the lectures given by our family friend Sharad Rao, an eminent lawyer and jurist. In 1933, Giridharilal Vidyarthi, the editor of the *Colonial Times*, was imprisoned for the slogan "Frank, Free and Fearless." In 1950, Makhan Singh was sent to prison for demanding "Uhuru sasa" (freedom now). He served 11 years in prison. Pio Gama Pinto, a charismatic friend and confidant of Kenyatta, was imprisoned as well and became a trusted advisor to the future President Kenyatta. Sadly, Pinto was assassinated in the prime of his life, caught in a web of political intrigue.

Pant, a Maharashtrian prince from the state of Aundh, was closely connected to the Marathi community in Nairobi. His wife, Nalinitai, was our family surgeon and took out my mother's appendix. As children, my friends and I had played ping-pong with the ambassador's son and daughter.

The British, greatly upset about the commissioner's unambiguous support for Kenyatta, forced the Indian government to recall him. Despite that history, India appointed him as its new ambassador to London some years later.

I had a memorable meeting with him in 1968.

****

Sir Evelyn Baring arrived as the Governor–General of Kenya in 1953, and announced that anyone administering the oath of the Mau Mau would be sentenced to death. The same year, another white settler was killed. Areas where the Kikuyu lived were cordoned off, and their movement was restricted even further.

In 1954, the Mau Mau burned down the famous tourist place called Treetops Lodge near Nyeri.

Two years later, two English boys were killed. The children of expatriates had never been targeted previously. The conflict had assumed a new and dangerous dimension.

The number of Africans killed in the nine-year conflict from 1951–1960 numbered in the thousands, although precise numbers vary based on the source. Countless others were imprisoned and tortured. Both sides committed atrocities. By 1959, most of the Mau Mau leaders — including Dedan Kimathi and "General China" — had been captured, killed in jungle battles, or executed. Others had escaped. The movement fizzled out.

Our elders must have been afraid too, but they allowed us to grow and play without many restrictions. We continued to walk to school unescorted. In general, we believed that the bad stuff happened to others.

DAR ES SALAM, Tanganyika

Four years after we had separated, my father went to Dar es Salam to work for a Swedish import/export company. His office was just off the beautiful beach and harbor. He was able to persuade my mother by letter to join him again after so many years apart. She debated the plan extensively, since she had already put in 11 years in the teaching job, which would give her a lifelong pension when she retired.

We were to live with Doctor Kaka, who had recently moved from Moshi to Dar es Salam. He was now the physician for the Aga Khan Clinic. The arrangement seemed beneficial for everyone.

We took off from Embakasi Airport on a cold Nairobi morning in June 1954. My mother and I had never been in a plane before. The small plane rose, pierced the white clouds, and leveled off. My 11-year-old eyes remained glued to the window. The clouds dissipated as we flew southeast. I kept a lookout for wild animals, even though common sense dictated that we would see none at this altitude.

Suddenly, Kilimanjaro appeared like a framed photograph on our right. My jaw dropped. I yelled, "Look, look!" embarrassing my mother and startling the sleepy European passengers. The pristine white snow at the peak sparkled in the sun. Massive gray glaciers lay awkwardly within the crater. The majesty of the mountain stunned me. This was the mountain my father had seen when he first arrived in Africa to become the manager of a coffee plantation. I took a photograph with my Kodak box camera.

We flew over the plains bypassing Lake Manyara, where lions climbed trees, upsetting the cheetahs and frightening the baboons. The landscape became more barren as the coastline of Tanganyika came into view. Coconut palms swayed gently in the breeze. The plane descended gracefully onto a narrow strip, and then the tires screeched as we came to an unceremonious halt, with profuse apologies from the captain. My mother made a Herculean effort to contain her retching.

Figure 6: Aerial View of Kilimanjaro (1954)

We were greeted with warm smiles by my father, Baba, whom I had not seen for five years and Doctor Kaka, whom I had never met before. There was little fanfare or melodrama. My father looked much thinner and darker.

Doctor Kaka was kind and soft-spoken. He was a bit taller than my father (who was almost 5"10'), built like an ox, with broad shoulders, and sported a crew cut with graying hair and a thin moustache. He smiled at me, surprising my parents. Beneath that smile, however, there appeared to be a longing, a hurt. He had been lonely, and the only people he spoke to were his patients. He had no time to make friends and was socially awkward. His gentle pat on my shoulder suggested that he cared. He was the brother of a grandfather whom I would never meet. It was special.

My mother and I felt at home, although the three-room apartment was dark, drab, and dusty and the furniture old and sparse. We cleaned the place up, exchanged the old bulbs for brighter ones, and bought new curtains. The barely used kitchen had few utensils. A kettle, a pan, and some plates, glasses, and cheap cutlery were all he needed for his occasional meals at home. There was no food in the house. Refrigerators had not yet entered Indian homes. Dining out, even if there had been an Indian restaurant in the area, was frowned upon.

Doctor Kaka asked me one evening to pull a large book off the top shelf of a bookcase. It was heavy and dusty and the pages had yellowed. Tiny silvery insects with flat chests the size of small caterpillars crawled out briskly from the pages and fell to the ground. Their slumber interrupted, they quickly slid under the chairs and carpets. I sneezed repeatedly, frightening the silver creatures even more. Doctor Kaka said he had studied this book as a medical student and suggested I look at the drawings and diagrams in this ancient copy of *Gray's Anatomy*, the title barely visible along the spine.

The doctor said he had grown up destitute and was privileged to attend medical school. By this time, I was convinced that every person in India was dirt-poor. He was evidently a self-made man whose family had few resources to support him. I was not sure why he was telling me all this, especially since he was a man of few words.

My father observed this bond that he had never been able to forge with his son. He had never heard his uncle speak so eloquently and with such passion. There was no boasting, just a statement of facts. My admiration for this man grew as I listened to him, fascinated.

Gray's Anatomy is an excruciatingly boring book. I saw bones, muscles, and blue-red channels that carried blood here and there. I did wonder why people had two sets of eyes, ears, kidneys, legs, and arms but just one nose, gall bladder, liver, spleen, and penis. My eyes widened at pictures of the female body. I had no idea they were so different. I wondered why we needed hair in places no one could see. I could understand the benefit of hair in the nose and ear to keep dust and pollen out. And if hair was good, why did men shave each day?

Wanting to impress him, I pretended to read the book whenever he was around or when I heard his car pull up. I wanted him to know that I was a good and obedient boy. He nodded and smiled. Soon everyone was convinced that I wanted to be a doctor just like him. Mild-mannered and immersed in his work, he never did anything to hurt our feelings. One of his sons, Shashi, somewhat older than me, also moved to Dar es Salam from Bombay and embraced me as a friend and family member.

In the evenings, after a full day in the clinic, Doctor Kaka always asked if I wanted to join him for his house calls, which was flattering. Soon enough, I knew the routine and stood at the door with his black bag, which contained his stethoscope, syringes, scissors, scalpels, rolled-up bandages, a few white pills and powders, and a rather large hammer with a rubber mallet. I did not know why doctors needed to carry such weapons.

He drove a large black car. We kept the windows open so we could feel the cool ocean breeze on our faces. Sometimes we went as far as the end of Oyster Bay, a stunning beach, which curved around the coastline for miles.

His patients, gentle Khoja Ismailia Muslims, were followers of the Aga Khan and from the same sect of Islam as the founder of Pakistan, Mohammed Ali Jinnah. I saw the healing touch of this unassuming man and the gratitude in the eyes of those he healed and treated with great compassion. They in turn showered him with gifts and praise. They loved this doctor. If they had met during the Partition of India, these individuals, in the heat of the moment, might have slaughtered each other.

We were welcomed warmly in each home. While he examined the sick family member, I was given a tray full of sliced mango, papaya, bananas, dates, grapes, or biscuits along with refreshing juice or coconut water. This happened in every home. My appetite was voracious and food was my weakness. I did not mind how many homes we needed to visit. I was always game — and always hungry!

I was enormously proud that he let me carry his black bag. No words were spoken, but we were comfortable in each other's company. I guessed he was at least 60 years old. The faded *Gray's Anatomy* textbook, the evening rounds, and the obvious affection his patients expressed for him profoundly influenced my decision to become a doctor.

I vowed one day to carry a similar bag. Doctor Kaka became my idol, my role model, and my first guru.

****

The Jangwani Primary School for Indian boys, segregated by race and gender, was situated near a creek. The classrooms were several huts with thatched roofs, each with an opening that served as the door. A dirt lane separated the huts from a stone building housing offices for the teachers and the principal and an examination hall.

One morning, a classmate let out a blood-curdling scream. He had seen a large green snake with whitish stripes. The reptile, perhaps four feet long, flicked its dark tongue as it slid skillfully along the rafters. We were transfixed. Panic took over when the creature decided to climb down one of the wooden support poles, smack in the middle of our desks. We made a run for the opening, the pot-bellied teacher not too far behind. Indeed, given the opportunity, he likely would have escaped first.

Its exit cut off by this horde of screaming Indians, the snake found an opening at the rear and rapidly slithered toward a grassy bank, leaving a track on the dusty ground, its green coated with brown dust.

We stood a safe distance away, surrounding the reptile. An African school aide arrived with a *panga* and, without any hesitation, severed its head. The head fell a few inches away from its still writhing back end. Irrational fear of this defenseless creature had resulted in its unnecessary slaughter. It was not necessary to kill the serpent. I remembered a story about a massive cobra that had once protected Lord Krishna during a storm and helped him cross a turbulent river to safety.

When all movement had ceased, curious students came closer but dared not touch the two lifeless pieces. Someone said snakes can pretend to be dead. Once the two reptilian body parts were safely disposed of in a trash can, we trickled back into the hut, glancing warily at the roof to make sure there were no snake siblings out to avenge the unnecessary murder of their loved green one.

****

Math, science, history, and geography were taught in Gujarati. I did very well in school, topping the class in every test. The family was together and happy, and I had many friends. One of them, Ashok Jamenis, and I sometimes walked to the beach to sit under a palm tree. A favorite sport was to see how far we could throw pebbles into the ocean and whether we could make them bounce off the water. We loved to glide over the silvery sandbanks into the blue ocean on sleds made from fallen coconut palm trunks and fronds. This was one of the happiest periods of my life.

****

One hot summer day, while walking aimlessly along the beach, I caught a glimpse of the ninth Sultan of Zanzibar. Originally from Muscat, Oman, the sultanate had transferred its capital to Zanzibar in the 19th century. This man had ruled Zanzibar and a 10-mile coastal strip in Kenya and Tanganyika since 1911.

He had arrived from Zanzibar by sea in his private motorized yacht instead of a dhow his ancestors used. I did not know his name then, but know now that he was Sayyid Sir Khalifa bin Harub Al-Said, who was to rule for 49 years until his death in 1960.

His motorcade made its way slowly and deliberately along the road that ran parallel to the palm-fringed coastline of the lovely harbor. I imagined he owned a second palace nearby, but I had not seen any. He was no more than 10 feet from where I stood. The first sultan I had ever seen, he could have been a character from *Ali Baba and the Forty Thieves*. Tall and thin, he wore a turban laced with shiny diamonds. His graying beard matched his flowing white robe and colorful sashes. He wore a pair of glasses that seemed too large for his thin face. He sat ramrod straight on a throne-like chair in his limousine with an open top. I could not see his royal feet or socks.

I had expected a large entourage, loud music, a harem of women in *burkhas* and veils, and a convoy of expensive cars. But there were just two cars and no women. The crowds were sparse and unenthusiastic, but he waved anyway, just as I had seen Arab kings do in the movies. People who reciprocated did so halfheartedly, out of courtesy rather than respect. Most did not know who the man was and did not care. The limousine moved at a snail's pace to allow his subjects, many of them descendants of slaves, to pay homage. Any disappointment at the tepid response did not register on his face.

I imagined Arabs coming in their *dhows*, paying local Indian traders to go inland with black middlemen to capture black slaves for them so they could be sold in foreign markets. The vision of thousands of shackled men and women, whipped, torn away from their villages and families by armed men, rowing large ships toward the market in Zanzibar where they would be sold, if still alive, made me very angry. The prosperity of Arab and European nations was created by the oppression of people like me—colored, poor, and unarmed. His opulent life was fed by the misery of slaves his ancestors had captured. The sultan had no way to know then that four years after his death in 1960, angry African mobs would go hunting for his descendants.

****

Folks in the coastal strip spoke fluent Swahili, a hybrid combination of Arabic and Bantu. One of my unpaid tutors was the servant's son. No one bothered to ask him his real name. He was simply called *Mtoto,* meaning a child. Though younger than me, we bonded immediately and spent hours together on hot afternoons when others were taking siestas.

With an exceptional talent for carving, he built a small wooden boat from a log he found nearby. His sharp knife moved deftly as he hummed an African song I did not recognize, and he neatly set aside the fine wood shavings. From scrap material, he whittled a mast and sails. An hour later, I beheld a gorgeous, miniature Arab *dhow*. I envied his skill and confidence.

I tried to do the same, but my effort fell far short. My boat was unlikely to float. Seeing my admiration for his artwork, Mtoto told me to hold on to it until he returned the next day. Even though he did not gloat, he was immensely pleased with himself. It had been so effortless for him. He declared that we would take the boats to the beach the next day.

That evening, in an unforgivable fit of envy, I set his boat on fire. The wood got charred, the sails were half burned, and the mast crumbled to the floor in an ugly black heap.

He returned the next day, excited. His eyes wandered to the remains of his boat. I had made no effort to hide my crime. His eyes, brimmed with tears, turned toward me with a silent accusation. I looked down, feeling awful. He was inconsolable. Now his face contorted in grotesque ways. Huge tears trickled down his ebony cheeks from his large and expressive black eyes. He sobbed uncontrollably. I tried to reach out, but he pushed me away, the hurt too deep and the injury to our friendship beyond repair.

His elderly father stepped out, took a quick look, shook his head slightly as he hugged and consoled his child. As they walked away, the father's hands on the child's shoulder, the boy shuddered, and gripped his father tightly. As servants, they had no recourse against the actions of the doctor's grandnephew.

My family heard the commotion, saw what had happened. Doctor Kaka ran after the boy, hugged him, and apologized, patting his head and whispering into the whimpering boy's ears. Looking to his father for permission, Mtoto accepted the 10-shilling note—a fortune.

Wedged between his father and his father's employer, he calmed down. I had breached a significant bond of friendship and trust, and got the silent treatment that day. Deeply ashamed, I apologized repeatedly. My family was extremely disappointed. These were not the values they had instilled in me. This transgression was my personal weakness; it would haunt me forever. My Swahili remained imperfect.

****

Baba remained sober. I am not sure what he did for the Swedish company. We had now been in Tanganyika for six months and, except for the sailboat incident, everything was going well. Our lives were normal again. My mother had adjusted to life as a homemaker. Doctor Kaka was grateful for the warm meals and company at dinnertime. He had obviously forgiven me for burning the boat and continued to ask me along for his evening rounds. I had feared that he would withdraw that privilege.

Indians of Maharashtrian origin had bought a small building with a concrete courtyard, which served as a meeting place and club. Nearby was Dhavale's ice cream shop, which offered two flavors: mango and vanilla. When we could not afford the ice cream, we settled for the free and unlimited ice-cold water. However, that practice stopped after an unpleasant experience.

A friend had dared me to drink five tall glasses of water in five minutes. Not one to shy away from a challenge, I accepted. The water caused an instant and unpleasant brain freeze, a strange headache that yielded to dizziness, loss of balance, and a frightening premonition of death. My mind was a blur. I felt I was falling rapidly and tottered toward a broken chair, hanging on for dear life. The feeling passed as suddenly as it had come. My vision cleared. My friends soon assumed their normal voices, shapes, and sizes. I had just experienced the body's incredible ability to adjust to a severe electrolyte imbalance.

The Pandit family owned a sports shop, where they sold tennis and badminton rackets, hockey sticks, shuttlecocks, balls, and bats. Window shopping was free. The owner, a Maharashtrian woman, tiring of our pitiful gaze day in and out, gave each of us a free badminton racket and three shuttlecocks. I learned that day that if you stared long enough at the object of your desire, you could get it, because there is compassion in every human heart.

There was an unwritten rule that boys did not mingle or socialize with girls. It was simply not done. Unaware of the existence of hormones, sex, or how babies came to be, we were nonetheless attracted to young female teenagers in the club, especially the three Thakur sisters. All eyes followed them as they walked in. They appeared taller than they were, regal in their colorful saris with their shiny, long black hair flowing down the back. They glided across the courtyard like graceful gazelles, their skin fair and flawless. We stared in wonder, making sure no one caught us. If the girls noticed, they did not say anything. For the most part, they ignored us.

At some point, we decided they were stuck-up, playing hard to get, and we stopped staring. I ran into one of the sisters in India many years later. Hearing of our childhood infatuation, she blushed and exclaimed, "But you were all so young!" She was still beautiful and was married to an Indian Air Force officer.

Ashok and I continued to visit the harbor and slide down the sandbanks on fronds of fallen coconut trees. Some evenings, families went to the harbor just to feel the cool air which carried the delightful fragrance of roasted *muhogo*, a potato-like tuber. Ships sailed in quietly but departed noisily, with black fumes arising from their chimneys and horns wailing, as though in protest of having to leave this idyllic place.

****

Nothing that good can last forever.

In December 1954, we assembled for the final sixth-grade math exam. It would be followed by a two-week break. The large exam room was just across the thatched huts, where we had witnessed the snake sliced in two. I was confident that I would once again top the class. I had an outstanding record. I found the test questions easy. There were no butterflies in my stomach.

The proctor, a teacher whom I had not seen before, paced up and down the rows to supervise. It was my intent to finish early and head for the beach. But that was not my destiny.

Chhagan, the burly bully and class dunce, sat right behind me. Before and during the test, he kicked my chair and "invited" me to share answers with him. I tried to ignore him, but he kept trying to draw my attention. His efforts became desperate. Just as I turned to ask him to stop, Mr. Prahlad approached us. I thought he would either warn

Chhagan or separate us. To my horror, he asked both of us to follow him to the principal's office. I protested loudly that I was almost done with the paper and had done nothing wrong. He announced to the principal, "They were copying."

We had always been taught that to cheat was a terrible sin. I had never done that. I could barely speak. Chhagan stood stoic, unfazed. He did not tell them I was innocent. I bit my lip to avoid crying. People would mock me. Our family name would be ruined.

The principal, relying on the teacher's word, expelled us both.

The school called Doctor Kaka to pick me up. He asked to see the exam papers. It was obvious that all my answers were correct and I was almost done. Chhagan had submitted a nearly blank sheet. Doctor Kaka's pleas were dismissed. The principal said it takes two to cheat. And rules are rules.

I hated the teachers. Doctor Kaka understood the finality of the decision, thanked the two men politely, and drove me home without a word. He did not look at me. I desperately wanted him to believe me. I had let him down. Was he angry? Had I broken his heart? My parents were devastated. They did not reprimand or console me. This lack of sympathy left an indelible mark on my well-being. I cried alone all night, my sobs muffled by the wet pillow.

NAIROBI AGAIN

A few days later, in early 1955, we packed our bags into a car that would take my mother and me back to Nairobi. It had been a brief, six-month sojourn. This time it was not my father but I who was responsible for the breakup.

My faith in an almighty God evaporated the day I was expelled. The God who had been my hero, whose stories I had read repeatedly, and who was a core of my Hindu being had abandoned me. The time spent reciting *shlokas* from the Gita, memorizing an entire chapter for a contest, reading the *"Ramayana"* and *"Mahabharata,"* had been a dreadful waste of time. I removed the images of Lord Krishna, Ram, and Sita from my room. They had all let me down. An innocent child who had suffered enough already, I did not want anything more to do with this God or any other. I wanted to be left alone. And if He did not leave me alone, well…I would leave Him.

I saw hypocrisy in every ritual, ceremony, and prayer in every temple, church, synagogue, and mosque.

I had hoped my elders would state explicitly that they believed me or explain, "This is a test of your resilience and strength." My mother said nothing. Not a word. I suffered alone. My integrity had been stolen from me by an unjust teacher and a principal.

My mother did not tell anyone what happened. It was too shameful, a truth to be buried forever. Perhaps she figured sharing that history might make it impossible for me to get into a good school in Nairobi. For the first time in my young life, I wondered, "Why me?"

I even thought of ending my life, but did not know how to do it. All the options frightened me.

****

My father remained in Dar es Salam so that at least one parent had a job. I was reenrolled in the seventh grade at the Desai Road

Primary School in Nairobi. My expulsion from Jangwani was not mentioned.

Finally, I was able to put that episode behind me. My grades remained good and my interest in extracurricular activities was rekindled. My parents did not make me feel guilty, ashamed, or unworthy. I felt they knew me well enough to know that I was a victim, not a villain. But I wished they had said that in so many words.

To this day, I feel an urge to find the teacher and principal at Jangwani to advise them of the injustice they perpetrated on an innocent child. They are certainly dead by now, but the indignant side of me continues to hope *May they rot in Hell forever.*

Nothing had changed at the school. Rules about speaking English remained intact. My head continued to do arithmetic in Gujarati. I found joy in learning; the teachers were good and extracurricular activities kept us busy. I was a happy child in school and sometimes also the class clown. I could get away with it because my grades remained excellent and the teachers knew my family.

The job my mother had held at the Duchess of Gloucester School (previously the Government Indian Girls' School) was now unavailable. So she joined the Arya Samaj Girls School, where Dada was the vice principal and my grandmother was a teacher. Arya Samaj is a sub sect of Hindus, who are mostly from Punjab. Her new job, we were to learn later, provided no long-term benefits such as a pension plan, and the salary was lower. She would teach math, English, and either history or geography to third-grade students. My mother always regretted the lack of a pension, which would have been helpful years later.

We were back in the joint family, who welcomed us warmly. We had matured, and the petty squabbles of old days were far less common. I progressed through the seventh grade without difficulty.

It was time to select a high school. The choice was between "technical" and "grammar" schools. The technical schools attracted those who wished to become engineers, craftsmen, builders, or architects. Those who chose medicine, law, or the arts generally chose the grammar schools.

The Duke of Gloucester School became my high school, where Bhau, my maternal uncle, had left a blazing trail of glory by winning the Kenya Open Scholarship, topping the scores of students of all races. In the era of apartheid, Bhau's achievement reminded us of Jesse Owens' victory at the Berlin Olympics in 1936, where Hitler — the most virulent racist of all — was disappointed to see a colored man win four races. This is the school where I developed lifelong friendships.

****

The first white people I ever saw at close range were our English teachers: Mr. Turnidge, a tall, unkempt, pompous red haired man with a big chip on his shoulder and Mr. Hood, a plump, kind, and gentle man who, during his energetic geography lessons, sprayed the class with ample amounts of spit. All other teachers were of Indian or Pakistani origin. After the Partition of India, they referred to all brown people as Asians rather than Indians.

Our uniform — gray trousers, white shirt, green tie with yellow stripes, and a green blazer — could not hide our Asian diversity and ancestry. An exceptional student leader got two extra yellow stripes on the blazer and the title of "prefect."

The day began with mandatory physical activity — running, jumping, cricket, soccer, or field hockey. In the evenings, we stayed behind to engage in an hour of non-mandatory sports. I never won a sports medal, but was often listed as one of the top 8 athletes in this school of over 600 hundred students.

Bhau attended some athletic meets to give me moral support. I knew that a dot in the distant stands was cheering me on. When I failed to win, he said, "You were selected out of 600, and that is so hard to do." He would then imitate a clumsy, inept athlete. We laughed, and all was well again.

Each year, the school held an awards ceremony for top students. The guest of honor was usually the wife of a senior British official. This year, it was the wife of the governor of Kenya, Sir Evelyn Baring, the man who had been posted to Kenya to eradicate Mau Mau. Hundreds of students had gathered in the courtyard where praise — and sometimes punishment — was delivered.

I recall bowing and receiving Victor Hugo's *Les Misérables* and Arthur Conan Doyle's *Sherlock Holmes* as the second-place prize for declamation and oratory. The tall woman in a flowery dress maintained a plastic smile throughout the entire ceremony.

She stretched her long arm, half covered with white gloves, to shake my hand. Cameras flashed. We were to smile and say, "Thank you, Your Excellency." We were not to linger. A small black-and-white photograph immortalized the moment and was available for purchase. This was the first time I had ever touched (or been touched by) a white woman, even though a pair of gloves had intervened. Were those white gloves a fashion statement, a matter of hygiene, or a barrier to prevent the touch of a colored hand? I had been forced to bow to a person whose race and rule had stolen my ancestors' freedom and caused the slaughter of millions. The brown teachers (with the exception of Mr. D.N. Khanna), in their desire to please the visitor, bent down so far that I thought they would lose balance, fall on their noses, and lie at her feet.

****

We feared our teachers. There were rumors that Mr. Khanna had suffered a personal tragedy during the Partition of India. He dressed immaculately in a dark suit and tie and spoke fluent English, caressing each word softly and clearly as though an errant pronunciation might cause grievous injury to the language. He was unusual in that he allowed us to choose the topic we wished to write about rather than impose one. He urged us to abandon caution, to write freely, without fear. This man commanded respect, pacing up and down with his head bowed and eyes focused on the floor, oblivious to the world. Sometimes he clenched his hands tightly behind his back and his knuckles turned white. That meant he was getting annoyed. Outside the classroom, he nodded briefly, without eye contact, when we greeted him. He sat alone during breaks.

One year, I wrote an essay on the world's population crisis with ideas borrowed freely from *Time* magazine, a habit learned from my father. The quotes (with proper attribution) made me look like a great scholar. The clincher was a mention of the Malthusian theory, which likely was unknown to anyone in the school, country, or continent. He held up the paper, with a score of 70% and three exclamation marks scrawled in red on the top right corner, and announced, "This is the highest score I have ever given to anyone." There was a smile on his thin lips. I almost burst with pride. I had crossed a threshold that had never been crossed before. Thereafter, I thought he smiled whenever I said, "Good morning, sir."

My love of the English language started here. That was odd, because I had deeply resented the fact that we were fined for speaking our mother tongues in school. I had hated speaking the language of those who had conquered India, beaten my grandfather, taken over all the good things in Kenya, and segregated us based on our skin color.

Mr. Chiplunkar, a Marathi teacher who knew my family, called me to the front of the class and told me that my score in math was pathetic, since it was not perfect. He said I needed to follow in the footsteps of my uncle Bhau, who had won the Kenya Open Scholarship, beating the scores of all students in Kenya. I promised to work harder. Word of my poor math score reached my mother. Before I could blink, my favorite sports sessions from 3:30-5:00 PM were canceled, and I ended up in the home of Mrs. Varma, who became my remedial math tutor. I was not happy.

The only way out was to improve my grades quickly. A tiny woman, she was quite stern. Were all Punjabi teachers brilliant yet strict? After each intense session, however, she brought me milk and cookies. How could someone to be so cold and mathematical yet so kind? I was grateful for the snack and wondered who paid for it. My scores did improve almost to perfection.

Through this experience, I learned a bitter lesson about our elders: they are never satisfied. If I got 96% on a test, they asked, "What happened to the other 4%?" It was impossible to please them. How about a pat on the back for my efforts? We were told that success was expected and failure was an opportunity to learn from our mistakes. There was no value in bragging about what we did well. (Many years later, I learned that this is a common theme in the safety culture of American hospitals. They call it "a healthy preoccupation with failure.")

Despite the spit spewing from his mouth, Mr. Hood taught me why rivers meander, why waterfalls recede, and how clouds form. Why the moon does what it does and why stars twinkle. He had a peculiar way of looking at everyone — and no one in particular — at the same time. Fascinated by his description of people and places, I could identify the chief export of every country and name its prime minister or the capital. Later, when the number of countries started increasing exponentially (usually through conflict), I lost interest.

I recalled how my father used to brag to guests how brilliant I was by asking me to spell *Czechoslovakia*. It was easy since we had rehearsed it a million times, but invariably made other children look less intelligent. This brought Baba immense joy. We watched for signs of approval from the now bored visitors who had heard all this before. I resolved one day to visit the place that no one could spell. When I did, I found they had split the country into two – the Czech Republic and Slovakia – to make the spelling easier for everyone. Luckily, they did not ask the British to draw the new borders.

Another Marathi teacher, who drank too much, taught geography, history, and current affairs. Naming the three non-aligned countries (Yugoslavia, Egypt, and India) was one exercise in his generally dull class. This teacher always stared straight at me when he spoke, in a monotone like the hum of a distant drone. He never had an unkind word for anyone. In a highly conservative society where interracial marriage was taboo, his wife made history by sleeping with her African servant and producing a child who did not resemble his three siblings. The teacher, always unkempt, sad, and stooped, disappeared one day. We heard he had died of shame (a euphemism for suicide) or from a broken heart, but I was never sure. The siblings brought up this mixed-race, brown and black child with love and kindness, in spite of the malicious stares of others.

One thing all Indian teachers had in common was resentment that Mr. Turnidge had been promoted to vice principal in spite of his short tenure and "lower" qualifications. They grumbled about "that unkempt, no talent Englishman with shabby suits and bad teeth." In his presence, they said "yes, sir" and "no, sir," for no brown man ever called a white man by his first name. The principal who allowed the promotion, they said, was looking out for his own hide or under pressure from higher authorities.

Mr. Turnidge adored Winston Churchill, the wartime leader who was generally disliked by Indians. We thought he was sloppy, arrogant, and fat, drank too much, and smoked stinking cigars. Not to mention that he was racist and opposed Indian independence. This man believed that Indians were buffoons with a "beastly religion" incapable of governing themselves and that Gandhi was a "naked *fakir*." The British, after looting India's treasures, were now stealing our words too. Words like *fakir*, bazaar, and thug.

We reluctantly agreed that Churchill's speeches, especially the one about "blood, toil, tears and sweat," were really good. The sentence about "fighting in the hills" — and everywhere else — came second. We knew the chap had saved Britain from defeat during the Second World War, but we were sure victory was the result of the two million Indian soldiers and the loot from India, rather than his words. Also, we were angry that the British had diverted food for their soldiers while millions of Indians starved to death during a famine in Bengal. Shashi Tharoor, in his book *Inglorious Empire*, published in 2017, wrote about Churchill's despicable role in creating conditions that led to the mass starvation.

William Shakespeare was forced upon us. There were rumors that the bard did not really exist. Or that someone else had written the stories for him. Similarly, a student claimed that he was the reincarnation of Kalidasa, a famous Hindu writer from centuries ago, who wrote in a language very few understood.

Indians have a unique way of connecting everything wonderful to India. Take the word *pushpak*, meaning airplane. Mentioned in ancient mythology, it was deemed as evidence that Indians had flown planes centuries before the steam engine was invented. Armies were transported rapidly by air, from North India to what is now Sri Lanka, to conquer demons who had abducted Lord Ram's wife, Sita. Why then do they show Lord Hanuman flying through the air without an aircraft? If the Chinese had not beaten us to it, we would have bragged we were the first to make ice cream or spaghetti.

And who had ever heard anyone speak like the characters in Shakespeare's plays? Even the English did not talk like that. We entered competitions where we were asked to stand on stage, raise a pretend dagger, and in our squeaky voices shout to an audience of bewildered Indian parents: "Is this a dagger I see before me…?" Of course, it was a dagger!

It was ludicrous to have these kids, some wearing turbans, make such ridiculous speeches. Worse, we were given a test to prove that we had understood what was said. Also imposed upon us were Macbeth and his nasty wife, the witches and their brew, Hamlet and his misery. We did like Romeo and Juliet, but thought that Indian movies had better love stories, songs, and dances. Indian women were prettier, especially when they wore saris and wove fragrant flowers into their long hair. We would rather read about *Laila Majnu* or *Heer Ranjha* - our precursors to Romeo and Juliet with the added ring of fact rather than fiction.

We were taught in school about the slave trade, but the emphasis was on how the British had been the first to abolish it. Always putting a spin on their evil deeds! We learned about a man named Stanley meeting another explorer near some lake in Tanganyika and asking, "Dr. Livingston, I presume?" when he damn well knew it was David Livingston.

I was bored to tears reading about Oliver Cromwell and the royals, who were somehow all related. Lacking imagination, all the kings were called William, George, Richard, or Charles and the queens were Mary or Elizabeth, with a single Victoria. They were a rather violent bunch, chopping heads off in the Tower of London. But rather than feeling shame, they made it a tourist spot!

They did not even have the decency to bury a king, one of the Richards, in a better place than under a future concrete parking lot, from where he would be unceremoniously dug up centuries later.

Then there was the fellow Sir Walter Raleigh, who ruined a perfectly good robe by throwing it over a puddle so his queen's shoes and gown would not get splashed with mud. All the monarch had to do was walk a few steps around the puddle. Such a flatterer the gallant knight was, and such were our travails, to read about the obvious, the mundane, and the uninteresting.

****

Hundreds of students in uniform stood quietly in neat rows in the school's central courtyard each morning. The Romans would have been proud. The principal summarized all the bad things we had been caught doing during the previous 24 hours and issued dire warnings about future infractions. Punishment was usually detention after class. The ultimate rebuke was being called to apologize at a school assembly. Rarely, someone was singled out for praise for exceptional academic brilliance or leadership.

We were forced to recite "God Save the Queen" on special occasions, such as when a British dignitary was visiting. Most Indian teachers, forgetting that their motherland was now free, became subservient, many bowing to the white dignitaries more deeply than necessary. Some students routinely substituted the word *save* with *shave*. If the dignitaries noticed, they probably assumed Indians could not differentiate between *sss* and *shh*, which was indeed true for some

Bengalis and Gujaratis. In reality, this was our defiance of the British Empire!

One year, the principal announced a field trip to greet the Queen Mother, one of the Elizabeths, who was on an official visit. We were herded like cattle into buses and taken to the agriculture grounds. The stadium was filled with children from every school in Kenya. This was the first time I could recall students from white, brown, and black schools coming together, but we stood in pavilions separated by race. We had been told to shout and cheer as the motorcade entered the grounds and to escalate the noise level when the car reached our pavilion. The event would last less than 10 seconds. They said that if the Queen Mother turned her head and acknowledged the Duke of Gloucester High School, we would get the following day off.

We were willing to do almost anything to get a day off. Initially, she waved to no one in particular, in the manner unique to kings, queens, and sultans. However, as the car approached our stand, perhaps alarmed by the amount of noise we made, she turned her royal head toward us. Seeing only jubilant schoolboys, Her Majesty's brown subjects in green blazers, she simply smiled as the motorcade proceeded to the next section, which was definitely not as boisterous. Our Indian teachers puffed out their chests in pride, eagerly seeking praise from their British supervisors, who acknowledged the effort with curt nods and deeper puffs on their pipes.

We should have had a day off, but did not. They had tricked us. Here I was—the grandson of Indian freedom fighters, a teenage supporter of Kenyan independence—cheering on those who had put my grandparents in prison! The British could not even keep their promise of a day off to youngsters who had screamed in vain to welcome their monarch's mother.

****

Bhau returned to Nairobi with an engineering degree from a British University in 1954, and joined an English firm. His marriage was arranged to Nalini, a 16-year-old high-school graduate, tall and beautiful, fair and freckled, and an accomplished cook. She was the daughter of Mr. Amrite, who had discarded the drums Anil now owned. To the elders, she was Nalu, but we called her Nalutai, the term *tai* meaning sister. The union of this handsome pair predictably produced two beautiful daughters, Asha and Varsha. I remained the only male grandchild in the home until Prakash was born to Bhau and Nalutai some years later.

The joint family, now a bit more prosperous, moved to a large bungalow in Parkland, a nice middle-class Asian area, to make room for the growing clan. Dada bought a white Ford Prefect, but repeatedly failed the driver's test. The man who had not feared brutal British beatings was petrified by the prospect of being in the driver's seat. Thus Bhau became the sole licensed driver in the family. We developed a scientific method to figure out how to fit the entire family in this vehicle. Laps of older children served as seats for the youngest. The car, dangerously overloaded, groaned as it grudgingly climbed the numerous hills in the area.

This was a household with much laughter, many pranks, ravenous appetites, and lots of music. Each day was an adventure, and we could not have been happier. We decided to get a puppy, a German shepherd we named Mastan. Loved by all, he grew more rapidly than anticipated and infringed on the limited space we had indoors, so we started keeping him outside on the veranda. The weather was always pleasant, so we did not think this was cruel, although his drooping tail and forlorn expression said otherwise.

Figure 7: Bhagwat-Panwalker Joint Family, Front row: Asha, Subhash, Mira, Second row: Bhau, my mother, Sudha, and Nalutai, Third row: Anil (holding Varsha), Dada and Mai, Fourth row: Author and Sharad

One night, we were awakened by a shrill sound we had never heard before. It pierced the quietness of the starry night. Mastan was surrounded by six spotted hyenas, which had strayed from the nearby forest. These deadly predators are not afraid to fight wounded lions and even elephants. They move in packs and rapidly tear the flesh from their prey in a feeding frenzy until just the bare bones remain. Easily identified by the dirty spots on their fur and their distinctive limp due to longer front legs, the animals are greatly feared, yet fearless.

Saliva dripped from their hungry mouths, exposing long pink tongues. Their tails stood straight up as they menacingly advanced inch by inch toward our pet. Mastan bared his teeth, snarling and whimpering at the same time, his tail securely wedged between his hind legs. His ears fell flat against his tense and stiff fur, eyes fully dilated. The hyenas took one step forward, and one back, all the time keeping a respectable distance. This dance continued until Mastan was cornered and exhausted.

As we peered through the window at the gallant battle being waged, Dada waved his short plump arms with threatening gestures and made grotesque sounds never heard before in this household. We did not dare go outside. We gathered flashlights, sticks, and knives and clanged pots and pans. Our collective yelling, screaming, and show of force scared the hyenas away, their tails now lodged between their hind legs. We were all shaken up, but we had proved that spotted hyenas are no match for frightened, screaming Indians and their dog.

Mastan, tremulous and still whimpering, gave us a "see what you have done" look and took his indoor corner again. His tail began to wag again, but the accusation of abandonment in his eyes did not leave until the following day. His demeanor reminded me of the dog in an anonymous poem quoted in John Kennedy's book "Profiles in Courage."

There was a dachshund once, so long
He hadn't any notion
How long it took to notify
His tail of his emotion.
And so it happened, while his eyes
Were filled with woe and sadness,
His little tail went wagging on
Because of previous gladness.

****

The growing family and limited space presented problems. The loss of privacy began to grate on tempers. A simmering feud about cooking and cleaning duties erupted. Invariably the jobs of the women in the home, the younger daughters were often exempted since they were students. The housework thus fell to Mai (who never complained about anything), my mother, and Nalutai. The men and the boys had no assigned chores and did not volunteer for any. That is simply the way it was. The women occasionally argued about who should go to movies and who would cook each evening.

One evening, my mother's resentment reached a boiling point, and she expressed her frustration openly to Dada and Mai, between tears and within earshot of others. I had not witnessed such tumultuous interactions in this household before.

Another time, someone yelled at Asha and Varsha, upsetting their mother greatly. There was quite a scene. On another occasion, one child was smacked on the arm and an argument followed. But the conflicts were typically resolved quickly, with a compromise or two.

Then there was the gripe water episode. Intended for the younger children to treat an occasional colic, the sweet purple fluid became a reason for frequent bathroom visits by the teenagers. We had no reason—or permission—to drink it. Each one took a swig and replaced the lost volume with tap water. Eventually the purple faded away to clear and the fluid tasted like water. At this point, a new bottle was produced. This went on for a while. The elders caught on soon enough and a more secure place was found for this elixir. We did not admit to the thefts until we were adults.

A telephone, a novelty in most homes, was purchased. The black instrument with a rotary dial sat on a small table covered by an embroidered silk cloth. There was no need for a "DO NOT TOUCH" sign. That was understood. Even Bhau, who had paid for the gadget, asked for permission before using it. Most of us had no one to call anyway. Dada or Mai dusted it frequently. The rest of us simply admired it and were easily startled when it rang occasionally. While we all agreed to the phone rules, an occasional call by unidentified persons caused an upset when the bill arrived.

A used black-and-white Sylvania television arrived next to supplement the radio and the gramophone already in the home. These signs of prosperity, mostly from the income Bhau earned from his engineering job, also caused problems. There were disagreements about which reruns of American programs we would watch.

The various sounds in our home-made solitude or contemplation impossible. Sharad's singing, the hum of the harmonium, the *dha dhin dhin dha* of the drums, songs blaring from the radio, scratchy vinyl records on the gramophone, Mastan's barking, the clatter of pots and pans in the kitchen. Sudha decided to learn how to sing. Mira, a gentle soul who was easily upset, cried often. Subhash became an expert bongo player. There was rarely any quiet in the home.

Underneath it all was the disquieting sense that things were not going well for everyone.

Dada had questioned my desire—my need—to see *Snow White and the Seven Dwarfs* because I had already been to another movie the week before. Movies, a potential source of bad ideas and an oft-cited reason for the loss of virtue, were barely tolerated and therefore censored. More than one movie a month was considered quite unnecessary, not to mention unaffordable. Since Dada's children (my uncles and aunts) had also seen a movie the week before and received permission for *Snow White*, I felt unjustly singled out. So I decided I would never go to any movie ever again. That was to be my personal civil disobedience—my *satyagraha*—against injustice, to shame the oppressor. And—unlike my grandfather who left India, abandoning the freedom movement—I was not going to give in until the guilty felt shame.

Nine months later, Dada—realizing the extent of my resolve—begged me to "forgive" him. I was deeply embarrassed when he asked if he should touch my feet. Elders never touch the feet of younger family members. I knew I had won and agreed to go to the movie *Junglee (The Savage)*, where I saw a most beautiful actress, Saira Banu, making her debut in movies and being chased by Shammi Kapoor, the perpetual Romeo of Indian Hindi movies, in a ritual of song and dance. This was possibly the "dirtiest" movie I had ever seen, where an unmarried man chased after an unmarried woman and touched her far too often.

Some months later, the elders held a strategic meeting and decided to break the family up into several units. There was no anger, just thoughtful negotiation about feasibility and affordability.

Bhau had changed jobs and moved to the free university quarters with his family; my mother and I went to a subsidized two-room apartment near the river; and Dada, Mai, and the remaining children (Sharad, Sudha, Anil, Mira, and Subhash) found a three-bedroom flat nearby.

Mastan was exiled to the village, where our servant's family lived. We heard later that he engaged in a vicious battle with a young leopard, leaving both dead.

Bhau and Mai looked back at the avocado tree with sadness as the car left its ample shade for the last time. They had acquired a taste for this green-black fruit with its creamy interior, although the rest of us hated it. We had carved our names on its massive trunk.

We moved into our separate new homes after tearful goodbyes. My mother and I were on our own for the first time.

****

Reports about my father reached us through the grapevine. He lost his job in Dar es Salam, started drinking again, and was somewhere in the northern desert of Kenya. I saw an occasional letter that my mother had forgotten to hide. He was tired, he said, and his life had no direction or meaning. He wanted permission to meet me. This permission was usually denied. I had no interest in eating a meal with him, even though the offer of ice cream and chicken *biryani* was tempting.

One afternoon on the school playground, I felt I was being watched. Turning toward a fence several feet away, I saw a tall man in a dark suit looking straight at me. Our eyes locked, and I knew it was my father. I knew he would want to talk to me. I hesitated and started to walk away. As my pace increased, he called out. I turned and he said he just wanted to talk to me, to ask me how I was doing. I mumbled that I was fine and ran away. A quick glance backward showed that he was deeply disappointed. He turned and walked away, hunched and looking very tired.

On my return home, I informed my mother about his visit. There was initial silence followed by a meeting of the elders. They were concerned about my security and fearful of a kidnapping...or worse. Bhau wrote to Baba, and they agreed that was not to happen again. Any future visits had to be coordinated with the family. Baba agreed and once again begged to be allowed to meet with me. Bhau understood my father's loneliness and despair. He felt sorry for his brother-in-law, who'd had a rough life and had his ambitions derailed.

A meeting was arranged. It was understood that Baba would have to abstain from drinking for the occasion. The lunch and ice cream session was to last no more than three hours.

My father was now a stranger to me. We had nothing to say to each other. I felt no fear or rancor. He took me to the Brilliant Hotel, where one of his Punjabi friends cooked a wonderful chicken curry, rice, and *roti*. The meal was topped off with delicious ice cream, quite a luxury in those days. But I could not bring myself to answer his questions with more than one word. I did not smile the whole time. Some of his friends dropped in to see him and made a big fuss about me. They wanted their friend's son to be happy during this rare and precious meeting.

A photograph from that day shows an exhausted father, a healed gash on his left temple, with his hands on the shoulder of an unsmiling son who looked straight ahead, lips pursed and brows furrowed. I was dropped off at the designated place and walked away without a word of gratitude.

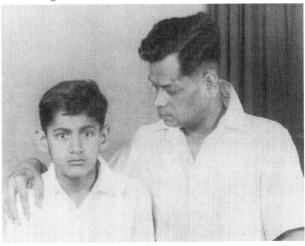

Figure 8: Lunch with my father

Bhau did not ask any questions, but he guessed that I did not want any future meetings, and even the bribe of a nice meal with ice cream would not sway my mind.

THE ESSAY

After four years of high school (in December 1959), we took the Senior Cambridge examination to test our skills in physics, chemistry, mathematics, history, geography, English language and literature, and Gujarati. The assignment for the English language examination was to write an essay about a person we admired the most. I had many heroes, but for reasons I cannot explain, I chose a famous sitar player, Ravi Shankar, as my subject. I knew very little about him except that he was famous.

Mr. Khanna had always taught us to write without fear, be honest, and let our imagination flow. He had not recommended fabrication of stories. I made up a story of a musical duet and duel. The synergy and banter between the melodious notes of the sitar and the pulsating drumbeat of the tabla intrigued me. This was an especially dangerous choice since the paper would be graded by an English person in Cambridge, UK. My recollection of what I wrote follows.

The revered Hindu sitar player and the Muslim master percussionist first bow to each other. The Islamic tenet that no man shall kneel or bow before anyone other than God is violated as each asks his own God to bestow blessings upon the other. They turn to the audience, bowing with folded hands, to honor the music aficionados who have packed the auditorium. A third person follows and sits behind a *tanpura*, which will provide the background hum. They sit down cross-legged on the ornate rug and caress their instruments while the audience waits.

A hammer gently hits the wooden struts of the tabla and fingers tighten the sitar strings No words are spoken. They take their time to get it right. They are dressed in colorful *kurtas* and matching pants. We have seen their pictures a thousand times, but here we are, sitting in the same auditorium, breathing the same air. They look up, thank us without words, and announce the first *raga* they will play and what the rhythm will be.

Pin-drop silence.

Pandit Ravi Shankar strikes the first note. We are in the presence of the world's greatest sitar player and a revered master of Indian classical music. It is like being with Perlman or Pavarotti. He strums the strings slowly, each note rebounding off the great hall's acoustic walls and ceilings. With an increasingly faster pace, the *jhala* ends in a crescendo of brilliant notes and sounds. He pauses, acknowledges the ovation, and signals silently to his tabla player that the two will now perform together in what is called a *jugalbandhi*.

The percussionist tunes his tabla once again. The first drumbeat *tin* rings through the hall like an electric shock, a bolt of lightning. The listeners now lean forward in anticipation because this man is no other than Ustad Alla Rakha, the legendary master of Indian rhythm and the father of child prodigy Ustad Zakir Hussain. The sitar and tabla engage in musical banter, mimicking each other — the artistes smiling, trying to trick the other into a rhythmic error and, not succeeding, applauding him. For the listeners, petty squabbles and rivalries become distant. Differences of age, religion, caste, and color and the pettiness of their daily prejudices are forgotten. The audience is mesmerized.

The artistes possess no written notes. They anticipate what the other will do at any given moment. They improvise. Because there are no rules for masters. Their spirits are high. It is Indian classical music but, like jazz, it allows unlimited freedom. Their hands become a blur as fingers move deftly over stretched leather or taut metal strings. At any time, one or the other can pause to take a sip of water or wipe the sweat off his brow. Spontaneous applause, permitted in Hindustani classical music, becomes frequent, an effort to release pent-up emotion. The masters acknowledge the applause and indeed welcome it. They continue as though there had been no interruption, now at a breakneck speed.

The synergy, and the mathematical crescendo, brings the audience to the edge of their seats.

The segment ends after one hour and is followed by a brief recital in another raga. Then they stand with folded hands, humble masters, bowing before the thrilled audience. Sustained applause continues as they depart the stage. The audience thirsts for more. "Encore, encore! Once more, once more!" they shout.

The two masters return, smile, bow with folded hands, sit down again, and perform a shorter raga, *Bhairavi*. The audience knows that this is a signal that there will be no further encores since this raga ends the night. It is a folksy and playful piece. One can feel in this music the cool air of the mountains and the gentle sound of a stream stumbling over rocks. The audience wishes it would never end. But end it must, and it does.

At that time, only 16 years old, I could not have foreseen that I would meet Ustad Zakir Hussain and his father at concerts in America.

I would not receive the exam results until March 1960. It was unclear what the future held in store for me. My friends left for India or England for further studies. It was decided that I should get a job and let the future unfold on its own. Perhaps I could get a scholarship.

Bhau called an Indian friend who worked at the Norwich Union Insurance Company in Nairobi. I was to start the next Monday as a filing clerk. I would be the only other Indian.

****

John Clark, the manager, came to the point quickly. He was going to train me, his youngest employee, to become an insurance agent. My salary would be 375 shillings a month with no benefits. I was to maintain and retrieve files as needed and to read the manuals he left on my desk. I quickly learned terms such as "actuarial," "premiums," "whole life," and "term life." Indians were leery about planning their own deaths. If they did buy insurance, it was with an Indian company so I saw no Indian names in the files I managed. Africans could not afford the premiums and likely did not know such things existed. Women knew they would outlive their husbands and wisely refrained from wasting their money.

Mr. Clark, a jovial, back-slapping type of bloke, was kind and welcoming. The staff respected and liked him. I concluded that, despite being white, he was a nice man.

There was no need for segregation at this workplace since there were only two Indians in a sea of white faces. The older Indian kept a watchful eye. He would have intervened if he thought I was about to do something idiotic. I sat at the very first desk behind the customer counter. Senior agents, mostly young Britons in their late 20s, sat in rows behind me. Not used to being in a multiracial setting, my interactions with others were generally awkward.

The only black employees were the cleaners, coffee servers, and those who ran errands to other offices in town. There were no female workers. The aroma of fresh Kenyan coffee, precisely at 10:00 AM and 2:00 PM, was said to be some of the world's best and was highly anticipated. People generally worked during breaks and lunchtime. Tongue-tied with no mutual topics to discuss, I remained silent most of the day. During my second month, Mr. Clark decided I deserved a raise of 25 shillings. I was now earning half as much as my mother was.

The city emptied in the evenings as the Mzungu went to their bungalows in the green hills of Muthaiga, the Muhindi to modest apartments in Parkland and elsewhere, and the blacks to the slums, where there was no electricity or running water.

On a particularly slow day, I asked Mr. Clark for permission to replace the tattered brown manila folders. Hundreds of new folders, a rubber stamp, and an inkpad were purchased. I diligently stamped and numbered each folder, working overtime until they chased me out at closing time. The file room, which was my own domain, looked brand new. I had impressed the team. Other workers warmed up to me. My confidence soared. I delved deeper into the insurance manuals. Perhaps this is what I was destined to do with my life.

I could be like Vinay Inamdar, who had made a ton of money selling insurance and had married a beautiful woman to boot! He was also a director who had cast a bunch of kids in a play at the magnificent National Theater. Our job in that play, he said, was to "die painful and miserable deaths during a famine." He said his reputation as a director of serious drama was at stake. That was the day I learned that grown-ups are weird and that dying on the stage is not that difficult.

The results of the Senior Cambridge examination were published in the *East African Standard* in March 1960. My name was among the few who had achieved the highest grade. I was disappointed nonetheless because I wanted to be the top student in my school. I had let Mr. Chiplunkar down. Not only did I not top my school, but I was far behind in my quest for a national scholarship.

The customary distribution of sweets to neighbors, friends, and families followed. The Ravi Shankar essay helped me to get a Distinction in the English language test. I knew Mr. Khanna would be proud. I also got a Distinction in mathematics thanks to my tutor, Mrs. Varma, and Mr. Chiplunkar, who had embarrassed me into excellence. I also did quite well in the other subjects.

Without a full scholarship, however, my future remained bleak. We did not have a penny to our name nor did we have a bank account. My mother had been repaying "debts" from the treachery 11 years earlier. An accountant suggested that we declare bankruptcy. On the day she did so in 1960, we felt shame and humiliation.

My friends knew the future path of their lives. They were either going to join their parents' businesses or study overseas. Oddly, these wealthy boys and I had become inseparable in school. During a recess, they went to the canteen for a Coke and a delicious piece of cake, which I could not afford. I lied and told them I did not like Coke or cake, then wandered off. It upset them; they did not understand why I was anti-social only during recess.

Norwich Union employees were surprised. Evidently, they did not think that people with good grades worked for insurance companies. I told them truthfully that I was unable to afford a higher education. A fellow named Seagram, whose first name escapes me, said to no one in particular, "He won't be here too long."

I ignored that comment at the time, but as it turned out, he was the only one to foretell the future!

****

A Maharashtrian officer in the Indian Embassy in Nairobi was a family acquaintance. He told us about a scholarship given annually to candidates with good grades, limited financial resources, and ancestral links to India. I provided the relevant documents and was certain I would be high on the list. The officer said I had a very good chance. But a few weeks later, we received a rejection letter. The winner's father was a rich and influential man in the community and also a family friend. I had better grades and my need was greater. We chalked it up to kismet.

****

In April, while pulling a file, I realized that I had mistakenly stamped the wrong end of hundreds of folders, which would make retrieval difficult. All I had to do was place a second stamp in the correct corner, cover the errant entry with tape, and tell Mr. Clark that I had made a mistake. It was not a grievous or costly error. But rational thought deserted me. I knew the error would be discovered soon. Would they reprimand me, fire me, or hold my wages?

Whenever there was a crisis in my life, I reached out to Bhau, the calm one. When I told him about the folders, he burst out into laughter. That is exactly what I was afraid of — ridicule.

"All you have to do is tell them what happened," said the wise one.

"They will laugh at me just like you did."

"Why does it matter? Anyone can make a mistake."

Did he understand the enormity of my error? I was not going back to that place to be the laughingstock of an entire office full of white men, one Indian, and a few blacks. I begged him to go tell Mr. Clark. He tried in vain to convince me that one must face up to such things in life. But I was not swayed.

Mr. Clark, hearing the story from Bhau the next day, burst out laughing as well and said not to worry, that I was a good worker and he wanted me back. He promised not to laugh and said he would order others not to either. But I refused. I decided I would rather lose wages for the month and not face the humiliation of being incompetent. It was a matter of personal pride and honor.

Mr. Clark, a man who had been so good to me, mailed my last check for the entire month with a small bonus added on. The Norwich Union staff possibly suspected that it was my plan to leave all along. And I had let down Bhau, who had gotten the job for me in the first place.

We had a family meeting at home. Bhau and my mother decided the best course was to apply to the Duke of Gloucester School for two years of advanced studies (equivalent to the British Advanced Level). The problem was that a whole term had passed while I was being trained as an insurance agent. Perhaps I would not be able to catch up.

I had been a good student, a prefect, and an athlete too. Bhau's plea to the principal, Mr. Sadiq, forced the issue. This was perhaps the first time that the school had bent its rules to allow someone to join so late.

GO BACK TO BOMBAY

Kenyatta's incarceration created a vacuum, which was quickly filled by two charismatic men, Tom Mboya and Oginga Odinga. They demanded freedom for Kenya and Kenyatta. Africans, who had remained silent for so long, were energized by their passion. The frenzied crowds grew larger. The speeches were laced with slogans like "Go back to Bombay!" (These words garnered sustained applause.) No one ever asked anyone to "Go back to London." Their words struck terror in the hearts of "Asians" a term used to lump all brown people from India and Pakistan together. Newspapers proclaimed "Mboya demands the immediate repatriation of all Asians." Those who had contemplated acquiring Kenyan citizenship, whenever freedom came, now had second thoughts. Would they become second-class citizens? They did not trust the British to protect them.

Mboya said true integration would not occur until Asians allowed their daughters to marry Africans. Already burdened by imported notions of caste, custom, and conservatism, Asians retorted that even in India people did not marry anyone who spoke a different language had a different caste or religion. How could they suddenly consent to interracial marriages? That type of assimilation was unacceptable to the Indian community at the time. Those who were servants today could not suddenly become sons-in-law tomorrow!

It was not just a matter of personal safety anymore. There was now a deep threat to tradition and culture. Daughters were dispatched to India in significant numbers to attend schools and colleges there. The Asian community, always segregated from others by law, could not tolerate social and sexual discourse with those of other races.

It was unsafe for Indians to attend rallies when leaders were threatening to drown them in the ocean. Their absence, however, was seen as a lack of commitment to Kenyan independence. No African leader ever mentioned the fact that Makhan Singh, an Indian labor union leader, was the first to demand independence for Kenya and was jailed from 1950–1961 for sedition. Or that the lawyers who defended Kenyatta at his trial included several Indians. Or that Pio Pinto, a fearless leader of the freedom movement, looked after and helped Kenyatta to settle down after he was released and became his confidant. Or that Dada sent a future African member of Parliament to study in India.

Day in and day out, newspapers reminded us that the future leaders of Kenya would not tolerate our continued presence. It did not matter whether one was born in Kenya or in India. It was a matter of color. We knew that if this rhetoric ever translated into action, the white minority would be protected by British fusiliers but we would be on our own.

I had admired Mboya, a handsome man with a round cherubic face, large intelligent eyes, and a flawless ebony complexion. He stood ramrod straight and spoke impeccable English. Later I learned that he had been to America and had stood on the same stage with Martin Luther King in 1959. Born in 1930 to Luo parents, he went to a Catholic school, then to Oxford University to study industrial engineering. He then became the treasurer of the Kenya African Union, founded by Jomo Kenyatta. Sharad wanted to join the Mboya team as a volunteer, but hesitated because of the anti Asian rhetoric emanating from angry black politicians.

Other joined the Asian-bashing game. They said that the Asians' prosperity and higher educational status was due to the exploitation of African naiveté and labor. While Asian employers often treated their domestic servants harshly, I was not sure how a shopkeeper exploited people by selling goods to them or how a teacher exploited the Africans by teaching in Indian schools. We felt very insecure. Sometimes, after the rallies, groups of Africans would beat up or rob an Asian or two.

The idea of uhuru gained ground rapidly. Britain reluctantly agreed to a desegregated joint legislative council. Mboya became one of 14 Africans selected to represent 6 million blacks. And 14 Europeans represented 60,000 white settlers. I forget if there was any Indian representation.

Asian families started making contingency plans.

****

After two years at the Duke of Gloucester School, I had planned to apply to Makerere University Medical College in Kampala, Uganda. It would be affordable and just a train ride away, and my chances of entry would be fairly good. This option had never been considered previously because the school was new and the political climate in Uganda was equally volatile.

Although the Duke of Gloucester was a boys' school, the two-year curriculum known as Form 5 and Form 6 was coed. This small class was a microcosm of Asian society in Kenya. There were people of all religions and all parts of India and Pakistan. The presence of 6 girls in a class of about 25 was disconcerting at first. Social norms did not allow dating. Several of the girls had attended coed private schools such as the Ribeiro Goan School -named after the famous doctor on the zebra- and were quite comfortable. I found myself quite ill at ease and awkward with the girls and fumbled the few words I had rehearsed. They quickly lost interest.

All the teachers were Indian. We were to learn advanced chemistry, physics, English language, and mathematics during the two years. My love for chemistry began when a short, rotund, and bald teacher from Madras, Mr. Raman, spoke passionately about acids and alkalis, atoms and molecules.

Our English teacher was a tall, perpetually angry Punjabi gentleman with an unpredictable temperament. We nicknamed him "Mathari," the name of an institution in Nairobi for the mentally ill. His yellow, protruding front teeth and long face gave him the appearance of a laughing rabbit. He never yelled at me, probably because he knew my family, but he was very mean to a Muslim student whose twin sisters were suspected prostitutes often seen soliciting near Ngara Road. The lanky girls made use of an upstairs apartment. Never having seen a prostitute, I noticed that they wore excessive makeup and very short skirts. The duo, both with flat chests, furtively propositioned Asian men. They smiled, taking anxious puffs from cigarettes hanging from scarlet lips. The lipstick was oddly out of place on their pockmarked brown faces. The dress, the makeup, and the smoking were completely alien to Indian and Muslim custom and culture.

Whenever the brother of the prostitutes raised his hand to ask a question, he received a barrage of verbal abuse with an invariable reference to his sisters' moral character. Some snickered, but most of us felt bad for him. Ultimately, he learned to be quiet in class. Shortly thereafter, he stopped speaking to anyone. When asked a question, he looked down and remained quiet. Occasionally, a tear would form and he would look away as though that might dry his glistening eyes. When we tried to cheer him up, he smiled weakly, thanked us, and then receded into his private world of suffering. The abusive teacher hailed from Punjab, where the terrors of partition had been most evident. I wondered if he had lost family members and this verbal abuse was his way of exacting revenge on this Muslim boy.

One day, two students (one of them my friend Ashok Shah) reported that their dissecting set had been lost or stolen. This was reported to the principal and, after an investigation, a Muslim boy—a star athlete—was determined to be the culprit. He was severely reprimanded but allowed to return to school. The extra yellow stripes on his green blazer, earned as a prefect, a mark of leadership and integrity, were stripped off by the principal in front of hundreds of silent students during the morning assembly a week later. The reason for the punishment was announced.

We felt terrible. He was never the same again. His academic performance suffered. He never participated in sports again. He spoke only when spoken to. His playful personality, the smile, and his dreadful rendition of Elvis Presley songs became a distant memory.

****

It was November 1960. A short, bald, and obese black man stood in the middle of the stage. He had a round, shiny face, large mischievous eyes, and a trumpet up to his lips. His cheeks expanded like stretched balloons with each exhaled note. Perspiring profusely, he wiped his face with a white handkerchief the size of a tablecloth. He laid the trumpet down and, in a cracked voice, said something about "marching saints" as he and his fellow musicians swayed on the stage.

I did not recognize any of the songs but was mesmerized by this performance. His playful banter with his musicians and the audience was endearing. Louis Armstrong, accompanied by his wife Lucille and fellow artists, including Danny Barcelona on the drums, had come to the Agriculture Grounds in Nairobi, the same place where we had greeted the Queen Mother. Thousands of Africans, a sprinkling of Europeans, and fewer Indians had temporarily forgotten about the color bar as they sat together.

These were the first Americans I had ever seen in my life. My thoughts wandered. Several generations ago, I imagined his ancestors were forcibly dragged from a sound sleep to waiting ships, to row themselves, shackles on their ankles, to an unknown land — to labor until they died a premature death. I visualized Armstrong being born to poor parents who had not yet recovered from the enslavement of their ancestors and still struggled in a racially segregated society. I wondered where he had stayed during this tour. The only black men we saw in posh hotels were cleaners, waiters, shoe shiners, and baggage handlers. Where did Satchmo sleep and eat in segregated Kenya?

Sharad, more a friend than an uncle even though he was older by eight years, had purchased the tickets. He did not say this, but I thought he felt sorry for me. I was grateful for his caring.

I had never imagined jazz could produce such sheer joy. We had no words to describe the experience. I saw in jazz not only the harmony, rhythm, and synchrony, but also a jarring reminder of apartheid and slavery.

****

It was highly unusual for Indians to attend a jazz concert. We did not understand or know western music. The only records we had at home, which we played on an old gramophone, were a few worn-out, vinyl 78 rpm records featuring Indian classical singers. The machine, cranked by hand, had the words His Master's Voice and a puppy etched on it.

The family had just acquired a harmonium, a kind of French organ with its legs cut off, so Indians could squat on the floor. Anil became a pro at playing it and gained fame locally. He also learned to play the tabla, a remarkable percussion instrument introduced into India centuries ago from Persia. Quite primitive in design, a hollow wooden cylinder covered by stretched leather, it was tuned by strokes of a metal mallet. Played well, it is mesmerizing. Anil had a natural genius for music. He always said it was because as a four-year-old he had sat in the lap of the famous vocalist, Hirabai Barodekar when she had visited our home in Nairobi. Anil and Sharad assembled a group of talented instrumentalists and formed the group Kala Niketan. Some of the orchestra members had previously performed on All India Radio.

Sharad aspired to become a movie star and playback singer, but that came to a screeching halt when Dada found out that instead of going to college in Bombay, Sharad was hanging out around movie studios and had befriended Mehmood, a popular comedian in Hindi movies. He was promptly summoned back home to Nairobi to work as a clerk for an English law firm. With his good looks and a great voice, he became a local musical hero, singing the songs of Kishore Kumar, a hugely popular playback singer for Bollywood movies. Much to Dada's chagrin, thousands attended his concerts. During public performances, he was often asked to sing the song "Tikdambaazi," which became his nickname. The shows, which were given to support charities, were sold out and became a staple of entertainment in Nairobi. They called Sharad the "Kishore Kumar of Nairobi." Their orchestra was homegrown with brilliant talent. Soon they were invited to sing commercial jingles on Kenya Radio, which had an Asian section, to advertise soap, saris, and sundries. My mother became the female voice in these jingles and later had her own solo performances with Kala Niketan.

Figure 9: Kala Niketan-Anil (accordian), Sharad and my mother (singers), Vinay Inamdar (director)

Sharad and I had a developed a special bond. I sat and listened as he rehearsed his songs. Sensing some boredom on my part, he devised a scheme to encourage me to stay. He asked me to accompany him on the tabla, especially when Anil was unavailable. Sharad knew the theory of rhythm but could not play the drums. So, he taught me a few rhythms. I became accustomed to 6, 8, 10, 12, or 16 beats called dadra, keherwa, japtal, ektal, and teental respectively. The odd number beats like roopak with seven beats were much harder for me. Anil would take over during the actual concerts.

The mathematics of rhythms fascinated me. The magic weaved by great masters like Ustad Zakir Hussain, his father Ustad Alla Rakha, and Pandit Shamta Prasad mesmerized me. The clear notes, the playful banter between the main instrument and the drum, the improvisation — much like jazz — were amazing. One day I hoped I would learn tabla from a master.

****

All-white schools already had swimming pools; Asian and African schools did not. Because we felt left out, our teachers decided that we ought to build a pool, even though most Indians could not swim. The exception was my father, who swam like a fish and could float on his back.

In a rare display of democracy, we were asked for fund-raising ideas. My idea of staging music concerts took hold. I thought the girls now looked at me with admiration! Energized, I asked my uncles if their band Kala Niketan could pitch in. They agreed instantly. Their instruments included a harmonium, accordion, violin, mandolin, flute, bongos, and tabla, and they had a variety of singers. Each artiste had a superb reputation in the community. A classmate, recruited her uncle, Mohammed Kassam, a western-trained violinist who had drifted toward Indian music with surprising ease.

Thousands of students from Indian schools in Nairobi and its vicinity paid a shilling each and attended, often with their parents, to listen to Hindustani pop music. Every show was sold out. They were ecstatic that their field trip was a music concert! They swayed and smiled as melodious songs filled the auditorium. Sharad stole each show with his medley of Kishore Kumar songs and received thunderous applause. Anil played the harmonium, accordion, or tabla and Subhash the bongos.

Dada and Mai had not been too happy with the choice of Bollywood songs or the effort to build a pool, but were swayed by pressure from the community. They thought this was a waste of precious time. They did not attend any of the concerts. "Is swimming more important than studies?" they asked. And why were we singing all these "vulgar" songs, meaning love songs from movies? What impression would the community have of our family? This was perhaps the only time when their will had not prevailed.

Since I led this fund-raising effort, Sharad thought that I should also be on the stage. The lighthearted Hindi song they chose for me was "Charandas ko peeneki jo adaat na hothi, to aaj Miya bahar or Bibi under na hothi" (If Charandas did not have a drinking habit, he would not be outside the home while his wife was indoors, refusing to let him in.)

It did not occur to me at the time that I was singing the story of my own life before thousands!

The pool was built after I graduated from the school in 1961, but I never learned to swim.

THE WIND OF CHANGE

Belgian Congo was granted its independence in 1960. It turned out to be a dreadful mistake. Belgium had not trained enough African administrators, army leaders, and professionals. The ensuing chaos should have been no surprise. One month after independence, several Europeans were dragged from their cars and shot to death in Elizabethville, now known as Lubumbashi. The resentment against Belgians, who had a legacy of ruthless subjugation, oppression, and violence against Africans, reached a feverish pitch.

Trainloads of Belgian refugees passed through Nairobi. They had hurriedly assembled their few belongings while the rampaging, murderous mobs roamed the streets unchecked. They clutched bewildered children to their chests as they ran for their lives. We saw haunting black-and-white images in the local newspapers. Curious, I walked to the railway station and saw trainloads of white refugees, once powerful rulers, now fleeing in fear. The exhausted, homeless, starving white families—victims of rage, rape, and shame—were leaving the country they had called home for so long. The silent acceptance of a new reality was reflected in their sad faces and empty eyes. Joyless, unkempt, and hopeless, their clothes tattered and stained, they were now just like the blacks they had oppressed and left behind. Their hearts and spirits were broken. Children cried softly as the mothers comforted them. Did the African coolies on the platform frighten them, reminding them of the Congolese who had violated their lives?

After an overnight journey to Mombasa, on the railroad that Indians had built, they would board ships to return them to Belgium, a country many had never known.

Things remained unstable for several years in Congo. In 1965, General Joseph Mobutu staged a *coup d'état* and ruled until his death in 1997. William Close, a surgeon who had been trapped in that country and served as Mobutu's personal physician for 16 years shared some of these stories with me after we developed a friendship which lasted many years until his death. He was the father of the well-known actress Glenn Close.

The events in Congo had a major impact on how Asians viewed their future in an independent Kenya. My family's decision to leave Kenya permanently, some years after the events in Congo, was shaped at least in part by this turmoil. There was a sense of foreboding about our future in Africa.

That concern was heightened by a speech made by a British prime minister in 1960.

****

Africa, the Dark Continent, had been carved up among western powers as spoils of distant wars. In this scramble for Africa, treaties were signed without the Africans' consent.

The successful independence struggle in India had rekindled the flames of nationalism all over the world. Ghana became free in 1957, proving that Africans were quite capable of governing themselves.

In February 1960, in a speech to members of Parliament in Cape Town, South Africa, Britain's prime minister, Harold Macmillan, spoke of the "wind of change" blowing through Africa. He received a frosty reception from white politicians after speaking frankly against the country's system of apartheid and of the right of Africans to vote and rule themselves.

The wind of change is blowing through this continent and, whether we like it or not, this growth of national consciousness is a political fact. We must all accept it as a fact, and our national policies must take account of it.

As I see it, the great issue in this second half of the 20th century is whether the uncommitted peoples of Asia and Africa will swing to the East or to the West. Will they be drawn into the Communist camp? Or will the great experiments of self-government that are now being made in Asia and Africa, especially within the commonwealth, prove so successful, and by their example so compelling, that the balance will come down in favour of freedom and order and justice?

White South African leaders were angry. But the fire had been lit, and its embers reached Kenya in early 1961. That year, Kenyatta was elected as the head of the Kenya African National Union (KANU) in absentia and released from nine years of incarceration. Africans were given more representation in the legislature. Other political parties with increasingly bold goals and national ambitions emerged.

At the Belgrade conference of non-aligned nations in September 1961, Nehru, the Indian prime minister, was uncharacteristically chastised by African leaders for not liberating Indian enclaves from Portuguese rule. It was felt that this hesitation by a powerful Indian Army was suppressing African ambitions for the liberation of Portuguese Angola and Mozambique. Perhaps in response, Indian troops moved in on December 18, 1961, and after minimal resistance, Daman, Diu, and Goa were liberated. A total of 34 Indians and 31 Portuguese soldiers died. Navy Commander Anand Badve, married to my cousin and childhood friend, Surekha (Sulu) Panvalkar, was on the front during that war. Both had grown up in East Africa.

Tanganyika became independent on December 9, 1961, in a peaceful transition.

Indians debated whether to keep their British passports. It was a strange feeling to root for African independence and yet fear the potential consequences of that freedom. The stirring within the bosom of Africa became an agitation that dramatically affected Asians in countless ways. There was great trepidation that Asians would be hunted down and hurt. Perhaps it was time for the future prey to flee and escape the clutches of a looming predator.

ON TOP OF THE WORLD

Mr. Agarwal, the first Kenyan ever to qualify for Wimbledon, and Mr. Turnidge decided to lead a party of students to Mount Kilimanjaro. Located just south of the equator, the snowcapped peak is 19,321 feet tall. Its aura of romance and mystery has tempted thousands to visit.

Gods must reside on this most magnificent mountain, the highest point in Africa.

All we needed was permission from our parents and a little bit of money to buy used sweaters, jackets, and shoes. I was a skinny 18-year-old who stood 6 feet tall and weighed 110 pounds. This would be my first time away from home. My mother conferred with the elders and signed the papers. But there was an unexpected hitch. An immigration agent, a friend of my father, insisted that my father would have to sign the release as well. That was a problem because he was in the remote north of Kenya doing something with the police force there. A telegram was sent. The reply read, "I give my son permission to climb Mount Kilimanjaro." I think my mother had hoped he would say no.

We set out in a roofless truck in April 1961 for the long and bumpy ride. Two white teachers sat in front with the driver. The Asian teachers including Mr. Agarwal and students retreated to wooden benches in the roofless back, exposed to the elements. Clothes and rations, packed in a rucksack, weighed less than 25 pounds. We had been told that only water and raisins were permitted during the ascent. There were no porters. We carried no medicines and knew nothing about mountain sickness. But we were armed with plenty of determination.

I was retracing my father's journey from 1941, when he had traveled to Nairobi.

There had been a terrible drought that year. The dust blew through the plains and settled in our hair, eyebrows, and ears. The heat and sweat created cakes of mud on our skin and clothes. Laundry facilities would be unavailable until we returned to Nairobi a week later, but no one minded since we were all equally dirty. Limbs of acacia trees hung limply. Vultures feasted on the carcasses of dehydrated animals strewn along the road.

Kilimanjaro loomed large in the background as we approached Arusha. A wide curtain of clouds parted to expose the peak, which was much higher than we had imagined. A total of 25 students shared 4 rooms in a low-budget hotel run by an Indian. The meal was potato and pea curry with *chapattis* (flatbreads), onions, and a slice of lemon. We bathed using cold water from a bucket.

The African guide arrived the following morning dressed in shorts. He apparently did not need all the fancy stuff others carried up the mountain. We selected long sticks from the nearby forest. The guide said our bed would be the floor of a cave. What about pillows? The backpacks!

Not trained in rock climbing, we chose the easier path that most tourists take. The first day was a breeze. We walked up smartly, whistling familiar tunes and wondering what all the fuss had been about climbing this "hill." We were on the lookout for animal poop, especially large poop, a sign of elephants. However, we saw no animals on the mountain.

We established camp that evening in a cave. I ate corned beef from a can, not knowing what it was, with coffee and bread. My family would have frowned upon the consumption of beef.

We slept well, but woke up stiff and cold. Our contempt for those who had told us this was a tough climb grew dramatically as the trek on the second day again brought very few challenges. As we climbed higher, the forest gave way to a large grassy plain. The air was now thinner and our progress noticeably slower. A beautiful blue lake, not a mirage, lay just to the left of where Kilimanjaro stood naked in all its glory, the sharp peak of Mawenzi on the right. It was Heaven on Earth. We made slow but steady progress. Our breathing became more labored.

We established camp that evening in a large natural cavern. I was nauseated and felt dizzy. A persistent headache became oppressive.

I lost my appetite. We lay down along the cold and damp walls of the cave, our bedroom without beds or blankets, in various states of distress.

Figure 10: Mt. Mawenzi on the way to Kilimanjaro

The teachers decided that I, along with a few others, needed to descend to a lower altitude. They did not want any deaths on their conscience. Through the haze in my brain, I heard the words "mountain sickness." I overheard a teacher discussing the logistics with someone else. The smell of canned meat was now sickening. My head was pounding. As the awful night wore on, I concluded that I might be better off dead.

I had prided myself on resilience and courage. It felt so rotten to give in. If only I could tough it out for one more night, climb to the top, and salvage my self-respect. As members of the RSS, we had been told to keep going regardless of the challenges ahead. Never give up, until your very last breath. Secretly, I hoped that a stretcher would take me down to safety.

A classmate, Shiraz Rabady, somehow convinced Mr. Turnidge to allow me to go on. He promised he would remain by my side through the night and the final ascent. I was still short of breath. The headache and nausea persisted and I had not slept at all. Although I had known him just for a year, we had become friends and shared meals in our

Nairobi homes. I recalled the history of the gentle Parsi people and their huge contributions to India, where they had found refuge centuries ago. This descendant of people who had been persecuted in Persia because of their Zoroastrian faith was now helping me selflessly.

The ascent began at 2:00 AM. A daytime start is demoralizing because one can then see how steep the final climb is. Two steps forward, gasp, catch your breath, and start again! Shiraz followed close behind, just like Sherpa Tensing had done for Edmund Hilary on Mount Everest. Undoubtedly, I slowed him down, but he stayed loyal and nudged me on. Without him, I would have bolted down the mountain.

Four arduous hours later, we reached the summit. We were the last to reach it. Only 14 of the 25 students made it to the top. Sadly, neither Shiraz nor I had a camera.

No one ever *conquers* this mountain; one falls in love with it. There was a small, metal box on the rim that contained a small notebook. Its brown, brittle pages were beginning to crumble. Many names were scribbled in that book. We added ours. Recent climbers whom I have met do not recall seeing such a box at the summit.

As we sat on the rim of this massive crater packed with glaciers, the majesty of Africa unfolded before our eyes. The sun rose, an orange ball of fire, casting a glow across the plains of the Serengeti. The gray ice shimmered with shades of white and orange. We said nothing. At that moment, perhaps the two of us occupied a spot higher than any other human on the entire planet. Shiraz Rabady and Anand Panwalker! What were the chances that anyone else would be sitting on a mountain over 19,300 feet high at 6:00 AM on a cold April day in 1961?

As though jealous of the attention Kilimanjaro was getting, Mawenzi rose from the fog to display a magnificent orange glow on its sharp peak. I looked northward for Mount Kenya, the second highest mountain in Africa, hundreds of miles away. But low clouds concealed the view.

I had climbed the mountain that had enchanted Ernest Hemingway and drawn my father to its foothills in 1938, and whose peak I had seen from a plane in 1954. Three generations of the Panwalker family had been touched by the magic of this mountain.

It had taken three days to climb up; the descent was far easier. Shiraz, whose generosity I never forgot, and I walked down the mountain in one day. Mr. Turnidge was surprised that I made it. Mr. Agarwal, a man of few words, simply nodded. Pictures were taken at the base camp where we were "crowned" by local tribes people with flower arrangements. The flowers, they said, were blessed by the Mungu, who lived on the mountain slopes. They looked like plastic but were real. Locals said they live forever.

****

As the years passed, the letters from my father became less frequent. I knew where they were hidden and sometimes peeked at the contents. Each letter asked about me. He spoke of loneliness, errors, and regrets and of a wasted life. He wanted another opportunity at fatherhood and promised, if given another chance, to be a better person. There was never any anger or excuse. He did not acknowledge that his alcoholism had caused our woes.

My mother did not respond. Yet he kept writing in a forlorn hope that we could be a family again. Bhau, when asked for his intervention, expressed empathy but made it clear to Baba that he did not want to risk yet another upheaval in our lives. He worried particularly about my well-being. I had become so used to not having my dad around that it did not matter anymore.

We were, however, getting assurances from reliable sources that my father was not drinking anymore, had lost much weight, and was unwell. He had also generated much goodwill by permitting me to climb Mt. Kilimanjaro.

One evening, many months after the last letter, Baba arrived at our two-room apartment with a single suitcase, all he had to show for 23 years in Africa. I had not seen him for six years. Tired, gaunt, and weather-beaten, he looked up at me, for I had grown taller. His awkward embrace suggested he had forgotten how to hug loved ones. I felt empty. Not sure how to react, I left the apartment. No one had shared this plan with me.

My bed, desk, and books in the living room were left alone. They rearranged the smaller bedroom, squeezing an extra bed into that space. They acted as though this was a routine reshuffle. The logistics of travel changed. My mother drove to her school. Baba found a clerical job in a small glass factory. As the only white collar employee, he told everyone that he was the manager. Baba and I had minimal interactions. It was as though a stranger had entered our home. He gave me no advice and I did not ask for any. On occasion, I snapped at him for trivial reasons. Our communication was brief and awkward. I was not sure whether I loved him. Deep down, I felt sorry for him — for us — but I wanted to move on.

Each morning, as the crowing roosters awakened us, my mother served me hot tea and *parathas* in bed while I read the *East African Standard.*

As my friend and I passed the bakery on our way to school, we looked for the long-gone dimpled, blue-eyed Italian beauty with olive skin and the shy smile. The fragrance of freshly baked bread remained, but she was gone. If God really did exist, she was one of His finest creations. Why then was her brother so mean and ugly?

****

Our municipal quarters, reserved for Asians, consisted of several comfortable stone buildings, each four stories high and containing eight flats. Large windows allowed us to peek into each other's homes. It was a big scandal if a teenage girl lingered just a bit longer than socially acceptable with a boy of a similar age. Gossip immediately ended that "relationship," or at least made it more discreet. Everyone was acutely aware of the secrets and scandals within each household.

In the building across our own lived a Sikh woman, whose husband had died when their children were rather young. She made ends meet by sewing clothes for others while her brother pitched in with cash. Mohan Sood, her eldest son, was a year ahead of me in school, and we began a friendship that endured for six decades. We were always together.

In the evenings, he and I walked several miles to downtown Nairobi to buy fish and chips, British style — in paper bags, with vinegar dripping from the bottom. The money came from a small weekly allowance we now received. We did not want to upset our mothers, so we told them we had eaten nothing since lunch and proceeded to enjoy the dinner prepared for us. Our stomachs were unending pits. Mohan's mother sent down delicious curries for me whenever she could afford to buy meat.

Zainab, the Bohra Muslim neighbor on the top floor, was married to a handsome, alcoholic auto mechanic, who would totter into their fourth-floor home every evening, swaying dangerously, barely hanging on to the railings as he climbed the stairs. He had long forgotten how he had once loved this graceful, cultured, and extremely beautiful woman with a divine smile who, through self-neglect, had become fat and flabby. When angered by trivial things, he beat her.

Zainab never lost hope that if she continued to serve him tasty meals, he might love her again. Their union had produced no offspring. She was all alone, far away from her own kith and kin in India, free to leave but with no place to go. Nursing his own personal demons and wounds, he was indifferent to her suffering. They rarely touched each other and slept in separate beds.

The delicious kebabs he refused to eat ended up on my plate four floors below. This was Zainab's excuse to visit my mother and share her misery. She was a simple and kind woman who bore her suffering with dignity. The two wounded souls developed a chemistry that required few words. They chatted animatedly about *samosas*, curries, and kebabs when I was within earshot. Occasionally, if I caught them off guard, their voices became whispers as tears welled in their eyes.

It struck me as ironic that despite the wounds of partition and the fractured freedom that India had gained, these two women — one Hindu and one Muslim, both staunch in their religious fervor — could share their grief with such ease. The suffering created by their broken homes pulled them together. Their humanity overcame any artificial boundaries set by others. Grief knows no religion.

****

The Mau Mau insurgency abated. The country now suffered from a general state of lawlessness. Robberies and assaults became commonplace. Neighborhood watches were established. Asian teenagers with hockey sticks patrolled the streets for a few hours after sunset. It was now dangerous for an Asian to be outside after dusk.

One evening, as Mohan and I walked the beat, hitting every light post noisily with a hockey stick (the din made us feel safer), I slipped on a puddle of sticky fluid and fell on a thin, short man who lay on the grassy strip next to the pathway. He had propped himself up against a light pole, leaving a trail of blood on the ground, and was mumbling incoherently. We approached the dim light of the streetlamp gingerly and saw blood oozing from his neck. Someone had slashed him with a *panga*.

My Red Cross first-aid training came in handy. I placed my hand on the nape of his neck and was astonished to feel the bones of his spine bathed in a slimy, bloody mess. The crevice was deep enough to hide half of my right hand. His neck was broken, his limbs lifeless. My heart started pounding. Mohan produced a white handkerchief, which I stuffed deep into the wound. Blood soaked it and seeped around the cloth in a steady trickle. The man lost consciousness. After a few minutes, I extracted my clot-covered hand from his neck and ran to my grandfather's home nearby.

Breathless and scared, I could barely utter the words and dragged Bhau, who was visiting Dada and Mai, to the spot. We placed his limp body in the back seat of Bhau's car. Lacking a stretcher or the ability to call an ambulance, this injured Indian had no chance if we did not act immediately. The clinic, a mile away, was nearly empty. The doctor on call thanked us, said we had done what we could, and he would now take over. I saw no hurry in his words and actions. Was the man dead already? Had I held a corpse in my lap? I shuddered.

Four spindly knees, Mohan's and mine, knocked against each other. We were forbidden from further patrols. Secretly, we were extremely relieved.

****

In December 1961, I took the final exams for the Cambridge Advanced Higher School Certificate, considered a prelude to college. The results were reported as Pass, Fail, Credit, or the much-coveted Distinction. Three months later, I was disappointed to receive just Credits in physics, chemistry, and biology. A Distinction in English language reduced the angst a bit. These were good grades, but I could have worked harder and done better. The knowledge that I might never go to a college had dulled my competitive spirit. I knew I would never carry a doctor's black bag.

The family debated my future in hushed tones. Pharmacy school, teacher training, a trade or skill, or a clerical position were all options. We sent an application to Makerere University Medical College in Kampala, Uganda. The response came quickly. I had missed the deadline by months. But the letter also mentioned that my grades were highly competitive and would I please consider applying for the class of 1963?

I secured a teaching position at a high school owned by an Indian. It offered morning sessions from 8:00 AM to 12:00 noon for Asian students. The afternoon sessions were for Africans. This was an interesting and novel method of segregation.

The Asian students, expelled from other schools, were the dregs of society. They behaved badly, had no interest in academics, were disruptive in class, threw paper planes at each other, and had no fear of authority. I endured the chaos for two days. I pleaded with them to focus, make their parents proud. Halfheartedly, I told them they could achieve anything they chose to do because they were bright and capable. They laughed. I tried to befriend them. After all they were about my age. Instead, they slapped me on the back, used foul language, and disrespected me. Many were bigger and stronger. Whenever I turned to write something on the blackboard, there were giggles and catcalls, and the air was filled with paper planes, candy, and other missiles. On the third day of this relentless torture, I'd had enough.

Throwing all caution to the wind, I banged my fist on the table and shouted something like, "Stop it. Stop it right now! This is idiotic. I will not tolerate this!"

There was a momentary silence as they pondered the consequences of defiance. This lull in action did not bode well for me. One student, his manner sweet and mocking, asked, "Sir, what will you do if we don't stop?"

I glared at him, speechless. They erupted in raucous laughter. Objects started flying again. One student stood up on his chair, clapped, and raised his hands in the air to encourage his fellow delinquents to join the escalating mutiny. The noise level increased, my dignity and self-respect severely challenged. The gauntlet had been thrown. My next action surprised me considerably. I threw an eraser at the student as he continued to shout from his high perch. It hit his left ear. Surprised, he reached for the ear and saw blood on his fingers. A smudge of blood stained his white shirt collar. He looked around at his friends, my tormentors, and sat down. The room was silent. The laughter stopped. The faces hardened. I was a skinny youth with barely any facial hair. Many of these students were taller, bigger, and older.

Not good, I said to myself. I debated whether to apologize, but in foolish defiance, I stood my ground. I remained very still. This was going to end badly. The tension was palpable. My heart beat faster than it ever had. My mouth was dry.

Sadrudin, one of the toughest troublemakers, stood up and — in the most bizarre scenario imaginable — said, "I challenge you to a game of badminton...Sir."

I had a dangerous habit of never refusing a challenge. I informed him, with some bravado, that he could choose the time and place and I would be there. I had forgotten how a young wrestler had beaten me into pulp years ago, when I had foolishly agreed to a match. Remarkably, that defused the tension. I hoped I was good enough to beat him and earn some respect. The students, as usual, filed out of the room before the bell rang.

We ended up in a gym a few days later, with a mob cheering their friend on. Sadrudin thrashed me in every game. Hope being eternal, I kept accepting challenges for another game, only to be beaten again. He raised his fist after each game. Then he felt sorry for me, and became less vicious. The students got tired of cheering their champion. They trickled out, muttering obscenities in whatever Indian language they spoke. They had had their revenge. I acknowledged defeat. Sadrudin was gracious in victory, shaking my hand, but then condescendingly patted my shoulder.

I had escaped death at the hands of these hooligans and lost a humiliating duel to someone who was supposed to learn from me and respect me. This was my *Blackboard Jungle*. But unlike the movie, their behavior never improved. I learned to endure the indignity of being a teacher for those who did not wish to learn. I gave them Fail grades most of the time, but they didn't care. Parents did not show up for parent-teacher meetings. They had given up on their offspring a long time ago. The students were happiest when I left them alone so they could read their comic books or simply daydream. They laughed when I asked a question, claiming it was "too tough" for their "pea-sized brains." They could not do simple math, knew no science, and were absolutely disinterested in language, literature, and the fine arts. They yawned much of the time. I got a good look at their uvulas daily. I asked my fellow Indian teachers how they managed this bunch. They shrugged and said to leave them alone. They were not worth the effort. The owner of the school was simply interested in the wealth that this school generated for him.

The afternoon sessions were attended by African students. I imagined that there were not enough high schools for black students and that is why they came here. The contrast with the Asian students was like night and day. The Africans wore khaki shorts, black belts, and white shirts, and filed in and out of classrooms in a single line. There was always pin-drop silence. Their shoes were shined, books were carried neatly in backpacks, pencils were sharpened and ready to write. In class, they sat quietly, erect, looking straight ahead while writing notes with outstanding penmanship. They rarely asked any questions, but were invariably polite. I was to teach them history.

The curriculum, for some odd reason, included ancient history featuring the great dynasties in India. Since I was unfamiliar with this subject, having learned British history in school, I read the chapter the night before and regurgitated it the following afternoon. They never gave the impression of being bored. How did they suppress their yawns? I knew that it was ridiculous to teach Kikuyu, Luo, and Mkamba children about the Indian emperor Chandragupta Maurya. (My family members were quite amused when they heard I was doing this.)

One day I decided to do something different. Tanganyika had just achieved its independence. I thought we could talk about current African affairs, emerging leaders, apartheid, and their aspirations for freedom. Secretly, I also wanted to know if they, like their leaders, wanted me to leave Kenya.

They looked at each other briefly and then, to my astonishment, sat silently with absolutely no expression on their faces. They were afraid to share an opinion about their own aspirations and desires. Were they suspicious of my motives? Were they afraid I might report any "subversive" comments to the authorities? Was it the master–servant complex? I never knew the answer. I abandoned the attempt to engage them, and continued teaching ancient Indian history to Africans. That is what I was paid to do.

I felt a deep compassion and respect for them. They were so eager to learn but were getting little in return. I resigned myself to simply showing up, doing the best I could, and collecting my monthly salary of 650 shillings. This income would be essential if I was ever to attend college. Three months later, I got tired of the hypocrisy and quit. I had now saved 1,950 shillings, but had failed in my duty as a teacher.

A DOCTOR IN NEED

Doctor Kaka informed us by mail that he was coming to Nairobi. We found this rather unusual since he had never done this before. The elders secretly hoped that he was coming to discuss my higher education plans. Perhaps he could help financially. In truth, my parents and I would never have asked for money from anyone. We were too proud to beg and too poor to repay any loans. We had accepted our destiny that I would not be able to pursue my dreams.

He arrived by car after a long journey from Dar es Salam. We were shocked to see a very ill man. He stooped and had lost a lot of weight. His skin was rough like the bark of an old tree. Flakes of dead skin, caked with dried blood, fell from his face and scalp. As we examined more closely, his entire body was covered with an unsightly rash from head to toe. Even my young eyes told me that this was some kind of allergic reaction. He hesitated to touch anyone. The man stood on the threshold of the home and no one knew what to say or do. I made the first move. I hugged him. It was clear he was not used to such expressions of affection. He smiled weakly and a tear arose in his right eye, trickling down over the facial scabs.

His embrace, initially tentative, became firm, and I knew he had forgiven me for my expulsion from that school in Dar es Salam. I had always wondered if he had believed I was innocent. It was important for me to know that those I loved and respected had believed my story about being a victim rather than a villain in that episode. Curiously, no one — including my parents — had ever expressed that to me directly.

Doctor Kaka, having no one to care for him in Dar es Salam, had ventured to Nairobi to see if the only folks he knew would give him shelter until he healed. Dada immediately decided that this guest belonged in a hospital, not at home. We promptly piled into a car and drove to the Aga Khan Hospital in Parkland. Doctor Kaka was an employee of the same hospital system in Dar es Salam, so there was no difficulty getting in and procuring him a single room. He changed into pajamas and sat nervously on the edge of the bed.

An Indian physician came in and they spoke privately for a few moments. A nurse brought in a jar full of Nivea cream, perhaps spiked with a steroid, which was to be applied three times a day to the entire body. The scabs, like thorns firmly embedded in his dark brown leathery skin, would hopefully soften and fall off. He tried applying the cream but failed to reach his back, scalp, or toes. He firmly refused my offer to help. Ultimately the spectacle became too painful to watch. I grabbed the jar and began to apply it to his body, starting with his scalp and going downwards. He made a feeble attempt to stop me and then relented. My mother and grandparents watched without a word. The patient seemed embarrassed. Scabs fell to the floor, some dry, some wet, some withered, and others bloody. As the cream entered the crevices and cooled his skin, he felt better. A nurse entered, drew up a liquid in a syringe and injected it into his arm. She said it was for pain and would help him sleep.

Over the next week, his skin condition improved and his pain diminished. He started eating better and informed us that he wanted to return to work. His short and awkward stay with the joint family was over quickly. Before he left, he passed me an envelope to open after he left. Enclosed within were five crisp 100-shilling bills, a fortune for us, but clearly not enough for five or more years of medical school. Curious, many heads peeked at the contents of the envelope. Perhaps they had expected a huge check but managed to keep from looking too disappointed.

I was just happy that I had seen my favorite Doctor Kaka once again. It had never entered my mind that he owed me anything. On the contrary, the honor of walking with my father's uncle was reward enough.

Any money received usually went into a communal coffer maintained by Dada. This gift was to be placed in a bank account for me. As the car sped away, I remembered the nights the doctor had taken me to see his sick patients in Dar es Salam — the Haven of Peace, where my own peace had been shattered so unexpectedly — allowing me to carry his black bag, suppressing a secret smile when he observed my huge appetite for the gifts of food his patients arranged for me, and his look of satisfaction that I was reading *Gray's Anatomy*.

The car became a blur enveloped in a cloud of dust. Doctor Kaka did not look back, but I kept waving even after the vehicle vanished. I was thrilled he had come and was healed under our care. I wanted so desperately to be like him.

We had the dreams, but not the means.

BOOK TWO:
The Land of My Ancestors

THE QUEST

My parents decided that if they lived even more frugally, their combined income just might cover the cost of my tuition, boarding, and lodging in India. Additionally, after my mother's declaration of bankruptcy in 1960, a badge of shame, there was a little more cash at hand.

Students with far lower scores were heading toward college overseas, and they understood my unspoken angst.

In early 1962, my father mailed typed letters to 50 medical schools in India requesting application forms. He used the finest paper. The letters were polite and professional. He checked the grammar and spelling and confirmed the addresses provided by the Indian Consulate. I thanked him awkwardly when he finally told me what he had been typing so feverishly for weeks.

We waited as days turned into weeks and then months, but still there was no response from any college. We assumed this was due partly to the laziness and ineptitude of Indian officials and the constant quest for bribes. My family finally decided to send me to Bombay to plead my case in person. Our relatives in India happily agreed to host and guide me.

I worried that Indian colleges would not be able to compare my grades from Cambridge University with the scores that Indians were accustomed to. I hoped, however, that my Maharashtrian ancestry, excellent school record, and letters might help. I now had the added distinction of having climbed Mount Kilimanjaro. Would that count?

On May 28, 1962, I boarded a train bound for Mombasa. Subhash, my younger maternal uncle, left for India four days ahead of me. This was the same train taken by Belgian refugees in 1960 as they escaped the chaos in Congo. At the railway station, I saw uncharacteristic tears in my grandfather's eyes. I did not know then that

I would never see him again. The women were bawling inconsolably. My mother bit her lip, but the tears defied her attempt to contain them. She wiped them with a corner of her sari. My father stood quietly on one side as he watched his son leave home for the first time, for a new country and an uncertain future.

Mombasa is a lovely town with its Arab and Portuguese history, gorgeous beaches, and graceful palm trees. There was a large Indian and Arab population here and race relations were good. My hosts, the Shah family, and I sat under great *baobab* trees eating roasted cassava and sipping fresh coconut water as a gentle sea breeze blew and large ships entered the harbor. The white strips of sand stretched as far as the eye could see. Fort Jesus, built in the 16th century, faced the ocean. It had protected much of the Portuguese empire and the slave trade on the east coast of Africa.

The steamship *Amra* would take me to Bombay in seven days. My wooden berth was in a third-class cabin below sea level. Narrow metal stairs led to the massive kitchen, where food for hundreds of (mostly Indian) passengers was cooked in huge pots. The air stood still and stale, as though it had passed many lungs before entering mine. The ordinarily welcome smell of spices and fried food was nauseating in that confined space. I was overcome by seasickness as the ship left the harbor. The college students, seasoned travelers all, were returning to India after a break in Kenya. Veterans of these voyages, they knew how to have a grand time on the upper deck. I heard distant sounds of music and celebration as I suffered alone on my bunk deep in the bowels of this enormous ship. The shared bathrooms were far away. I started vomiting into empty bottles and cans, leaving a disgusting smell. The nausea was followed by a severe headache. It was relentless, nonstop agony for three days.

I knew I had to get some fresh air, food, and fluids. Someone left me a full bottle of ginger ale. I felt better and ventured up to the deck after three days of starvation. A Hindi movie was being shown on a large screen, perhaps a bed sheet, on the deck under the dark, starry sky. Large waves lapped on the bulwarks of the ship. The teenagers were singing, dancing, and sipping gallons of soft drinks. A few smoked cigarettes now that they had escaped the scrutiny of their elders. I was surprised how the boys and girls mingled together. They flirted but kept a respectable distance at all times. There was no touching. All of this felt unreal.

On the fourth day, a childhood friend, a veteran of several voyages, Kaustubh Kolhatkar, took one look at me and shepherded me to a higher deck where the air was fresher. There were very few people at this level. We sat on a wooden picnic table.

In short order, a highly dignified family appeared. The regal and handsome gentleman was accompanied by an extraordinarily beautiful woman and two small children. The children peered at us curiously. The couple looked like movie stars. They welcomed us in impeccable English and asked us to join them for dinner. Kaustubh apparently knew them. Awkwardly, I said, "Yes, thank you."

What followed was a delicious western meal that ended with cakes and cookies. It was my first meal on the ship. I hoped they would invite us again. To my delight, they did.

These Pakistani immigrants to Kenya were heading to Karachi to meet their extended family. I never discovered their names and do not remember thanking them for their hospitality. We never paid a penny for the meals, but they expected nothing in return. I learned about Muslim hospitality from this gracious family. One of my regrets in life was not getting their contact information so I could send them a heartfelt note of thanks. The family knew we were Indian, Hindu, and from the lower decks, but it did not seem to matter. I tried to reconcile the kindness of this Pakistani couple with the atrocities during the partition.

I felt stronger and well hydrated, and was thriving on cakes and ginger ale. I did not return to the lower deck with its acrid smell of fried food, vomit, stale air, and dried sweat. I slept on the deck, in the open air under the stars, for the next few days. Occasionally I would dart down for a change of clothes and escape from that hell as quickly as possible. I do not recall bathing.

One day, the shoreline of Seychelles came into view. It was enchanting. The blue ocean with a tinge of turquoise green, the miles of sandy beaches, and the lush palms were even more beautiful than Bamburi Beach near Mombasa. We went ashore on small boats and walked around town. It was strangely quiet that afternoon and the shops were closed. We saw little shacks that pretended to be restaurants and bigger structures that masqueraded as shops. Hungry, we peeked in one door that could have been a private home or a small eatery. A handwritten sign offered bread and tea for a low price. We ate the dry bread, without butter, dipped it in the sweet tea, and left grateful for a good meal. The locals were unlike any I had seen before. Their light skin and gray eyes betrayed their mixed ancestry. Kenya did have a small population of Seychellois, but we had little contact with them.

We reached Karachi. A taxi driver promised me an affordable tour. We passed President Ayub Khan's palace on the oceanfront. The driver, sensing I was Hindu, took me to a deserted temple. It was tiny and clean but housed no priest, bells, or idols. It occurred to me that this might be a propaganda tour to convince the world that Pakistan, the "land of the pure," was tolerant. I felt nervous. Why had he brought me here? I told him in Hindi that I no longer wanted a tour and would be grateful if he could take me to the center of the city. I just wanted to be amid a lot of people so I might blend in as a local. After all, there was no real way of telling that I was Hindu by my appearance. He dropped me off on a busy street, in a business district that had the hustle and bustle of commerce.

I saw a huge, tattered poster of a white man with a deep dimple on his chin. I entered the theater to watch *Spartacus*. The theater was dingy, the seats old and musty, and some were broken. Pakistanis in pajamas cheered every time Kirk Douglas appeared. I joined in.

At sundown, I took a cab back to the ship.

The final stretch would take us through the Arabian Sea toward Bombay. I was three years old when my mother had taken me to India and knew that all my relatives would be strangers. As we approached, I was struck by an overwhelming sense of belonging. We were approaching the land of my ancestors—the birthplace of Hinduism, Buddhism, Jainism, and Sikhism; of Gandhi and Nehru; Bose and Bhagat Singh; Tilak and Tansen; Savarkar and Shivaji Maharaj; Akbar and Birbal; Rana Pratap and Govind Singh.

It was a land where martyrs gave their lives for freedom, the land of art and music. A great civilization, where my flesh and blood was formed. Where people looked like me and spoke my mother tongue, and where nobody could tell me to leave because of my skin color or my religion. That feeling never left me.

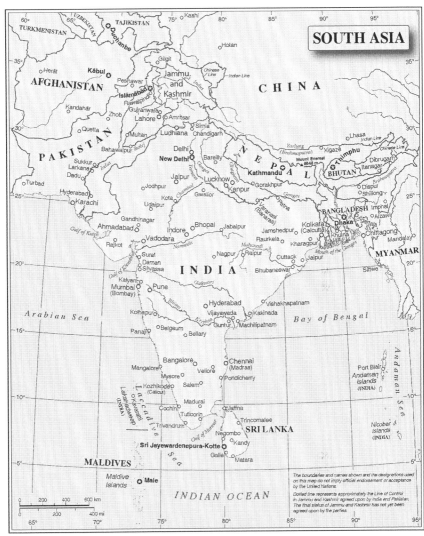

Figure 11: South Asia (with permission from the UN)

****

The weary and smelly passengers congregated at the rails, looking down at the ground below. Porters, little ants in red uniforms, ran toward the ship so they could approach the wealthy first-class passengers first. My father had stated simply that the family would find me when I disembarked. I scanned the little dots below from my high perch on the deck. My eyes focused onto a small cluster consisting of two tall men, the taller one with an old-fashioned turban and three very fair children. I felt at home even though those dots were strangers to me.

I had been warned about customs—the inefficiency, corrupt officials, pickpockets, and other miseries. But the officer smiled, said a few words in Marathi, and simply waved me through.

I had laid my British passport on the counter to sign some papers. When I turned around, it was gone. I was frightened. How would I travel again? How would I prove to anyone that I had a British passport in the first place? The officer calmly suggested that I file a police report. Had he taken it?

I touched the feet of the two men. The tall man with the turban was Gurjar Kaka, my father's sister's husband. The other man—fair, handsome, and with chiseled features—was my uncle Dinkar Kaka. His three children, my cousins, checked me out briefly and converged upon me for a collective hug. They did not seem to mind the grime or the smell. They hailed a cab and we managed to fit everyone into the yellow car. No one said a word. I was aware that all eyes were on me. I wondered why they all had such fair skin and nice features when I did not. After a while, bored with what they saw, they began to survey the scene outside the cab.

Almost an hour later, we reached Dadar, where my grandmother Aji lived. It was the same dilapidated *chawl* where my father and his siblings had been born, the home that my father had left in 1938, unannounced and unexpectedly, and where I had complained about the slice of mango at age three.

Figure 12: Aji

Any stranger entering these grounds was noticed immediately. I sensed a thousand eyes on me as I climbed up the rickety stairs to the fourth floor, my cousins fighting over who would carry my bag. Nothing had changed here for decades. The inner room served as a kitchen, dining room, and place for a bath. A small curtain provided privacy. One had to make do with half a bucket of warm water. The living room had a single bed. At night, mattresses appeared miraculously and every inch of real estate was used, women in the inner room and the men outside. In the morning, everyone folded up their stuff, stored it under the single bed, and went about their business. Just outside the living room was a common path leading to the toilet, which were basically holes in the concrete floor and a can of water to clean up. Rows of such two-room apartments housed hundreds of people from several generations. People had lived and loved in this stark setting, content with their coexistence and with little ambition for anything better.

I stared at my grandmother. I could recall nothing about my visit in 1946. She had become widowed during the flu epidemic of 1918 and had single-handedly raised her three children. Dinkar Kaka had still been in her womb when her husband had died. Mean people, gossipmongers, wondered how she came to bear this baby. The struggle had sucked all the joy out of her life. She had aged prematurely, bent over her tiny frame, and her white hair was unkempt. Her wrinkles conveyed the misery of decades. An unhappy widow, she was unable to sense the misery in others. For her, it was normal to suffer silently, to accept her lot in life.

But as I clumsily touched her feet, a divine smile lit up her face. Perhaps she saw in me the son who had vanished without permission in 1938, married without her knowledge, and produced this child who was now touching her feet.

The other woman present in the room embraced me as though I were her own child. She was Sunder Atya (aunt), my father's older sister, who had married Gurjar Kaka. They had no children of their own.

Dinkar Kaka, my uncle, who had never met his brother (my father), had married a beauty from the Ratnagiri district named Chandu Mirashi. A striking woman with goddess-like features, she was the most beautiful woman in our family. Old touched-up photographs show a woman with high cheekbones, a perfectly symmetrical oval face, and brown eyes the size of almonds. The genes encoding her somewhat dark complexion had not been passed on. The children were as fair as their father.

Figure 13: Sunder Atya and Dinkar Kaka

He was a good-looking man too, rugged, fairer than my father, with deep furrows on his forehead, brown eyes, black hair, and the physique of an athlete (although he was not athletic). They made a fine couple. Their moments of passion indeed had produced three beautiful children, whom I came to love deeply in years to come.

My aunt Chandu felt trapped by her existence in a dilapidated home with an essentially absent husband who needed to work double shifts as a railway engine driver to make ends meet. Profoundly unhappy in this stifling environment, she had committed suicide by means unknown.

I remember watching my father break down in tears when that awful news reached Nairobi.

Dinkar Kaka had suffered the loss bravely. He immersed himself deeper into his job as an engine driver for the Indian Railways. He sold cloth at night as a side business. The work distracted him from worries about his motherless children, whose upbringing was left to others. With an absent father and a deceased mother, the two older children were farmed out to relatives.

The youngest, Pramila, went to an inexpensive boarding school because she was unmanageable—a volatile and wounded tigress, eyes full of fire and fury. When calm, she was very pretty. Although she was only 12, I was afraid of provoking her and therefore tried to avoid her. Pratibha (13) had inherited her mother's beauty and height. She could be feisty when the occasion demanded. She was sent to live with Sunder Atya, who had no children of her own. That worked out for intermittent periods of time, but the child had to be shuttled to and fro for a variety of reasons. Prakash (14), the eldest of the three and a Tony Curtis look-alike, was gentle, kind, and Aji's favorite. She adored him and bestowed on him the rare smile that she had given me only once. Prakash lived with Aji and cared for her until she died.

Dinkar Kaka remarried and moved to quarters provided by the Indian Railways. His second wife gave birth to a boy they named Pramod.

These strangers were part of my flesh and blood.

The arduous voyage to Bombay, the adjustment to new people and a new place, the crowds, the unending murmur of Marathi voices, the blaring radios — it was all too much to get accustomed to. My mind was a whirlwind of emotions.

Perhaps Tom Mboya had been right after all. I really belonged here in Bombay, India. I was awed by its history, culture, and traditions, as well as my ancestral and emotional bonds to the country. My lifelong love affair with India had begun even as I worried about my lost British passport which was eventually replaced by a new one.

****

The letter was addressed to Aji. It stated that Dada had died in Nairobi of a massive heart attack on May 28, 1962, the day I departed from the railway station in Nairobi. He had died rather quickly at home before medical help arrived. Everyone said that stress killed him. Although Dada had been upset by the earlier departure of his youngest son, Subhash, and then my own four days later, it was likely that the high blood pressure, obesity, and poorly controlled diabetes contributed more to his demise than our departures had.

It was my second day in Bombay. Aji sat next to me, speechless, on that single bed, watching me anxiously. She had been asked to break this news gently because I was very close to my grandfather. I looked at the letter, then at her, not completely comprehending what had happened. She said nothing, but I saw deep compassion in those exhausted eyes.

Subhash, just 16 then, had been whisked away from the port in Bombay to Ahmedabad in Gujarat to be cared for by relatives of the Bhagwat and Deshpande families.

I passed out.

It occurred to me later that doing numerous sit-ups at a RSS camp or reading bad news could make one pass out, become feverish, and end up in the laps of strangers.

****

I had passed out once before, at age 10, during a rehearsal of *Jana Mana Gana*, India's national anthem, before a program to celebrate Independence Day in Nairobi. Our family doctor's wife, Mrs. Sumati Patwardhan, a staunch anti-British nationalist and a RSS supporter like her husband, was our tutor. I had always been afraid of her, but I am not sure why. A perfectionist, she demanded that each note be just right. I had passed out after singing the same anthem a dozen times in that small, hot, and crowded room on her second floor. Shocked, she froze. When I came to, I was wedged between her thighs, my head on her chest and her handkerchief wiping the sweat off my brows. I extricated myself awkwardly, told her I was fine, and stood in line again with those who had not yet fallen.

She declared that we had sung well and there was no need to rehearse anymore. The half dozen children, relieved, ran out giggling.

"How did you do that?" they teased.

"Anything to get out of a rehearsal!"

The children laughed.

****

Now in Bombay, having passed out for the third time in my life, I woke to find a young stranger placing cool milk poultices on my forehead as the Panvalkar clan looked on. I had never seen this man before. He informed me that he was Shrinivas Deshpande, that his mother was Dada's sister, also named Sunder. His father, Pandurang Ganesh Deshpande, was Dada's childhood friend, and they lived in Ahmedabad. He was going to take me there. I thought it would be good to be with Subhash again.

The next day, we boarded a train to meet a totally new set of relatives, all strangers to me. Unlike my Marathi-speaking relatives in Bombay, folks here were fluent in Gujarati. These amazing strangers informed me immediately that there was no need for formalities. I was a member of the family, their flesh and blood. Their home was my home. But I was disappointed not to see Subhash there.

Shrinivas was the only male among seven siblings. A short, stocky, good-looking man with gray eyes, he was a student at India's prestigious Indian Institute of Technology near Bombay. Gandhian principles of equality applied in this household, and he was required to share chores equally with his six sisters. Men in Nairobi did not do that.

The kindest and nicest people I had ever met, they healed my physical ailment and the trauma of my grandfather's passing. Pandurang Kaka, the patriarch, said very little but exuded serenity. He had led an austere, disciplined, and principled life. In 1974, he completed a Gujarati to English translation of a dictionary for the University Book Production Board in Ahmedabad, and in 1989 translated the 24th edition of the *Universal English–Gujarati Dictionary* for Oxford University, 940 pages long, the standard for such scholarly books. Later, as an individual who knew and had fought for freedom with Gandhi, Pandurang Kaka was asked by India's government to do some scholarly work on the life of the Mahatma. He was fair, tall, and distinguished with an aura of royalty, and he wore *khadi*, the locally made cotton goods that Gandhi had espoused. He had taken to heart the high principles of freedom, dignity, absolute honesty, and the emancipation of women.

Sunder Atya, with a heart of gold, was a great mother and mentor to seven children, who became renowed scholars, professors, and highly principled citizens of free India. They were so patriotic that, in 1962, after the India–China war over a border dispute, they stopped eating sugar because it was called *chini* in Hindi!

Their home was simple, clean, and practical. A swing screeched on the patio where the family gathered in the evening to share stories. The conversation was always about serious matters. They wanted to do great things for India. No one, and nothing, was going to hinder their dreams. They were going to be the architects of a new India, proud and resilient, and would build a great nation, strong and free from poverty, famine, and disease. They were highly regarded in town, and each evening, authors, poets, chancellors, scholars, and politicians gathered, sitting cross-legged on a lawn in front of one of the homes, to discuss matters of great import. I had never imagined that one day I would sit with such famous men. It was an overwhelming privilege.

I needed to get back to Bombay to pursue my dream of securing a seat in a medical school. I decided to visit Mira, my mother's youngest sister, who was studying in Baroda. Although I did not know it then, that trip would dramatically alter the course of my life.

On a hot day in late June, I took a train to Baroda, my mother's birthplace, just 60 miles from Ahmedabad. The lovely town, an interesting mix of bilingual Gujarati- and Marathi-speaking people, was known for its progressive rulers. The great university was named after the maharajas and attracted many Indian students from Kenya.

Mira, just about my age, was studying zoology. We shared our grief about Dada and what he had meant to us. Her hostel was close by the railway station and Kamati Garden. Vinod Shah, a childhood friend from Nairobi, hosted me for two nights in the men's hostel.

The next day, I met Mira's friend and roommate, Asha Sathe. I did not know why she was there. She said little and I asked her nothing. Dressed in a plain cotton sari, wearing no makeup, her shiny black hair reaching her waist, she had large brown eyes that betrayed shyness. She maintained proper decorum by making sure Mira walked between the two of us at all times as we walked around the garden, where peacocks were known to put on quite a show during their mating season.

I did not expect to ever see Asha again.

Vinod and I ate at the railway station cafeteria, where I was introduced to tandoori chicken, *pullao* (rice), and Tootie Fruity (ice cream with fruit). I met friends who had spent two years in college in India and were now entering the local medical school.

A letter from my parents informed me that none of the 50 medical schools had responded to my father's request for application forms. They urged me to personally visit schools in Baroda and Bombay.

The admissions office of the medical school in Baroda had no record of any letter. They also told me (kindly) that even if they could find the application, my Cambridge University certification, my British citizenship, and the stiff competition for limited seats made it highly unlikely that I would be accepted. They had received thousands of applications.

Discouraged and running out of money, I took the next train out to Bombay.

THE INTERVIEW

Back in Bombay, a huge and unfamiliar city, I walked to Grant Medical College. The clerk brusquely informed me that he had not seen my application. He asked me to spell my last name and to hurry up. He raised his eyebrows upon hearing "Panwalker." Was he trying to figure out if I was a Brahmin or a "scheduled caste"? He asked me if I knew a certain doctor Panvalkar, who was well known at the hospital. I said no. That ended the conversation.

He did not search for my application, but impatiently waved me away. He immersed himself in a massive pile of dusty and crumbling papers. I knew that somewhere in that pile was a carefully composed letter, typed on expensive stationery, from my father. I stood by awkwardly, hoping to catch his attention. Finally, he turned to me with great irritation, rebuking me in Marathi for still being there. His absolute power and arrogance stunned me. Was he just having a bad day or was he looking for a bribe? Had my caste upset him? Was he simply lazy, mean, or overworked? I decided I would not go to any other schools and suffer similar indignities again.

Dinkar Kaka implied that he had connections. But he was a railway engine driver, working two jobs and selling fabric on the side, so I was quite skeptical. In his research, he said, he had discovered that one of our very distant relatives with the same last name was a senior police officer in Bombay. Surely, he would have major influence. He sent a post card to the inspector. The officer and his wife invited us to lunch. In an era without telephones in most homes and before the advent of email, it was rather remarkable how people communicated so efficiently. People sent 3 x 5 postcards to get in touch.

Their small apartment was in a fancy neighborhood at the foothills of Malabar Hill. We ate lunch the old-fashioned way, sitting on a flat wooden slab on the floor. Tall, strong, and fair, he spoke with distinguished authority. I was convinced that this man could help me.

He said he would look into my predicament, but asked for no paperwork, no copies of my résumé or application, and did not tell us what exactly he was going to look into.

I had mixed feelings about using influence to bypass the system. It did not seem fair to deprive a more deserving person. Yet I was desperate. I had also been told that no one gets into medical school in India on merit alone. One almost always had to have either influence or money or both. My uncle reassured me that everyone uses these methods to gain entry into medical and engineering schools. I did not really believe that every Indian doctor had bribed their way to get accepted. Torn between principle and my desire to become a doctor, I said nothing, so the two of us became silent co-conspirators. Weeks passed and we heard nothing from the police official. The lunch was the only courtesy he would extend to a distant relative.

Days passed, and the June monsoon was in full swing. The ferocity of wind and water inverted umbrellas and shredded our cotton clothes into tatters. On one such dreary day, we received a postcard inviting me to meet a Mr. Patel and his family. They lived on the same Malabar Hill where the rich and mighty live, overlooking the Arabian Sea and Chowpatty Beach in Bombay. My uncle and I were ushered into this opulent, multilevel mansion with marble floors. I felt like a peasant entering a forbidden palace. A woman, who we assumed was Mrs. Patel, greeted us and offered us lunch. We ate quietly and uncomfortably. From the spotlessly clean large windows, we could see the cars and chauffeurs, the well-tended gardens and uniformed workers bustling by. Another servant asked if we wanted a second helping, informing us that the well-dressed woman who had served us lunch was in fact a housekeeper. We were eating in a room set aside for servants.

After the meal, a squat, obese, but jovial man guided us to a smaller room with deep leather sofas. He told us in Gujarati how my grandfather (Dada) had a huge influence on his life and how he was eternally grateful for the education and success, which would have been impossible without his guru. Dinkar Kaka, who did not understand a word of Gujarati, nodded whenever I did. The tycoon had apparently built a large enterprise, escaping poverty, thanks to Dada's inspiration. He was so sorry to learn that he had passed on. Mr. Patel said he had received a letter, written just a few days before Dada's death, urging him to look after his only grandson. That is why we had been invited to this mansion. My uncle's eyes lit up. This was an important man. His body language suggested power and control. But I became increasingly uncomfortable. Dada had told us to earn what we got and not beg for it or peddle influence. Why would he write such a letter to this man?

Secretly, I hoped Patel would produce a magic wand or pick up his phone and announce my admission to a medical school. We did see some stylish women dressed as though they were going to a party but it was just after noon. Perhaps they always dressed this way. We were not introduced to the rest of the family. After a few niceties, he dismissed us, graciously promising to keep in touch. He said he was so glad to see the grandson of his guru, and that it was his *kartavya* (duty) to help me. I thought he might cry, so authentic was his demeanor. However, I did not hear from this family again. There was no magic wand. Letters from Nairobi informed us that Mr. Patel had written how delighted he was to see his guru's grandson, "a fine young man," and how he was so flattered that the Bhagwat family had not forgotten him after all these years in Africa.

As we rode the double-decker bus back, my uncle urged me not to lose heart, that he had other connections. I protested that I did not want to do this anymore. He then used a word I had never heard before. He said, "*Vashila* (influence) is a way of life here."

This man, my father's brother, a thoroughly honest man, was telling me it was okay for him to do that on my behalf. I felt intense gratitude that he would be willing to violate his own principles to help me, his 19-year-old nephew, even though my family had never done anything for him.

We went back to his flat in Byculla in the Railway Quarters, where he lived with his second wife and a one-year-old son, Pramod. This child was accepted without much affection by his step-siblings. This would be my home for the next few weeks, since it had a little more space than the home where Aji lived.

It was a hot and wet monsoon summer in Bombay. The rain ruined the few clothes I had. The tatters were replaced by white trousers and white shirts made from the fine fabric that my uncle had failed to sell in his spare time. A man with great integrity but a terrible salesman, he admitted to customers that more expensive fabrics were no better than the cheaper variety he had stocked in his living room.

The railway apartments, ours being on the 16th floor, had been constructed with shoddy workmanship. Rain slanted under the balcony door. Rags were placed near each window and door to block the water. Opening windows for fresh air was not an option since they were often stuck, rotted, or broken. Bedbugs thrived in this hot and humid home. Their bites left itchy welts on our hot, wet skin. Plucking them off the seams of mattresses and drowning them in little containers of oil was a full-time job. Fans whirred overhead all day and night, in a futile attempt to cool our skin and dry soggy towels and clothes. The air was stale and sickening. Geckoes darted across the ceiling, some white and transparent, showing their innards. I remembered that Baba used to describe extremely fair Indian women with bluish veins as *"pandhri pal"* (transparent lizards)

I learned later that these apartments had been designed by my future father-in-law, a decent and honest senior engineer in the railways, who could not possibly control the many shortcuts the workers and contractors took. Trains carrying thousands of passengers passed by every few minutes on the tracks directly behind the high-rise buildings. The screaming whistles of commuter trains, part of the largest rail system in the world, announced their presence with annoying regularity.

Not used to being cooped up in such dreary settings and yearning for the fresh clean air of Nairobi, I ventured out and walked for miles in Bombay. I felt comfortable outside. The people looked like me, they spoke my language, and I felt safe at all times.

Prakash, Pratibha, and I bonded quickly. Both held my hand and took me to see places in Bombay. Pramila remained alone. Their step-mother had given up her efforts to be a good mother to all the children after being rebuffed so often. My uncle did not intervene in the quarrels he overheard.

All of them had an irritating habit of talking about the past in wistful terms, how reasonable they had been in spite of the things others had done to them. Each one had gripes about the other. They told the same stories repeatedly to make sure the listener had not missed a single word or forgotten each nuance.

Once a month, their step-mother refused to enter the kitchen for four days, so my uncle took over the cooking and other chores. On occasion, she would ask me to fetch a pail of warm water for her bath while she sat naked in the bathroom. She said something about "*sola,*" which I learned later had something to do with menstruation. We had never practiced such restrictions in Nairobi. I found this behavior very odd.

My dreary situation was never too far from my thoughts. It gnawed at me. My hosts were always generous. No one ever suggested that I had overstayed my welcome. Days passed, then weeks, as it became apparent that I would have to return to Kenya and find a job. I borrowed money and booked my ticket for the return voyage for late August 1962. I dreaded the prospect of getting seasick again. It was too much to hope that the gracious Pakistani family from my last journey would choose the same travel dates and be on the same ship.

****

I decided to visit my father's sister, the other Sunder Atya, and my father's brother-in-law, Gurjar Kaka. They lived two long train rides away in a little town called Amalner. The childless couple had looked after my father for several years in his youth. I was the only passenger to disembark at this tiny station, which was deserted except for a *tanga* (a carriage) driver, who was taking a nap as his horse rested.

"Can you take me to Gurjar Kaka's home?"

"Of course, everyone knows him!" He quickly grabbed my suitcase, cleaned the seat, and smiled.

The *clip clap* of horse hooves reminded me of Hindi songs composed by a famous music composer, O. P. Nayyar. There was a rhythm to everything in India. We reached an exceptionally clean two-room home within minutes. The *tanga wallah* refused to accept money for the ride. The warm embrace of those who would be my hosts for the next three days made me feel right at home.

Folks in this little town had known my father in his youth. I was taken to the home of a "compounder," the only pharmacist in town. He exclaimed, "Prabhaker cha mulga!" (Prabhaker's son) and held me tight as though he was making up for lost years.

Dr. Sen's mansion, a jarring sign of opulence in a town with mostly simple homes, was our next stop. I stepped inside to a truly warm welcome and touched Dr. Sen's feet. He was the only doctor in town. His son, Gautam, an extraordinarily handsome young man, informed me excitedly that he was nearly done with medical school, but was uncertain whether he would stay in the big city or take over his father's practice. The ambassador car in their driveway seemed oddly out of place in this little town with no paved roads and where buffalo roamed free. Where was the gas station?

Dr. Sen suggested that I meet a local politician, Mr. C, whose brother was the Minister for Health for the State of Maharashtra. Perhaps he could help me get into medical school. Once again, the tension emerged between principle and influence peddling.

We trooped toward the modest home on a mud road that led to a river. Wet buffalo waded in and out carelessly. Women thrashed their dirty laundry against rocks smoothened by decades of such rhythmic assaults. Sparkling white shirts and colorful garments fluttered gently in the languid breeze as they dried under the hot sun.

In this place, no one ever asked for permission to visit. There were no appointments; anyone at the doorstep was welcomed inside. The politician, a very pleasant man, had also known my father as a youngster. He was more than willing, even eager, to give me a letter of support. After the customary cup of tea, he handed me an envelope, which evidently contained a note for his brother, the Minister of Health, in Bombay. He promised to call his brother soon. I guessed the phone was in another room.

Is that how Gautam got into medical school?

I was now quite certain that my fortunes had turned and I would have the happy task of canceling my voyage back to Mombasa. I placed the letter carefully into my shirt pocket. High principles would have to wait. This was an opportunity I was not going to throw away. Dada had passed away and he would never know. I figured I did not need to tell others how I got into medical school.

****

On my return, I went straight to the Ministry of Health in central Bombay, a huge two-story brick building. I was told I needed an appointment, so I returned a few days later at the appointed time. It was a lovely day and my fortunes were about to change. I hummed a song. There was a spring in my step.

A little scruffy peon walked up to me and asked gruffly, in Marathi, what I wanted. He was dressed in a shabby, wrinkled khaki shirt and shorts, the typical uniform of government workers at the lowest levels of the hierarchy. I said I had an appointment to meet Minister C, and showed him the letter from Amalner.

He stared at the envelope, turned it over, held it up to the light and asked, "Where is the seal on the envelope?"

"What seal?"

"There has to be a red wax seal with a stamp so we know you have not opened this and altered it."

"This is a personal letter from the minister's brother and he is expecting it. He will know when he opens it. We are family friends." I lied. Wisely, I refrained from claiming to be the minister's nephew.

Puzzled, he disappeared for a few minutes, then returned shaking his head. He could not find my name in the ledger for any appointment. I knew that bribes escalate as time passes and the visitor gets desperate. The peons outside, the clerks and the security staff inside, are all lined up for their share of the loot. They tell you to sit or stand, and you do it like a trained dog. They are officious and serious at all times, but they are doing nothing important. They avoid eye contact. When someone looks you in the eye, it means a serious conversation about the *bakshish* (bribe) is about to begin.

I watched in amusement this ameba-like movement as the low-level workers extracted bribes. If you took too long to get the hint, they just disappeared until, in desperation, you begged for help. They are all acutely aware of your discomfort and pretend to be very busy. Through chinks in various doors, you see the lounging officials gossiping and enjoying endless cups of tea as the nation waits for them to do their job.

I waited. The appointment hour had passed a long time ago. The worker returned after the promised consultations with his *sahib*. He said the boss might be able to squeeze me in. I was getting angry. In one of my most fluent sentences in Marathi, I informed him that the minister would be extremely angry that a family friend's son had been treated this way. The man, now nervous, uncertain and apologetic, went back for further consultations, then finally returned and ushered me into the minister's office.

A fat man with a Gandhi cap sat at a clean, almost empty, desk. He did not smile. He rocked just a little in his chair, staring at the ceiling as though hypnotized by the slowly whirling blades of the fan overhead.

I greeted him with a traditional *namaskar*, with folded hands and a bow.

He glanced at me quickly, and in an exasperated manner asked, "Huh, aaz mee tumchi kashi madat karoo?" (How can I help you today?)

I replied, "Sir, maza Marathi weak ahe. Mee English madhe boloo?" (Sir, my Marathi is weak, may I speak in English?) I had given away my foreign status. Many Indians, envious of the success of their countrymen abroad, resented and disliked these "traitors" who had abandoned the nation for money. In their minds, we were mercenaries.

A flicker of sarcasm. His face hardened, lips curled upward. In a thick English–Indian accent, he retorted, "Some of us in India understand and can even speak a few words of English."

I had inadvertently offended him. Perhaps he thought I equated him with his brother in the village who spoke no English. Had I also offended him, as many nonresident Indians do, by implying a western sophistication, which he neither possessed nor cared for? It certainly was not my intent to anger him. My future depended on his willingness to get someone to open my files at the five medical schools in Bombay.

I apologized and decided to speak in Marathi, with an admixture of English words when I did not know the exact translation. Stooping forward a little, he simply stared at me while tapping his fat fingers on the desk. He had no reaction when I told him I had just met his brother in Amalner, that his brother was my father's childhood friend, and that Dr. Sen had been our connection. I informed him that I was seeking a place in medical school, that my parents were Maharashtrians born in India, and that I had received no response to any of my applications. Still no reaction. Could he please help me to activate my applications? I lied and told him I was not seeking any special favors, just a chance to have my application reviewed. Actually, I had hoped he would pick up the phone and secure me a spot immediately!

He sighed and leaned back in his large leather chair.

"I will see what I can do," he muttered and dismissed me with a wave of his hand. The meeting had lasted barely five minutes. He asked me nothing about my father. I wondered if his brother had sent him a blank sheet of paper. I thanked him and left the room, dejected. I looked back once, hoping for some encouraging words, but he was busy shuffling some papers on his shiny clean desk.

The meeting had been cold and brief. He had not greeted me, had never gotten out of his chair, and had not even asked for my contact information. The official had every right to be fed up with all these people seeking favors.

I stepped out of the massive building. As though on cue, the clear skies gave way to dark, ominous clouds. A steady drizzle, which had replaced the fury of the monsoons, dampened my spirits and chilled my bones. I shivered even though the day was hot and humid.

I told Dinkar Kaka the interview had gone well. No need to upset him. It was getting close to the end of August 1962. There were still no responses from the schools I had applied to.

The only alternative now was to return to Kenya, find a job, and apply to Makerere University for admission to the class of 1963.

****

I planned to spend a few days with my grandmother before returning to Nairobi, where I hoped John Clark would allow me to rejoin the Norwich Union Insurance Company.

Aji rarely received any mail, so we were surprised to find a brown 3 x 5 postcard addressed to me. It was a handwritten invitation to appear for an admission interview at the Christian Medical College (CMC) in Ludhiana, a thousand miles north in the plains of Punjab. Wilson College in Bombay was one of four interview venues.

It felt like a death sentence had been commuted. I had protested when Baba had shown me the list of medical schools he had written to. Not knowing a thing about CMC, I was quite upset that he would apply to such an obscure college. He had said calmly that it would not hurt, and the postage was just a few pennies.

No one in my family had ever heard of Ludhiana. It was a dusty city known as "the Manchester of India." Ludhianites were particularly well known for the mass production of wool sweaters. My family was anxious about me living with rather rowdy and robust Punjabis, but that did not bother me because I had grown up among them.

CMC had started as a missionary medical school for women around 1894 and became a coed institution in 1953. The odds of getting in were formidable, with 6,000 applicants vying for 50 slots. Half had to be women and half of Punjabi origin. Religious quotas were illegal, but a disproportionate number of students were Christians. A few foreign students from Malaysia, Singapore, and East Africa qualified for "Punjab seats" based on their parents' residence. I was competing for one of 25 male seats. I was not Punjabi, not Christian, a foreign student with no connections. My heart sank. There was no way they would select me. Rumors that an occasional student converted to Christianity to gain admission were probably false. I had written "Hindu" all over the admission forms.

A week later, dressed in all white, I entered a large hall. Nervous applicants, some wearing jackets and ties — attire quite unsuitable for such a hot and humid day — engaged in small talk, secretly wishing that the others would disappear.

The venerable Wilson College, at the foothills of Malabar Hill, is across the street from Chowpatty Beach, well known for its *bhel* and *puri* kiosks, coconut water vendors, and little ice cream shops. Marine Drive, a beautiful curved road, skirts the beach as tall buildings tower over the stone ramparts built to protect the asphalt from the murky waters of the Arabian Sea. Young families and couples frolic on the beach or silently contemplate the sound and fury of frothy waves lashing the concrete barriers. Occasional couples held hands discreetly while gazing at the sea.

Dada had graduated from Wilson College in the 1920s, before joining the independence movement. I wondered if he, in his heavenly abode, was aware that his grandson was walking on the same hallowed ground he had once trod. I silently asked for his blessings. I was not nervous; I had been through too much in my life. I was prepared for another disappointment.

There would be a written test followed by an interview. We were to describe the life of *Ameba histolytica* within 30 minutes. Fortunately, I was familiar with this topic and had ample time to tidy up my drawings of an ameba swallowing a red blood cell. We waited to be called for the interview.

Dr. Laxmi Rao looked up as I entered the room. Seated behind a small desk, she wore a blue sari, Maharashtrian style. Her oval face, brown eyes, and lovely features could have been chiseled out of granite by a skilled sculptor. She must have been a dark beauty in her younger days. Her friendly manner and soft smile put me at ease immediately.

She understood the tension, the potential for dashed hopes, and the suffering that might ensue. If she had the power, I thought, she would admit all the applicants in the room. She spoke fluent English with just a hint of a British-Indian accent.

Was she Maharashtrian, a Hindu, a Brahmin, a Christian, an Anglo-Indian? Did she go to a convent school? Was she a medical doctor or a PhD? I wondered if the paper in front of her was the essay I had written. She introduced herself as a professor of microbiology and the dean of the college. It was obvious that she had conducted such interviews for many years. She made sure I was Anand Panwalker, pronouncing my last name perfectly as a Maharashtrian might.

"Why do you want to be a doctor?" she asked.

I had rehearsed the answer, but I was not going to give her a corny, canned, cock-and-bull story about helping humanity. It was true, but everyone would say that. I muttered something about how, at age 11, I used to ride in a large black car with Doctor Kaka to make house calls every evening in Dar es Salaam. The words flowed effortlessly.

"He asked me each evening if I wanted to go with him. I think he had been lonely for so long and liked the quiet company I provided. And I felt important carrying his black bag. Besides, I enjoyed the beautiful ocean drive and the moist breeze stroking my face. While he did his healing in an inner room, I was offered food and fruit. I initially said no because I was unsure and shy. However, after a few visits, I decided it was rude to make a fuss each time and simply accepted the plate gratefully. I especially loved the mangoes. In order not to appear gluttonous, I ate slowly and politely, but fast enough to finish the offerings before my kaka would come out. If they insisted, and the healing was taking longer, they offered a second helping. And so it was, from home to home. The drive home, late in the evening, was wordless. This ritual became a daily affair and something that is branded into my being as one of the most influential things in my life. That, Dr. Rao, was my introduction to medicine."

The dean appeared to be in a trance. Was she asleep?

"One day, he asked me to pull out a dusty volume of *Gray's Anatomy*. The pages were yellowing and crumbling. I looked at the drawings and placed a bookmark so he knew I was actually reading it. It was terribly boring, but I did not want to hurt his feelings. I wanted to be the kind of healer he was, one who cared about people, not money.

He never sent a bill. Some paid him in cash, some in kind, and there were those who could pay nothing at all, unless the snacks they gave me counted as a fee. He had no clue who paid and who did not!"

Dr. Rao looked at me intently for a few seconds. Was she bored?

Just as quickly, she turned away and asked, "What would you do if we did not admit you?"

"I will apply again next semester." I told her that CMC was the only college, one out of 50, that had had the courtesy of responding to my application, and I was hopeful that my Cambridge certificate was not a barrier.

"What if you are rejected again?"

"I will keep trying until I get in," I replied, without much conviction.

"What would you do in the meantime while waiting for admission?"

I told her it would be an opportunity to find some work to support my tuition and ease the financial burden on my family. I told her about my work as an insurance clerk and a schoolteacher in Nairobi. She changed course.

"What is the most exciting thing you have ever done in your life?"

"Climbing Mount Kilimanjaro, watching the sunrise over the plains of Africa."

She sensed my joy and pride. She paused for a moment, seemingly out of questions, then smiled and said I would learn the decision within two weeks by mail.

She stood and shook my hand. "Good luck, Anand."

The way she said "Anand" gave me hope. She had listened patiently without interruption. My instinct said she liked me and I would be accepted. I thought I had done well to describe my motivation, my background, determination, and financial straits. Also, I knew I had written an excellent essay.

Was she as nice to everyone? Had she perfected the art of keeping hope alive?

It was now late afternoon. I crossed the street to the beach and sat on the stone wall watching the waves. Vendors offered snacks and sodas. Beggars begged. Families frolicked. Children cried when denied a second helping of ice cream. I watched the voluptuous curve of Marine Drive holding the Arabian Sea at bay. Malabar Hill stood guard, as it had for ages.

A feeling of belonging overwhelmed me. I knew I loved India and its people. They were like me, spoke my language, and did not want to throw me out of the country like Tom Mboya had. I felt a sense of exhilaration after a summer of anxiety and despair.

Hope surged within me that I would go to CMC, a thousand miles north of Bombay and thousands more from Nairobi. Colors appeared brighter. It stopped raining. The clouds parted. I walked back to my grandma's place in Dadar rather than take a bus. It took over an hour of brisk walking, but by now I knew my way around. And, unlike in Nairobi, I never felt afraid here.

Two weeks later, another 3 x 5 card appeared in the mail. It looked exactly the same as the first one. I was going to be a medical student at CMC, starting September 1962. My father's persistence and remarkable foresight in sending the application to this "forlorn place," in spite of my objections, had borne fruit.

I canceled my booking for the return voyage to Kenya. Feeling obligated to protect me from unknown dangers, Dinkar Kaka got free third-class rail passes and traveled with me to Ludhiana. All my earthly belongings and my favorite transistor radio fit into a small suitcase.

Wiry coolies wearing red turbans and sashes around their waists clawed their way in to find two open spots for us. Carrying delicately balanced bags on their heads, in their hands, and under their armpits, they negotiated the crowd without any mishaps. It was quite a feat. Such men, I imagined, had gone to Kenya to build the railway.

Ultimately, the chaos subsided. Conversations began cautiously. Passengers asked what our "good name" was, where we were going and why, our occupation, income, marital status, whether we had "issues" (meaning children), how much the transistor radio cost, were we "from foreign." No subject was off-limits. Why, they asked, was I going to medical school in Punjab when I was of Maharashtrian origin? Is it because of poor scores? How would I communicate with the Punjabis? Oh, so you speak Hindi and can understand Punjabi? How come? What does your uncle do? The sharp Indian eye quickly detected that the shoes were "foreign."

Pickpockets in India are said to be the most accomplished in the world. One moment of friendship, and the next your wallet is missing. They were so deft and quick. You NEVER kept your money in an outside pocket. You had to find ingenious hiding places, often close to your underwear. You never flaunted money in public.

Proximity to others is a fact of life in India, especially in third-class compartments. The smell, the sweat, and the lack of privacy can get on one's nerves if the journey is long, as mine was. Soon people began to doze off. Others played cards with total strangers. Before long, passengers were sharing food. The folks who had been shouting and shoving just a few hours ago were now generous and chivalrous, especially to the elderly, women, and small children.

The sounds of the train were interrupted by the shouts of *chaiwallahs* and vendors of baked and fried goods as we approached a major station. I especially loved the sound as the train crossed a long bridge over a river, its engine billowing black smoke from its nostrils. The train lurched to a halt at several stations. Some passengers disembarked to stretch their legs and drank sweet tea from small clay cups, an ecologic marvel, which enhanced the taste of the beverage. As the train spurted to life again, ticket less entertainers—singers, comedians, jugglers —and beggars entered the cabins. They had an uncanny ability to evade the ticket collector. Their amazing talent garnered meager collections, but perhaps just enough to feed their families for the day. Blind singers, lame instrumentalists, and limbless beggars tugged at your sleeve for alms. They assured the generous *sahibs* of God's blessings.

I saw heart-wrenching poverty and suffering in India. I had been shielded from Africans' suffering in Kenya, but to see people who looked like me go hungry and beg on the streets was a terrible shock. I remembered the story about Buddha, who had walked out of a princely life after observing the suffering of the old, the poor, the crippled, and the feeble, seeking an answer to why there was such suffering. I now understood why Buddha had done what he did.

Hubert Humphrey's words, at the dedication of the building named after him, on November 1, 1977, come to mind.

It was once said that the moral test of government is how that government treats those who are in the dawn of life, the children; those who are in the twilight of life, the elderly; and those who are in the shadows of life—the sick, the needy and the handicapped.

India's immense poverty brought tears to my eyes. When I handed a coin to one pathetic child, a swarm of deformed beggars, an endless sea of helpless humanity, suddenly descended upon me like bees to pollen. It was heartbreaking. Endless promises to end poverty, "garibi hatau," had not been kept.

Lacking toilets, men and women lined up along the slopes near railway tracks doing their best to hurry up before the train passed by, in a gallant effort to preserve their last vestiges of dignity. As one left the towns and cities, the stench created by the squatting and defecating masses near the rail lines receded. The slums and squalor were then replaced by verdant farms and oxen-led equipment tilling the land.

Disembarking in Agra, we found a cheap room for the night.

The Taj Mahal, built by the Emperor Shah Jahan to honor his wife, stands on the banks of the Yamuna River, a serene and extraordinarily beautiful tomb where both are buried, a monument to an emperor's love for his queen. The story that the architects' hands were cut off so that such a mausoleum would never be replicated is largely fiction; an attempt by someone with great imagination to suggest that love and savagery co-existed in this bastion of the Moghuls.

We boarded a packed train the next day with great difficulty. The occupants were far less accommodating and gracious than our previous companions. My uncle said Punjabis are far more aggressive and that the queue system, implying civilized behavior, exists only in Bombay.

We reached Delhi after a short ride. This is where Nehru had made his speech about the "tryst with destiny," where Mahatma Gandhi had been assassinated, and where the Moghuls had held court for centuries.

We did not have time to stop in Delhi and boarded yet another train, which would take us across the fertile plains of Punjab. Punjab's farmers, hard workers with a zest for life, fed the nation, and its soldiers fought India's enemies. These were the people who had bravely battled Alexander's army and, even though they had lost, won the hearts of the Greeks. Alexander was so impressed by King Porous that he returned the kingdom to him after the battle. It felt amazing to be on the grounds where great armies had fought. Many Greeks stayed behind even as Alexander continued on his travels through what is now Pakistan. He died before he could take his tired and depleted army back to his homeland.

We passed Kurukshetra. Bewildered, I asked my uncle whether this was the place where the famous battles described in the epic poem *Mahabharata* had occurred. Yes, he said, this was indeed that hallowed ground. This is where Lord Krishna had spoken to Arjun and told him to do his duty in the battle against his evil kith and kin, immortalized in the epic line starting with the words "Karmanaye vadhikaraste..." in the holy book, the *Bhagavad Gita*. I was speechless.

Ludhiana, a dusty little town, had no character, charm, or beauty. A rickshaw powered by a frail human carried us two miles to the hostel, named after Ronald Ross, the man who was a pioneer in malaria research. We were dropped off in front of an entrance with a curved arch. A cobbler sitting near the steps gave us a respectful smile and salute.

RITES OF INITIATION

We were met immediately by a friendly senior medical student. Short, podgy, and very fair, he was already bald. Smiling, he stretched his right hand forward. As I reciprocated, he quickly withdrew the hand and put his right foot up instead. My uncle was astonished at this extreme breach of etiquette. Enraged, I kicked the student. His face turned purple with rage. Three more men emerged, aroused from their siesta by the ruckus their comrade was making. My nightmare was about to begin. I, a freshman, had disrespected a senior. I was going to get special treatment.

I did not want my uncle to witness that. I hugged him and urged him to leave. Uncertain, he looked back over his shoulder once, waved a final goodbye, and took the train back to Bombay the same evening.

I had never heard of hazing. Insults, food, and sleep deprivation, lewd comments and raucous laughter, and teasing and humiliation persisted for five days. This was a little longer than average because I refused to apologize for the kick. They went through my belongings and found my transistor, which reinforced their stereotype of the rich Indian kid from abroad.

"Fake *Angrez* (Englishman)! Bloody colonial stooge!"

"You stink. When was your last bath?" They held their noses in mock disgust.

I soon learned that silence was the best strategy. Any other response provoked them. Eventually they lost interest or found new victims. A senior medical student from Kashmir, Atul Bhan, took pity on me, hiding me in his room and smuggling food in. This kind man would go on to become a Harvard professor.

I was to share a room with Ranjit Singh from Malaysia and Thomas Vettath from Singapore. We were now permitted to venture out to the dining halls and the recreation room, or to step out into the town that would be my home for the next five years.

After the ordeal was over, my tormentors asked if I wanted to play a game of table tennis with them! The seniors said the hazing was just for fun and they hoped there were no hard feelings. We were told we would get to pick our victims the following year. I thought the whole thing was downright stupid and uncivilized.

****

The college campus, a short walk from Ross Hostel, housed the classrooms, a canteen, and the women's residence. Nearby was Brown Memorial Hospital, honoring Edith Brown, the founder of what was originally a women's college.

The buildings, old brown brick structures, included a large anatomy hall on the ground floor. Small rooms upstairs were reserved for basic science lectures. Dr. Rao, the dean, and Dr. Constable, the principal, had small offices across the canteen. There were a few residential apartments for faculty. A chapel welcomed people of all faiths, but only Christians entered. A surprisingly large auditorium was used for graduations, plays, and concerts. Tiny gardens with flowering shrubs brightened the scene.

The summer heat was so oppressive that the air shimmered and mirages formed on the tar roads. A siesta followed lunch daily. Not even a bird flew during this period of inactivity. Afternoon lectures began at 3:00 PM and ended at 6:00.

I saw no Muslims on this campus. A few students with Hindu or Muslim-sounding names were actually Christian. There was a Hindu girl from Pakistan. Anglo–Indians, children of marriages between Englishmen and Indian women, had names like Oliver, David, or Desmond. They looked like all other Indians. Occasionally, we were startled to see a green-eyed Indian with brown skin.

They came from many states and from many countries. Brahmins, "untouchables," offspring of generals, nephews and nieces of film stars, the rich and poor — all intermingled seamlessly. North Indians were typically fair, good-looking, tall, and proud, perhaps reflective of the intermingling with Greek and Moghul invaders. There were Sikhs with turbans and those without. The Kenyan turban was more stylish than the one from the Malay Peninsula. Students from Malaysia,

Singapore, and Thailand dressed in smart, drip-dry, polyester clothes, while the Indians wore baggy cottons. Christians from Kerala in the south and Uttar Pradesh in the north were overrepresented, defying national demographics.

Most of the lecturers were Indians, primarily from Kerala and Bengal. There were white expatriates from the United States, Britain, and New Zealand who spent six months learning Hindi and Punjabi. The Indian professors were feared but highly regarded. Dr. Samuel, with his big eyes and thick glasses; Mary Mathews, who never smiled; and Joshi, who whispered softly. Others barked out questions, reserving a brief smile only for those who knew the answer. The ignoramuses, the majority of us, were aware of the low esteem we were held in. These great clinicians were intolerant of minor infractions, and their stares were enough to frighten. We knew they had the power to halt our careers if we offended them.

The first two years of the five-year curriculum were dedicated to anatomy and physiology. Each day began with the dissection of a cadaver, which was shared by four students at each table. Attendance was mandatory for all sessions. A student had to be on their death bed to take the day off.

The physiology professor, who was the warden as well, lived with us in Ross Hostel. No one feared him. He was a little man with elephant ears, preposterously large bulging eyes, and a pot belly. God had been unkind to him. Students mocked him. They teased him mercilessly, encouraging him to get married and produce a litter of little physiology professors for the next generation. Fearing retribution, he did not report the illegal hazing, or his own mistreatment, to authorities. One memorable day, he broke out into sobs. Some of us tried to console him. No one understood his loneliness. He looked at us in despair, tears in his eyes, and walked away, accusing us of being hypocrites.

Our white professors were approachable and enjoyed a little banter. They laughed at our jokes. The atmosphere was respectful but not tense. There were "no stupid questions," they said, a view they did not share with their Indian counterparts. We were courteous and respectful at all times, addressing everyone as "Sir" or "Madam."

My budget, 300 rupees a month, was a significant chunk of our family income. My parents lived a frugal life to ensure I did not lack.

The tuition was low, and I bought secondhand books. The food was inexpensive and plentiful.

The dining room, called the mess, served vegetarian, non-vegetarian, or South Indian cuisine. A few had a private room for western food. It cost more, but included daily meat and desserts. We were jealous and said they were stuck-up, rich snobs. In the evenings, we surrounded the cook, who made fresh *rotis* for the whole mess, and hijacked many of them soon after they left the oven. Sikhs and Punjabis often took control and intimidated those who protested the pilferage of their pickles. The perpetrators were my friends but I forgave their shameful transgressions because the food tasted better when mixed with the illegally procured condiments.

In this subculture of the North versus the South, Punjabis called everyone south of Delhi a "Madrasi," implying that those generally dark-skinned people were timid, gutless, or both. It did not matter that they were really from Kerala, the state with 100% literacy and a communist government. The southerners muttered under their breath how uncouth and uncivilized the northerners (those who lived anywhere north of Trivandrum) were.

I became a dark member of the fairer northern clan because I spoke Hindi and Punjabi. There was a rumor that some southerners passed secrets to Christian professors during chapel services. At least one Christian professor thought that northerners were a bad influence because they partied too much, spending valuable time in restaurants, in movie theaters, or with girlfriends instead of studying and praying. Despite these unspoken tensions, the campus had a happy atmosphere.

I was in seventh Heaven.

****

The corpses lay on a metal table surrounded by two boys on one side and two girls on the other. Younus Masih, the son of a poor Christian laborer, was my tablemate. He told me that a woman in Kansas had supported his education through a monthly gift of $15 to the Christian Children's Fund. He went on to a brilliant career in India and then America, and provided a home for his parents and education for his five siblings. We have maintained our bonds of friendship for decades.

Across the table was a Hindu woman with a toothy smile and a well-endowed figure. She enjoyed the attention from male students. She would later marry an Anglo–Indian classmate, then migrate to America and build a home on a cliff off the Pacific Ocean.

The other girl, a Christian, was a shy but attractive woman. She was teased for her last name, which translated into "red chili pepper." She was one of the nicest girls I had ever known.

Every morning we waited for a skinny old man, who looked like a cadaver himself, to pull the stiff bodies from their resting place—a huge tank full of formalin, which helped to preserve the bodies—using ropes and pulleys. He had pet names for each, and knew which table they belonged to. Our eyes smarted as the dripping dead were hoisted up and dropped onto our metal work tables.

As the day wore on, the thin, yellow fat layer around the puny muscles melted in the heat of the Indian summer, its acrid smell permeating the lab and clinging to our clothes. Our anatomy professors, walking with their hands behind their backs, helped us identify the tiny nerves, blood vessels, and muscles. There was to be no levity or inattention. We were not to stare at the girls. If the assignment was to study the brachial artery, we had better not touch the femoral artery. We were not to talk at the table unless it was a matter concerning the anatomy of the deceased. Dr. J. C. Saha enforced these rules with an eagle eye.

Who were these dead people, we wondered? Did they have families? Were the bodies donated? Did they die of disease or hunger? Could they not afford a decent cremation or burial? Had a poor family sold them in order to feed the lucrative market for skeletons locally and overseas? The cadaver at my table was a tiny, thin man with a straight nose, large ears, poorly aligned rotten teeth, and evidence of poor nutrition. He might well have frozen to death during one of the brutal winter nights. His uncircumcised penis suggested to us that he was a Hindu. The initial revulsion we felt sitting next to a corpse faded as he became part of the team. It took great effort to get rid of the putrefied and formalin-tinged fat embedded under our nails. At noon, the bodies were again immersed in the formalin tank, their resting place for a full two years.

Each evening, after the lectures, we gathered for a cup of tea in the canteen. Dinner followed. After sunset, we sat on the terrace of the Ross Hostel to watch the starlit sky over Punjab, the land of five rivers.

****

In 1959, the Dalai Lama sought refuge in India after Chinese forces occupied Tibet. Three years later, China invaded India in an effort to assert its claim over disputed territory in the Himalayas, but also to punish India for sheltering the spiritual leader. The Indian Army was ill-prepared. Chinese soldiers rapidly entered Tejpur, 80 miles inside the Indian territory of Assam. Krishna Menon, the flamboyant Minister for Foreign Affairs and a man with communist leanings, was vilified. Indians rued the day they had chanted, "Hindi Chini, bhai bhai" (Indians and Chinese are brothers) when Chou en Lai had visited some years earlier. Jawaharlal Nehru was devastated by this Chinese subterfuge. People spoke of the "Yellow Peril," a xenophobic term coined by Wilhelm Kaiser II in 1895 to describe the treachery of a race of colored people from East Asia, who dreamt of world dominance.

The nation was galvanized. Funds, food, clothes, and blankets were collected to send to our troops. Trenches were dug in Punjab, even though the foe was a thousand miles to the east. Western powers looked on but did nothing. Their silence emboldened the communists. There was no realistic expectation that India could defeat China in an all-out war. The enemy subsisted on minimal rations and had trained for high-altitude warfare. Indian soldiers were ill-equipped, cold, hungry, and unable to fight in the rarified air of the mountains.

It was during this time that we got to know Dr. Banerjee, a Bengali physiology professor and ex-major in the Indian Army, who became our cheerleader whenever our spirits flagged.

To everyone's surprise, the Chinese withdrew quickly. They had simply wanted to teach India a lesson to stop the skirmishes across the disputed border.

A few days later, a classmate, after a brief look at my jaundiced eyes, declared: "Anand, you are the Yellow Peril now!" Neither of us understood that this was a racist and xenophobic term.

"But I feel well," I protested as the clinic physician diagnosed Hepatitis A. We knew this was a rather common and benign condition related to contaminated food and water. However, another jaundiced student had gone into a deep coma, had required massive transfusions to replace his infected blood, and had nearly died. I was promptly admitted to the hospital. Treatment in those days included complete bed rest and bland food such as cakes and sweets. Fried food was forbidden. I was not to walk around unassisted. The very strict nurses, whom we feared even more than the professors, were called "sisters," even though none of them was related to us.

This lifestyle pleased me. How could one not be happy with cakes, cookies, and care? A few girls, some quite attractive, came to see me, but my awkwardness ensured no return visits. I did not inform my parents; they would worry too much.

This state of nirvana was not to last long.

On the third day, Dr. L. M. Dickson, a British anatomy professor who had just returned to India from her sabbatical, introduced herself. I was flattered, but unprepared for what came next. She declared that she would tutor me for one hour every evening so I would not fall behind the rest of the class. I was touched, but frankly I had been happier having no tutor or homework!

Each evening, we turned the pages of the dreadful *Gray's Anatomy*. I used a yellow marker for important Latin names, red for arteries, and blue for veins. Nerves were left white and muscles were brown. This gentle teacher's kindness challenged my generalizations about the British. Her persistence touched me. I resolved to pay her back by doing well in the upcoming examination. She brought the exam papers to me afterward. I had received the highest score in my class.

Competitors, alarmed by my success, gave grudging approval. They relaxed as my grades returned to average over time. Easily distracted from my studies, I preferred to read a novel, go to movies, eat good food at roadside kiosks, or simply hang out with my friends. Sometimes, when the cool evening air replaced the oppressive afternoon heat, we gathered on the roof of the four-story hostel to tell tall stories or suck mangoes placed in a bucket half filled with ice. From the roof, we also hoped to get a peek at the student nurses through the open windows in their quarters across the street. These young women, who had still not become fearsome "sisters," feigned anger and pulled the curtains down. If they saw us on the campus, their giggles told us they were not displeased by the attention.

THE MISSING SPIRITS

Dr. Banerjee almost ended our careers in an episode we called "The Matter of the Missing Spirits."

I had been elected Class Representative by our second-year class and was assigned to work with the Assistant Representative, Parminder Kaur, the female counterpart. It was a surprise, because I did not want the job and did not think of myself as a leader. Neither of us understood our responsibilities and thought it was simply an honor without any duties. Ten students, two for each class, represented the entire CMC student body.

The challenge came almost immediately.

The happy campus turned hostile. Our actions made headlines in the state of Punjab. Dr. Banerjee had been fired by the administration for stealing alcohol meant for the physiology class. The major told senior leaders of the student body that he had been framed. He insisted this was a plot to remove him since he was an ardent critic of the administration dominated by white Christian "foreigners."

"Who drinks 70% alcohol?" he asked, throwing up his hands in anger and disbelief.

"Who drinks 70% alcohol?" We agreed, like parrots.

He enlisted the student leadership to lodge protests targeting Dr. Constable and Dr. Scott, the principal and director. In effect, Banerjee stated that "Indian independence had once again been stolen by the British." He invited us to his home, where he told stories about his army days and how his family had fought for Indian freedom. He praised us for our courage – although we had displayed none thus far – and reminded us how, led by him, we had dug trenches to fight the advancing Chinese armies a thousand miles away, and how we had joined the National Cadet Corps (NCC), a national college organization much like the Reserve Officers' Training Core (ROTC) in America.

He omitted the part about how we were given old, rusty rifles to carry during the drills but were never taught to actually use the weapons, and the fact that we had never seen or touched a bullet. We had shouted patriotic slogans and dared the Chinese to come to Punjab, knowing full well that it was highly unlikely. I had learned then, thanks to Dr. Banerjee, that there is nothing like a war to unite a country. Even the most dysfunctional and corrupt officials came together.

His rather attractive wife won our sympathy by wailing and insisting that they would become destitute if he was fired. They served us unlimited Darjeeling tea, snacks, and *mithai* (sweets). Punjab, Banerjee said, is the land where the British General Dyer had ordered his troops to shoot unarmed peaceful protestors in 1919, leaving hundreds dead in what is called the Jallianwalla Bagh massacre. It did not occur to us that those murders were not the same things as an accusation of theft, or that the people who wielded the guns were Indian *sepoys* (soldiers).

We were young and impressionable, and had an inbuilt bias against the British. Brainwashed, the 10 student officers met and called a strike. We did not ask for a meeting with the "foreigners." We demanded the immediate reinstatement of Dr. Banerjee and the expulsion of foreign staff from India. Parminder and I, as junior members, said little. Parvez and his brother, Dalavez, both final year students, became ringleaders. I saw how a rabble's fury can be aroused. Dr. Banerjee felt buoyed by the strike. Laxmi Rao, the dean who had interviewed me, was not the target of our ire. In fact, some of us wished she would become the new principal. Her status was now deeply compromised.

On reflection, I realize how ludicrous this was. Here I was—a Hindu born in Kenya, carrying a British passport, studying medicine in Punjab, joining the Indian NCC, preparing to go to war with China, a thousand miles away with a useless weapon on his shoulder—and asking foreigners to go back wherever they came from, exactly the stuff that had oppressed me in Kenya!

Classrooms were empty, with wary teachers staring at unoccupied desks. The cadavers were spared further dissection and rested in their formalin baths. Punjabi newspapers picked up the story. Each headline rejuvenated our resolve. We marched in the streets of Ludhiana. The registrar sent the student leaders a letter stating that he had resigned and demanded a written apology for the offensive language used. We ignored the letter. Fed up, board members of CMC voted to close the college. In effect, we had been expelled and were no longer medical students. The classrooms were padlocked. We were told to expect letters informing us of the decision to close what was then a 68-year-old college. This action caused outrage throughout the state.

Well-connected parents of the expelled students were agitated and joined a highly public campaign to put political pressure on the foreign missionaries. The chancellor of Punjab University, which CMC was part of, tried to mediate. VIPs descended upon the campus to threaten the besieged board members. Eventually, the Chief Minister of Punjab ordered the college to reopen, warning that all CMC assets would be confiscated if the college board disobeyed.

The college reopened and we rejoined classes. We saw this as a victory. There was to be an independent inquiry about the missing spirits. Things returned to normal two weeks into the strike. The foreign faculty never gave an indication that they were hurt by allegations of racism or our vile behavior. They had forgiven us and simply got back to work.

Dr. Banerjee left the campus and we never saw him again. We never learned the outcome of the inquiry. Had he really stolen something? Why did he leave with a whimper rather than a roar? Was the independent inquiry a cover-up designed to end the matter in a politically correct manner? Was our behavior unfair, unjust, and possibly even racist?

Dr. Dickson changed her plans to live and die in India, doing what she loved to do. Instead, she returned to England permanently. The entire student body was at the railway station to say goodbye.

We had painted this gentle woman with the same brush used for racists and bigots. It was unjust.

****

In 1963, they needed a tabla player for the annual variety show to celebrate Christmas. I was surprised that I was the only one available. Word spread that a student from East Africa knew most of the popular Hindi tunes and rhythms. That, however, did not help me win the election to become the president of the CMC Music Association. The bright side was that some of my supporters, Younus Masih, Raj Bala Bansal and Nalini Sharma, became lifelong friends.

Dr. Saha, the anatomy professor, walked up to me, and asked me to come to his home one evening. It sounded like an order. On arrival, Younus Masih and I found his wife all decked out in a lovely sari, with a big red dot on her forehead and red *sindoor* sprinkled in her hair, looking very much like a Bengali bride. A harmonium and a pair of tablas had been dusted off prior to our arrival. She planned to sing the songs of Rabindranath Tagore, the great Indian poet, author of a collection of poems titled *Geetanjali* and a Nobel prizewinner for literature.

The woman had a round face adorned by thick glasses, quite unlike the extraordinarily beautiful Bengali actresses on movie screens, whose voices had to be dubbed since they did not speak Hindi. When Mrs. Saha spoke, the word *samosa* sounded more like *shamosha*. *She* became *sea* and *sham* became *sam*.

She went on for nearly two hours. The songs were sweet but similar, with identical rhythms. Our impending yawns had to be stifled quickly. After each song, we clapped politely, fearful that any lack of appreciation might lower our anatomy scores.

Her husband's stern, inscrutable frown from the anatomy lab was replaced with a smile. Pleased that he had fulfilled his wife's dream, he allowed himself some levity. Finally, she too tired of the songs and offered us "shnacks" and tea. We were tempted but declined, afraid that she might catch a second wind and sing again. She insisted we take home at least one cookie each. We were escorted out.

Two weeks later, I was summoned again. Younus was invited too, but he had sworn never to return. He would rather fail his anatomy test. I pretended I had hurt my right index finger. The invitations stopped.

Dr. Saha expressed his gratitude by lingering around our dissection table longer than necessary, and he continued to guide us with the detachment only an anatomy professor can display, but the mask now smiled occasionally.

The girls at our table, unaware of the music sessions, wondered why our table was getting extra attention.

****

In March 1963, I was quite surprised to receive a birthday card from Asha Sathe, Mira's roommate in Baroda. How did she know my birth date? Why would she write almost nine months after we had first met and barely knew each other? I wrote back to thank her. I thought that was the end of it, but two weeks later I received a letter thanking me for the thank-you note I had sent. This mutual gratitude ballooned into a regular correspondence. Over time, the frequency of letters increased. I began to anticipate them and became fretful when one was delayed. We shared stories about our backgrounds and interests. The letters became deeply personal over time. We would not meet again until 1966.

Her father was a gentleman, scholar, and chief engineer for the Central Railways of India. The family traveled in style in a specially equipped, three-bedroom salon hitched to the train. He would become a member of the Railway Board of India, the body that controlled the largest railway system in the world. He had received his postgraduate engineering degree in London in 1934, ate *chapattis* with a fork and knife, wore a hat, and carried a walking stick whenever he stepped out. He was Asha's most favorite person on the planet.

Her mother, the daughter of a former judge in the Lahore High Court in pre-partition India, had borne four children.

Her elder brother, Suresh, preferred to read books rather than work, causing anguish for his parents.

Kumud — an older sister and a college graduate, active in music, drama, and the arts — was married to an engineer and lived in Calcutta. They raised their three sons to become successful engineers.

The younger brother, Vijay, had gone to the United States for further studies.

The Panwalkers and Sathes were decent and honest people, but the similarities ended there. My parents were poor high-school graduates, hard workers who were unable to attend college. Asha's family, affluent and educated, had cars, lived in nice homes, and enjoyed a high social status.

I was the son of an alcoholic father and bankrupt parents who could barely support me in an Indian college. For the Sathes, there were no such inhibitions or obstacles.

In a class- and caste-conscious society, it was fortunate that both families were Brahmin, thus removing one potential obstacle. While my family had always hated the concept of "untouchables" or the subjugation of the "lower castes" by Brahmins, I was relieved to know that I was a Karhade Brahmin, a minority in a sea of Kokanastha Brahmins like the Sathe family.

I was worried but not intimidated. We knew we would marry each other.

CRICKET AND KENNEDY

Our team had somehow clawed its way to the finals of the Punjab Division 2 Cricket Championship match. I owed my last-minute selection as the wicketkeeper to a fellow who'd had a falling out with the captain about the batting order and had walked out the night before.

Figure 14: CMC Cricket team 1963

It was a cold fall day in November 1963. We were to play against Architecture College in Chandigarh, 60 miles to the east and about an hour and a half bus ride from Ludhiana. This city, designed by French architect Le Corbusier, was to be the future capital of Punjab and a model for Punjab and India. But state squabbles had made it a joint capital of two states. It was a lovely city, still being built, divided into several self-sufficient sectors. The modern buildings were surrounded by well-tended lawns. It was spotlessly clean and shone like a jewel on a gorgeous, sunny day.

Raj Bala Bansal, my classmate and a brilliant student who hailed from Chandigarh, invited us for a meal with her extremely gracious family. Her father was a prosperous businessman, and I was to develop bonds of a lifelong friendship with her and her family members.

I had played "street cricket" in Nairobi with a soft tennis ball, but this was different. A wicketkeeper is like a catcher in baseball. Up and down. Up and down. Constantly alert. The hard ball, hurled at an unbelievable speed by ferocious bowlers, is a veritable missile. The gloves, shin pads, and knee pads reduced the impact, but left the hands sore nonetheless.

The large crowd roared as the players, all wearing white, entered. Our captain chose to bat first. The players positioned themselves. Half way into the game, we saw officials hurrying to the field from the pavilion. There was a hush as they announced over a loudspeaker that John Kennedy had been assassinated hours earlier in Dallas, Texas. The Indian tricolor flag, hanging proudly from the ramparts of the Architecture College, was clumsily lowered to half-mast. The match was postponed.

Earlier in his presidency, Kennedy's wife had visited India and left an indelible impression on Indians. They loved her smile, dignity, and warmth. Nehru and Jackie Kennedy had developed a special chemistry. She had single-handedly erased the anger American politicians had aroused in India by their ambivalence toward the largest democracy the world had ever known. America's stance had driven the three non-aligned nations — Egypt, Yugoslavia, and India — to repeatedly vote against it at the United Nations.

Although the US provided much needed food aid to India, there was a perception that America had an ideological and military tilt toward Pakistan. This was deeply resented by Indians. It was bolstered by the SEATO (Southeast Asian Treaty Organization) treaty, which made the United States and Pakistan military allies. This distrust drove India into the warm and welcoming lap of the Russians, who were engaged in a Cold War with the United States.

Jackie's grief became India's grief. Millions turned to their radios. In this moment of solidarity with America, cinema halls were closed. Those that remained open were stoned and forced to shutter up.

Every store, school, and business closed. It was front-page news. Nationwide, flags flew at half-mast. We mourned for Jackie, her children, and America. She, more than anyone else, had improved Indo–American relations.

A few weeks later, we lost the rescheduled match and received the smaller trophy. A photograph was taken for posterity.

UHURU

Kenya became free on December 12, 1963. Black citizens of an independent Kenya now saw the faces of their white and brown oppressors in a new light. Most of the wrath was directed toward those of Asian origin.

I had held on to my British passport as a security blanket. My father and a small minority of Asians, including the eminent judge Sharad Rao, had chosen Kenyan citizenship because of their conviction that things would be fine. Most did not feel safe in a free black nation. A non-Kenyan passport would allow us to escape whenever that became necessary. Our ambivalence was seen as proof of our disloyalty.

We had felt secure in our segregated neighborhoods. With independence, the racial barrier to housing would break down; the Asian way of life would be disrupted. Africans now eyed Asian property and wealth with anger and envy. They had not forgotten how Asians had treated them as servants. It was time for payback.

A few months later, a Marathi couple, expatriates on a short-term assignment to Kenya for an Indian bank, were stabbed to death in their home. Their daughter, an obstetrician, had just returned to India after a vacation. My parents knew this family and were considerably shaken up.

The word *Africanization* crept into our vocabulary. This policy gave priority to qualified blacks in all jobs and businesses. The few Indians who had become Kenyan citizens now felt like second-class citizens. Those who held British or Indian passports were asked to obtain work permits. These were usually granted only to doctors, architects, engineers, teachers, professors, and administrators. Others had to bribe high officials or find a way to leave Kenya. Rumors of extortion by highly placed Africans became a reality. Shopkeepers forced to sell their shops could find no buyers. Sham partnerships became commonplace. Often the African "partner," and majority owner, did not have any business skills. The oppressed now became the oppressors.

Fearing a large influx of immigrants, Britain enacted new rules in 1968, allowing entry only to those born in the UK or to those whose parents were born there. This effectively cut off most people of color. Enoch Powell made his famous "Rivers of Blood" speech, warning that immigration of colored people would endanger the British way of life. There were rumblings that large numbers of Chinese from Hong Kong and Singapore were also planning to flock to the UK before the doors closed. The Indian government denied entry to Indians holding British passports, even if they were born in India, rightly insisting that this was Britain's responsibility.

Jomo Kenyatta, the new president, declared an amnesty to all who had been accused of atrocities during the Mau Mau rebellion. My family members, all British citizens except for my father, became stateless after the new British laws were enacted. Asians were unwelcome in Kenya, Britain and India. My parents received job permits, but renewal was not guaranteed. Our future now hung by a precarious thread. There was the continued danger of physical harm to Asians in Kenya.

A ROSE IN THE LAPEL

Soon after Kenya became independent, I went to visit Shrinivas Deshpande, the one who had taken me to Ahmedabad when I received news of my grandfather's death, and his father in New Delhi. His father had been asked by India's government to come to Delhi to work on documents related to Mahatma Gandhi's life. They woke up early, had cold-water baths, and prepared breakfast. I was embarrassed to awaken hours later to find a bucket of hot water for my own bath. It was not proper to allow elders to do such favors for younger folks.

Jawaharlal Nehru, the prime minister, was to speak in the evening near the historic Red Fort. A murmur rose from the massive crowd as his motorcade arrived exactly on time. Thousands had come to see this man who, with Gandhi, had won independence for India. I had read the letters he had written to his daughter while in prison, as well as parts of his monumental *Discovery of India*.

He ascended a few wooden steps, a red rose in his lapel, and was quickly surrounded by citizens, who placed huge garlands on his neck. We sat on the ground perhaps 50 feet away. I saw little security. He spoke in Hindi, but I knew he was more fluent in English. He started by greeting the "brothers and sisters" who had gathered. It was only 16 years prior that he had spoken of India's "tryst with destiny" and of his dreams. He saw the Chinese invasion in 1962 as a great betrayal, which weighed heavily on his heart. He appeared tired, sad, and defeated.

As handsome as ever, the sparkle was gone and he stooped a bit. In a hoarse voice, he urged the nation to regroup and face its enormous challenges with kindness, wisdom, and determination. The 45-minute speech ended far too early.

This is the man whose photograph had hung on our living room wall in Nairobi. He was a living legend and the pride of India. He was my hero. In 1964, I saw his motorcade pass by in Bombay and his unmistakable silhouette framed against the window. I imagined that our eyes had met.

A beacon of hope for millions, a beloved figure in the history of India, Nehru, a broken man, his spirits dampened by the 1962 Chinese invasion, died unexpectedly later that year.

****

Already active in extracurricular activities, Dr. Rao invited me to participate in the annual play titled *Charlie's Aunt*. Next year, she said, I could perhaps portray Abraham Lincoln, since I had that tall, thin, cadaverous look. I anticipated rehearsing great speeches about freedom, courage, and the equality of all men, especially the one about "four score and seven years…"

A few weeks later, Dr. Rao shared the contents of a letter my parents had sent her. Apparently, word had gotten around that I was having "too much fun" in college and needed to focus more on studies. They were worried. I had not failed any examinations, but if I failed the most difficult exam, the third part of the MBBS (Bachelor of Medicine, Bachelor of Surgery), my graduation would be delayed by at least six months. That would be a huge burden on the family.

Dr. Rao encouraged me to honor their wishes. My parents were not entirely wrong. They had made huge sacrifices and had a vested interest in my success. I understood their anxiety. Perhaps it was difficult for them to understand the excitement of college life. I was upset, but withdrew from all campus activities. I assumed there were unknown spies in our midst.

TROUBLE IN PARADISE

Our anxiety about events in Kenya was compounded by terrible things happening in Zanzibar. The country, just off the east coast of Africa, had played an important role in the history of the slave trade. It was well known to Arab, Asian, and Persian traders. Unguja and Pemba, two islands that comprise Zanzibar, with an area of just 565 square miles, were lush and lovely. As one approached Unguja, a strong whiff of cloves wafted over the swaying palms and blue sea.

Arab traders regularly raided villages, accompanied by Swahili-speaking Bantu intermediaries, to capture hundreds of local inhabitants, often with the permission of Bantu chiefs. Some were transported to Oman and Arabia as slaves. Others were taken to the new American colonies or West Indian islands. Indian merchants sometimes financed these Arab incursions.

I had visited Zanzibar in 1954, at age 11. The narrow streets reminded me of Arab cities we had seen in movies and magazines, minus the belly dancers. The streets were clean, the people friendly. The air was fresh, the ocean water a brilliant blue.

Underneath this façade of tranquility, however, was a simmering pot of discontent and anger. As independence drew closer, Africans saw this as an opportunity to exact revenge for centuries of persecution and servitude. Zanzibar became independent on December 10, 1963. The new government was overthrown on January 4, 1964. Mass killings began eight days later. In an orgy of ethnic cleansing, thousands of Arabs and Indians were slaughtered. Estimates of those killed vary between 13,000 and 20,000. Arab and Indian girls were sought, caught, and married off to Africans. Those who resisted were raped and killed. Thousands were expelled. Some essential workers such as doctors were forced to stay.

The tenth and last Sultan of Zanzibar, Sayyid Sir Jamshid bin Abdullah Al-Said, escaped in his royal yacht and found a way to Britain, leaving his helpless citizens behind to be slaughtered.

The simmering pot of discontent in Africa had boiled over. The echoes of hate, distrust, and racial prejudice in Zanzibar would impact my family's decisions in later years.

A MATTER OF THE HEART

Our clinical rotations began in the third year of medical school. Each morning was spent following the professors around the hospital. Unlike the American medical system, where interns and residents make most clinical decisions, the primary caregiver at CMC, and indeed all over India, was an experienced and often brilliant attending physician. We followed like sheep, with a mix of trepidation and excitement. The Sikh surgeon, an intellectual and physical giant, wore a white turban, which enhanced his height of at least 6 feet 4 inches. His broad shoulders and large hands always made us wonder if he had a hormonal imbalance. He was a good man and an accomplished surgeon.

He had a particular interest in young people with rheumatic heart disease. A 20-year-old girl was brought in by her worried parents because she had difficulty breathing. Her blue nails and tongue were markers of her misery. Her creamy complexion, innocent brown eyes, and shy demeanor endeared her to the medical students on rotation with the surgeon. She had spent much of her life gasping for air. Sometimes she coughed up bright, red blood. This was initially mistaken as an early symptom of tuberculosis.

She was quickly found to have a murmur due to a tightening of a heart valve. A valve replacement or enlargement of that opening was vital. Otherwise, the fluid might back up and flood her lungs. A decision was made to operate and widen the opening around the valve, so more blood could rush into the ventricle and perhaps relieve her air hunger. Her situation was dire, and this was a going to be a last-ditch effort. Her parents watched with great admiration as this fellow Sikh softly soothed their anxieties. He assured them they would pay nothing.

This was to be the first major heart procedure at CMC, in an era when the concept of intensive care units did not exist.

On the designated day, after some blood tests and an electrocardiogram (EKG) she was taken to the operating room. I vaguely remember holding the retractor for a few minutes — a great honor for a student — as this fine surgeon expertly cut through the breast bone, dissected through the tissues, and exposed the heart. I did not quite understand the functions of the machines carrying blood from one place to another, and dared not ask lest I distract the operator. The anesthesiologist and other team members did not speak. Almost two hours later, we were done, she was stitched back together, and there was a collective sigh of relief. Everything had gone as planned.

I was assigned to sit by her bedside all night, my first official night call. Her parents, simple farmers covered with shawls, sat nearby. I had become somewhat proficient in Punjabi and assured them that all was well. They nodded gratefully, saying, "Jite raho, putar" (Live long, son).

Her tongue was not as blue. Her flat chest heaved normally. She seemed comfortable, her delicate features almost angelic. A feeling of sheer joy overwhelmed me. I knew I was in the right profession. One day I would acquire the same knowledge and skills as these masters of medicine and surgery. I would be admired and respected, loved and sought-after by the rich and poor, and I would provide my services free to the needy.

I dozed off to the gentle sound of her breathing, awakened only by the occasional visit from the nurse who took vital signs every hour. The surgeon stopped by to ask how the patient was, and I assured him all was going well. He spoke gently to the grateful parents, who stood up with folded hands, bending slightly in a display of profound respect and gratitude.

Her parents were reassured by my presence. In truth, I had no idea what I would do if something were to go wrong. I knew I was to keep watch for any change in her breathing or vital signs.

It happened suddenly.

She raised her head, opened her eyes briefly, turned blue, and had a spasm of cough followed by a rattle in her chest, which pierced the quiet of the night and frightened me. She rolled her eyes and stopped breathing. I checked her wrist for a pulse; there was none. The skin was cool. The EKG strip flat. I had learned first aid in Nairobi some years ago, but this was a real situation, not a dummy, and I feared breaking the sutures if I pumped on her chest. We had no defibrillator and, even if we'd had one, I would not have known how to use it. I ran for help. My voice deserted me. I squeaked something unintelligible to the nearest nurse, who raised an alarm. Distraught, I watched my first real CPR (cardiopulmonary resuscitation) that day, as this beautiful angel left us.

Her parents, with tears in their eyes and gratitude in their hearts for the efforts we had made, left the room. They murmured "Raab di marzee" (It is the Lord's will) with palms facing upward to the sky. I felt anger toward the God they praised. Why would He make His people suffer this way?

The surgeon was stoic. We knew these were high-risk procedures, and the absence of modern intensive care units, machines, and highly trained personnel did not help. I had never seen a human being die before, except for the man slashed with a *panga* in Nairobi. The doctor placed a hand on my shoulder. The gesture expressed what no words could.

I was no longer sure about our power to heal. My already shaky faith in God was strained further. The ability of people to accept illness and injustice as the will of God infuriated me. An overwhelming sense of grief and futility overcame me. I saw this girl's face, even after her death, that night and the next, night after night—during my waking hours and in my sleep. She was serene in death—forgiving, grateful, and beautiful.

ANOTHER WAR

Our studies were interrupted by yet another war in 1965. India accused Pakistan of attacking its troops on two fronts, in Kutch and in Kashmir. We saw convoys of trucks carrying soldiers to the front. Politicians shouted patriotic slogans. Movie stars and musicians, beggars and billionaires, Hindus and Muslims all united against this common enemy. Wealthy merchants weighed dignitaries and donated the equivalent of their weight in gold. The fatter the dignitary, the better for the cause! Women tore off their jewelry, including *mangalsutras*, which were to be worn at all times to honor their husbands and marriages. Families proudly and tearfully sent their sons to the war zone.

Film songs gave way to patriotic songs. Stories of courage filled the airwaves. To die for your country, to become a martyr, or *shaheed*, was the ultimate sacrifice. Being very close to the border, we tuned in to radio stations in Lahore and were dismayed to hear Noor Jehan, the melody queen of pre-partition India, now singing patriotic Pakistani songs.

A curfew was imposed in most northern cities. All lights went out at night. Even the flicker of a lighter, it was said, could be seen from miles away by enemy planes. The skies over Ludhiana were regularly penetrated by the sound of jets as the Indian Air Force responded to incursions from their bases in Punjab. Occasionally, we saw plumes of smoke from our rooftop perch. Amritsar, the site of the holy Golden Temple of the Sikhs, was on high alert.

The two armies, once a single fighting force of pre-partition India, were now bitter enemies. Officers who had trained together were now in opposite camps.

We darkened our rooms with bedsheets and cardboard. We lit candles so we could study for the upcoming exams, but this light was easily seen from the outside and people from the street yelled or pounded on our doors until we extinguished them. We pleaded with school officials to postpone exams so we could focus on shouting slogans. They agreed.

Indian troops entered Pakistan and came close to Lahore. To prove they had entered enemy territory, Indians displayed tanks and buses captured from the city. Pakistanis reciprocated. Much of the news was propaganda and we could never tell what the truth was. The rest of the world remained silent. Eventually, both countries ran out of ammunition. A cease fire was announced, and a treaty was signed in Tashkent, with the Russians serving as intermediaries.

When Lal Bahadur Shastri, the Indian prime minister, died unexpectedly in Tashkent a day after the conference, on January 11, 1966, many Indians believed that he had been poisoned. An incorruptible and decent man, he left nothing for his wife and family. After the initial hoopla, Shastri and his family were forgotten. His widow was left to fend for herself. Gratitude apparently ends after the last bullet has been fired and a document is signed.

The end of the war also reminded the CMC administrators that an important exam was now overdue.

In the spring of 1966, we decided to visit the picturesque Kulu Valley in North India. We had heard of snow-covered mountain peaks connected by makeshift bridges overlooking deep gorges. It would be nice to get away from the bustle of the city and perhaps climb a mountain or two. Postcards showed photographs of good-looking people whose womenfolk often had large goiters on their necks due to dietary deficiencies of iodine. I became the natural leader, because I had bragged about climbing Kilimanjaro.

Unfortunately, the revered teacher Gurjar from Amalner developed a large, bleeding stomach ulcer and threw up enormous amounts of fresh blood. By the time he reached Bombay, it was too late. He bled to death. Sunder Atya, my father's sister, became a widow. Instead of going to the Kulu Valley, I rushed to be by her side. She wept softly, surrounded by family and friends. I was proud of her regal bearing. I disliked scenes where widows and others bawled and screamed hysterically.

Asha, who was pursuing a postgraduate degree at the highly renowned All India Institute of Hygiene and Public Health in Calcutta, was in Bombay to visit her parents. It had been four years since we had first met. Our correspondence had matured to a level where we knew we would marry. We decided to meet. Asha, unaware that there had been a death in the family, was surprised to see the gathering and hesitated a bit before coming forward to greet me. The family, unaware of our romance, stared at this intruder. I excused myself to be with her.

We walked and talked for hours, catching up. How could one be so happy in the midst of a family tragedy? Later that evening, Asha and I thought it prudent to ask the cab driver to stop a block away from her home in Marine Lines, a bastion of the rich and connected, since her family was also unaware of our romance. I did not go inside.

Uncomfortable with such secrecy, I wrote to my parents to let them know that I had met, corresponded with, and wished to marry a girl from a wealthy and well-known family in Bombay, and asked for their blessing. Asha had simultaneously broached the subject with her parents. We hoped that the elders would not object.

Both families began maneuvering in the background. Asha's parents made inquiries of family contacts they discovered in Nairobi. My parents, with far more limited contacts in India, heard generally good things about the Sathe family. A horoscope, initiated by her family, revealed that the alignment of stars was appropriate.

I wrote to her father, explaining my background, my family difficulties, and my aspirations. I wanted them to know that their daughter would be going to a joint family in Kenya that included my parents. Not realizing that he already knew, I also informed him about my father's addiction and how we had made peace after many years of separation. That had been a very difficult letter to write to a stranger. He wrote back that he appreciated my honesty.

There was a PS: "Would it not be best for you and Asha to live separately in Nairobi after marriage?"

I responded to say that was not an option.

I got the sense that the Sathe family had accepted the reality, but was not particularly happy about their daughter's choice. Understandably, they might have preferred she marry a local Indian, a fair-skinned and better-looking groom, or a rich Kokanastha Brahmin without a history of family dysfunction.

I did not know then that her eldest brother, Suresh, who had never met me, believed that Asha was marrying a "third-class fellow." Coming from a man who had never worked a day in his life, gave his parents a really hard time, and pretended to be a great scholar because he read books on philosophy, he had passed judgment on me from afar. It made me wonder what others in the family (her parents, another sister, and brother) thought about me. I was deeply angered and hurt.

****

Asha's father, whom everyone called Kaka, invited me to join their family on vacation at a railway bungalow in Shimla. It was an ill-disguised ruse to get to know me better, to check me out.

The British used to retreat to this hill station, their summer capital, when the heat in Delhi became oppressive. Only the high and mighty went to this haven of coolness. It was the playground of the rich, the elite, the well-connected, and rich tourists. The scenery was breathtaking.

The overcrowded bus, packed with farmers, peasants, and laborers, negotiated the narrow mountainous roads with stomach-churning turns. The luggage, balanced on top of the bus in remarkably high stacks, dangerously upset the vehicle's center of gravity. Even as the driver sped up the steep roads at a reckless pace, he told passengers how buses occasionally plunged down the sheer cliffs at certain key turns, sending victims to a fiery death in the deep gorge below.

In contrast, Kaka—who had risen quite high in the Indian Railways hierarchy—traveled in style in a saloon car with two or three bedrooms, a private bathroom, and a shower. A secretary catered to his needs. They stayed in bungalows reserved for the exclusive use of high government officials.

Upon arrival, I was disappointed to see Suresh. Something about his body language and the smirk on his face ruined my mood. A slight, thin man with prematurely gray hair, he wore shabby clothes with his shirt hanging out of the trousers. I could sense his contempt for me. Our distaste for each other was clear. As I stood alone on the balcony of the bungalow, admiring the sheer beauty of India's mountains and plains, he came and stood next to me. I ignored him.

After a few moments, he asked, "How was the bus ride?"

I read in that question a statement about how people traveled like cattle in those buses. He presumably came in the salon car furnished by Indian Railways.

"Fine," I replied through pursed lips. An uncomfortable silence followed. I felt suffocated. He waited for a while and then walked back inside. We did not exchange a word after that.

To my horror, I realized there was just one large room with two enormous beds. I wondered what the sleeping arrangement would be. All options seemed awkward. Asha and her mother shared one bed. Suresh and I were to flank Kaka in the middle of the second bed. Almost like the two wings of Pakistan on each side of India!

I brushed my teeth twice. Worried that a little movement might disturb the other men, I remained stiff and awake all night. I hoped I had not snored and wished I had a nightgown to wear over my old pajamas. I suspect this is the only time in the history of mankind that a groom has slept in the same bed with his future father-in-law and brother-in-law. What a relief it was to get out of that bed.

Kaka was soft-spoken, polite, and incredibly formal. He neither smoked nor drank alcohol. This was not a family that expressed affection in public.

Asha's mother, Indutai, was gentle and quiet and had an extremely fair complexion. I called her "Aai" (mother), as did others. She was used to a sophisticated, wealthy life. Her father had been a distinguished judge in Lahore (now Pakistan) before the partition and had moved to India, perhaps in anticipation of troubles ahead. I liked her a lot.

It also occurred to me that this family, like most others, was content with the British occupation of India and had possibly wished they had stayed on. They were typical of the Indian elite. After two days of strolling in the lovely hill station, I took the bus back to the dusty plains of Punjab.

Did they like me? Was I a suitable partner for their daughter? Only time would tell.

My mother wrote that she had not seen Calcutta and was keen to visit the city. No one in their right mind actually goes to Calcutta to sightsee. It was a poorly disguised plan to "check out the girl." Christmas would be a good time, I suggested, since I would be off for two weeks. She flew to Bombay (probably with borrowed money) in December 1966, and we took a train to Calcutta.

We arrived after a very tiring journey to be received by Asha and her friend Sumita (pronounced *Shumita*) Chakravorti, the daughter of a distinguished Bengali diplomat who later posted to the Indian Consulate in New York City. My mother and I rented a small room in the center of the bustling city.

Asha's sister, Kumutai, who lived in Calcutta, came over to invite us for dinner. Gentle and soft-spoken with her father's aquiline nose and warm brown eyes, she looked elegant in a sari and greeted us warmly.

We gratefully accepted her invitation. I suspect her husband, whom I had never met before, did not approve. Something had annoyed him. She was caught in a bind. It is traditional to invite future in-laws for a meal and very rude not to do so. Caught in this conundrum, she apparently had made a unilateral decision. To our surprise, he rushed out of his posh bungalow just as our cab arrived, hissed a very perfunctory "hullo" without a smile, then got into his car and sped off, tires screeching, in a cloud of dust. His exit was perfectly timed to insult us. He probably went to his club for a stiff drink. My relationship with him remained frosty over the years because of this incident. In later years, there was a formal cordiality and he stayed with us for a few days in America. I also saw his generous side when he helped me with financial transactions involving my mother's property in India.

I was not sorry to leave Calcutta. The huge metropolis depressed me with its teeming masses, its damp and dark skies, and its mostly unfriendly people. We returned to Bombay by train, and my mother flew back to Nairobi. My mother did not articulate her feelings about Asha, but did contact her parents. If there was underlying anxiety, she did not reveal it. She knew I could be very stubborn and that this is what I wanted.

Soon after, I was invited to Marine Lines in Bombay, where Asha and I were engaged in a brief ceremony attended by Kaka, Aai, and no one else. Suresh was absent, and the younger brother, Vijay, had gone to America for further studies. We exchanged rings, but I have no memory of purchasing one. The purpose of the engagement, I supposed, was to provide societal approval for Asha and me to be seen together in public without tongues wagging. The wedding date would come later and was contingent on my passing my final exam.

****

My five years in India had deepened my love for the country and its people. I had been accepted and felt at home. There was no color bar to worry about. No one knew that I had been born abroad, although astute Indians could tell from accents, clothes, or shoes that we had lived abroad. I did not want to leave India.

Affected by the wars with China and Pakistan, I considered joining the Indian armed forces. I grew a large moustache and twirled its tips like I had seen military officers do in movies like *Hum Dono*, in which Dev Anand, the evergreen movie star, wore such a moustache and got the pretty girl as well. A tailor made me a camouflage jacket from some cheap, thick, brownish-green canvas. I wrote to army recruiters and asked if I my British nationality would be a problem. Easy to become an Indian citizen, they said. The salary was great and one could retire after 20 years of service. Between wars, there was little to do.

I wrote to my parents asking for their permission. The response came immediately. I was not to join the army. What would happen to them, they asked, if I died in battle? I argued that I had not known of any doctor who had died in the Medical Corps. I would simply be putting on bandages. They sent no additional response.

Learning that Asha was visiting New Delhi, I took the train down to meet her. She saw my fierce moustache and told me in no uncertain terms that she did not want to marry a military officer, certainly not one with hair on his lips. To emphasize the point, she hinted that an air force officer had once written to her hoping to get a date, but she had written back that there was someone else in her life. I forgot to ask if he had stubble on his upper lip.

Staying in India was not an option if I could not join the army. I could not finance a private practice. And even if I were to land an extremely competitive residency position for further training in India, the low salary would make it impossible for us to manage.

I had no choice but to return to Kenya, a country that did not want me.

****

I had sailed through the first two exams with little difficulty and now faced the final hurdle to earn the MBBS degree. The last year of college was crucial. I placed all extracurricular activities on hold to focus on my studies.

In May 1967, two men from Delhi and one from Chandigarh came to proctor the final exams. Their intent, I thought, was to intimidate us into a nervous panic so we would say stupid things. Then they could justify giving us failing grades. An important portion of the oral exam included five short unknown cases. We were to examine the designated area of the body, ask or say nothing, and come up with a diagnosis. It was nerve-wracking. The generally illiterate patients let us know, with their body language, whether we had passed or failed. A slight sideways tilt of the head indicated that we were on the wrong track.

For the "long case," I was asked to see a young patient with evidence of weight loss and a lump in the right lower quadrant of the abdomen. This was easily palpable. An internal examiner grilled me about the differential diagnosis. I thought both tuberculosis of the intestine in the ileo-colic area or a malignancy were possible. I tried to defend my clinical choices. He frowned, paused, smirked, and repeatedly asked, "Are you sure?" until I was forced to say, "No, sir." That final answer appeared to please him more than all the others.

Paranoia set in. This Christian professor was going to fail me because I had "diverted" his nephew, my classmate, from the path of Christ and had never entered the chapel. When the results were announced, I learned that I had fallen short on the long case. But my perfect score in the five short cases with external examiners had saved me.

All I had to do now before they would hand over my Bachelor of Medicine and Surgery certificate was a six-month internship.

Kaka, who was now in Delhi, took me to meet a revered surgeon when I made a trip to meet them. Colonel Mirajkar was known all over India and was an occasional examiner for our medical school. A number of junior surgeons, all sitting a level lower than their mentor, were assembled to hear words of wisdom from their guru. As I touched his feet, and Kaka introduced me as his future son-in-law, the colonel asked where I had trained. Upon hearing I was from CMC, he asked if I was a Christian. I believe he would have been disappointed if he had learned that Asha was going to marry a non-Hindu.

****

Four of us were posted to Lalto Kalan, a small village a dozen miles from the main hospital, where a thousand people lived on rich agricultural land, tended to buffalo, and grew more wheat per acre than the rest of the country. American agriculturalists had taught Indians how to use better seeds and fertilizers and to irrigate the land properly, ushering in the so-called Green Revolution. The mostly Sikh residents lived in homes with the inner walls caked with mud and cow dung, and covered with thatched roofs. Water came from deep wells. Electricity had reached the area through the massive Bhakhra Nangal dam. In spite of their humble homes, these people were not poor. They had plenty to eat and share. There were no beggars, and the men and women were sturdy and content. A few stone houses belonged to émigrés who had traveled abroad and returned home. All spoke Punjabi.

This clinic had minimal supplies and essentially no medication. A senior doctor supervised our work during the day. We were on our own at night and on weekends. The villagers may have had an inkling of our inexperience and insecurity, but we maintained a façade of competence. We were real doctors, we told ourselves.

The cook welcomed us with a feast. The menu was developed by a fellow intern named Bhalla, who was best known for throwing live sticks of dynamite "borrowed" from his army father into the nearby irrigation canal, thus stunning the fish. The dazed creatures floated to the surface and were scooped up for dinner. This night he had coaxed the cook to fry the fish and some *bhajias* laced with hashish.

I took a bite and felt faint. Everything became blurred. The room started spinning. I held on to the wall and sat down. I thought my head would explode. Everyone else laughed until their bellies hurt.

We began our internship the next day. The first patient, a thin young Sikh girl, complained that she was coughing up sputum tinged with blood and was running a fever. With no diagnostic resources at hand, we decided the patient had tuberculosis (TB) of the lung and therefore should be started on TB medicines, including an injection. The first doses were purchased and given. The family was delighted that we had chosen an injection in addition to the white pills. The next day Dr. Donald Wysham, the cardiologist, decided she had a simple "walking pneumonia." The family was upset that the *Angrez* doctor had taken away the injection and substituted our big pills for tetracycline. But she recovered quickly.

An eight-year-old boy who had a very high fever and was toxic was given aspirin, since we could not find any specific infection. His temperature plummeted within hours, but the child looked worse, ashen and exhausted. He was the son of the village head, or *sirpanch*. Scared, we transported him to the hospital in Ludhiana. Professor Samuels, one of the brilliant senior doctors who had terrorized us as students, noticed redness along the edge of his tongue, felt a slightly enlarged spleen, and informed us it was typhoid fever. The clue was the rapid drop in his temperature after a single aspirin. The correct antibiotic was started, and the cultures confirmed the diagnosis. The grateful parents brought us a gallon of buffalo milk and invited all of us for a meal of a curry, *roti*, and buttermilk. It did not matter that we had missed the diagnosis and almost killed the boy. I was reminded once again of the Sikhs' hospitality.

We knew that most Indians chose home therapy before they came to see "real doctors" like us, but we considered this akin to voodoo. We had little respect for Ayurveda, an ancient practice rooted in the beliefs of our ancestors. One day, our cockiness was rudely shattered.

We had seen a young boy several times for a terribly disfiguring and itchy rash on both legs. It had worsened over months, and the skin resembled tree bark. We applied our western creams and ointments for two weeks with no improvement. One day, he did not show up and we forgot about him. While strolling through the little village weeks later, we saw him playing soccer. I recognized him and was astonished to see that his legs looked absolutely normal! His parents had chosen to take him to an Ayurvedic doctor in a nearby town. He told us his treatment had been a paste made up of an ash-like powder mixed with milk and applied twice daily. The dead skin had peeled off in less than four days.

We were embarrassed. I have never underestimated the power of "alternative medicine" since. In a study we did of veterans in Delaware and Pittsburgh several decades later, we found that 30% of our HIV-infected patients were taking "alternative" medicine, supplements, and nutritional additives but, fearing criticism, chose not to tell their western-trained doctors about it.

On our last day, the young boy cured of typhoid came riding up on a magnificent white horse with a beautiful mane, to invite us to his home for another meal in gratitude for his care.

The two months ended as abruptly as they had started. I spent a week working with Charles Rambo, a well-known missionary and ophthalmologist from Philadelphia, in a leprosy colony in Ludhiana, dressing wounds and learning about the lives of these dejected, deformed, and deeply depressed Indians. We completed our internship after four months at the main hospital. A date for the graduation ceremony was announced. I, however, was heading home and would miss the event.

I had finally become a doctor, thanks to my parents' sacrifices and my father's foresight in applying to CMC, one of the most highly rated medical schools in India in that era and to this day.

MARRIAGE

I left Ludhiana with a heavy heart. It had been a wonderful experience to live and learn in Punjab and to develop such great friendships. The smoke, the dust, and the glorious orange hue of streetlights in the setting sun receded as the train gathered speed. I strained to see my friends on the platform for the last time, but saw only the waves of anonymous hands. Irritated by flecks of errant charcoal and soot in my eyes, I entered the cabin from my precarious perch on the steps just outside the door.

I found a space for my little suitcase, which held all my worldly possessions, and looked around. The women immediately turned their heads and covered their faces; the men checked me out. Eventually one man decided it was safe to make a little space for me on the bench seat. Soon we were sharing food.

It was a cool day in Baroda. I was to stay with my grandmother, Mai, who had moved to India in 1966. Asha's father had retired and moved to Baroda as well. My parents could not afford to travel to India for the wedding, so Mai had volunteered to be our official representative. Kaka strongly "suggested" that my parents should attend the wedding and indicated that "the marriage is off if they cannot come." I felt bullied. Perhaps I should have put my foot down and asked them to pay the airfare if it was so critical, but Mai and I said nothing. My parents took a loan, or tapped their savings, and arrived in Bombay. A night train brought them to Baroda.

The Sathe clan was already in Baroda. Kumutai came from Calcutta without her husband. Suresh was there, but Vijay was in America.

At Kaka's request, I made a courtesy visit to see his father, Asha's grandfather. They called him Mothe Kaka (elder uncle). He had an eerie resemblance to Suresh: the same height, facial expression, baggy and shabby clothes. I touched his feet. He looked away. He had been to Nairobi in the 1940s, he said.

Then turning halfway toward some strangers in the room, he smirked and with a mocking laugh asked me in Marathi, "Do people in Africa still live in trees like monkeys?"

I took deep offence at this comment. It was unnecessary and uncalled for—an affront to the people and land of my birth, condescending, and racist. Not having seen anyone live in trees, except Tarzan and Jane in the movies and western tourists at Treetops in Nyeri, I retorted in fluent Marathi: "No, sir, they live in better homes than people here, are cleaner, and do not starve like the beggars I just saw outside your home."

I was quivering with rage. Was it so difficult to bless us? He simply stared. Kaka, sensing an escalation, gently steered me by the elbow toward another room, an apology in his eyes. It was clear to me that some—or all—in this family did not approve of me. What had I done to deserve this treatment?

The hall where Brahmins typically got married was booked for December 27, 1967. A whole day of rituals and Sanskrit prayers was to follow. Nalutai, who had moved to the UK with Bhau and their two daughters, arrived for the wedding with their third child, two year old Prakash. He held my hand and insisted on making the seven circles around the fire with me and Asha Sathe.

Hundreds watched as Asha married a 25-year-old and a two-year-old simultaneously!

The priest demanded we pay attention, even though I could not understand what he was chanting. We marveled at his ability to speak and sing nonstop for what seemed like a whole day. How did he remember all this stuff? I was convinced that Hindu marriages last forever because no one wants to go through that torture ever again!

The dozens of elders from both sides watched silently, perched comfortably on small mattresses, while the chanting and the smoke from the fire rose to the high ceiling. Everyone was dressed up. I had on a new pin-striped polyester suit, recently ordered from the UK, with narrow tapered trousers—quite unsuitable for the heat.

Figure 15: Our marriage

There were many group photographs. My father asked if we could take a picture of all the Panwalkers in attendance. Thinking it was impossible to take a picture with so many people, I brushed his request aside. Hurt, he retreated to his chair. I immediately regretted my thoughtless action, when his request was quite reasonable. He had been ignored for much of the day by others. I wondered if my pent-up anger was finally expressing itself.

From the corner of my eye, I saw Asha's father speaking to my grandmother, Mai. It did not appear to be a friendly chat. Apparently, more Panwalkers had shown up for the wedding than planned. Word got out that there were too few chairs and not enough food. The Panwalker and Bhagwat clan had made a mess of the meticulous Sathe plan. His meticulously calculated plans lay in ruins but they managed to find a mutually acceptable solution. Everyone dispersed. My parents flew back to Nairobi, on a flight financed by more borrowed money.

Asha and I rented a small room a short distance from Mai's home. This was because she had only two rooms without curtains or doors, so a newly married couple would not have sufficient privacy. We consummated our marriage in a room the size of a large American closet. We were truly in love and immune to the discord around us.

A mini train took us to Matheran for our honeymoon. This gorgeous place, a playground for rich Indians, is on a hill with verdant plains below. The lovely sunsets, the famous *chikki* (peanut brittle), and pony rides were the highlights. A cook was assigned to us in the Indian Railways bungalow, thanks to the perks Asha's father received.

The rich in India, I thought, lived very well.

I was acutely aware that while I was having fun doing nothing, my parents were back in Kenya toiling away, trying to make ends meet and repay their loans. It was time to return to Nairobi.

Asha secured a British passport based on my citizenship so she could follow me. Her grandfather passed away soon after the wedding, but I could not bring myself to attend the funeral.

BOOK THREE:
Back to Africa

NYERI, Kenya

There were no hassles at Embakasi Airport when I returned in March 1968. Any concerns about my British passport, lack of a job, or being Indian dissipated when the officer responded cheerfully to my greeting "Jambo, habari yako?" It had been almost five years since my last visit. My parents and I said little as we drove home. I gazed out the window, hoping to see animals that might have strayed from Nairobi National Park. It was good to breathe the cool air of a free nation, to hear the sounds of its streams, rivers, and mountains, to see the cloudless blue sky.

My parents looked older and tired. They had postponed their dreams so I would not suffer hardships. It was my intention to make their life easier. Anticipating the need for more space, we moved from the municipal quarters to a larger, two-bedroom apartment in Parkland.

Much had changed. The joint family had dissolved. Dada had passed away in 1962. Anticipating drastic changes in British immigration rules, Bhau and Nalutai had moved to London where Anil joined them. Sharad and his wife (also named Sudha) followed soon after. Mai had left for India to be with her youngest son, Subhash, who was still in college in India. Sudha, the middle sister, married a teacher in India, returned to Kenya and landed in Ottawa, Canada, via London. Mira had married a PhD student in Fargo, North Dakota, and had left for the US.

These frantic movements were precipitated by the fear, before and during 1968, of proposed curbs on immigration to the UK and the likelihood that work permits would be denied in Kenya. None of my relatives had any significant assets when they left.

Most of my classmates were overseas. I had arrived at a time when most were trying to leave. Some said I was a fool to return. We were trapped by circumstances. I still hoped I could remain in Kenya forever.

****

My medical diploma arrived in the mail, folded twice, crumpled, and squeezed into an undersized envelope. Armed with this piece of paper, my father and I arrived at the Ministry of Health, expecting a comfortable job in Nairobi. I was stunned to hear that to get a medical license, I would have to serve a one-year internship in Nyeri, 100 miles to the north. Take it or leave it. My Indian internship did not count. My hopes of joining the esteemed Kenyatta Hospital in Nairobi were dashed.

Nyeri was a medical wilderness on the slopes of Mt. Kenya. It was a beautiful little town with lush, green forests and red, fertile soil. On a typical sunny day, the majestic mountain pierced the white cloud cover to expose the snow-covered twin peaks of Batian and Nelion. Steep and rugged, it was said that the gods rested here during visits to their people. A drive around the perimeter of this mountain revealed the unimaginable beauty of this area. This was the heart and soul of the Kikuyu tribe. "Facing Mount Kenya" — an anthropologic thesis by Jomo Kenyatta with a foreword by his mentor, the eminent scholar B. Malinowski, at the London School of Economics — provides much insight about the area and its people.

Nearby Treetops Lodge, the hotel in the trees where Princess Elizabeth first heard of her father's death in 1952, is a famous tourist spot, which was burned down by Mau Mau and rebuilt some years later.

Lord Baden Powell, founder of the scouting movement, who wrote "the nearer to Nyeri, the nearer to bliss," was buried here. William Holden owned a safari ranch a few miles away. The Mau Mau leaders Dedan Kimathi and Waruhio Itote (more commonly known as General China) had operated in the Aberdares Forest nearby.

Wangari Mathaai, the first and only Kenyan to ever win a Nobel Prize, was a local Kikuyu from this area. The town had few shops or restaurants, no theaters, and few Indian neighbors to socialize with. Africans gathered in pubs in the evenings to listen to music and drink beer.

The beauty of the area notwithstanding, I was crushed that I would be so far away. I suspected that Indian doctors were sent to remote places while African and European physicians secured spots at the Kenyatta Hospital in Nairobi.

I accepted the job with a disappointingly low salary of 800 shillings per month, not much more than I made as a novice teacher in 1962. With the current exchange rate, it would have been worth $12 per month. There were no perks or allowances except housing, which consisted of one room and a shared kitchen. I was to start immediately.

My mother let me borrow her Fiat 500. The only time I had driven a car was at age 17, when I had "borrowed" the same car, taking my nervous friend Mohan Sood along. I accelerated when I really wanted to apply the brakes and vice versa. I did not know how to use the clutch or change gears. The car lurched, swerved, screeched, and made hideous sounds, its tires screaming at every turn. Miraculously, I managed to bring the car back without a scratch. When I got out, my thin knees knocked against each other. Mohan, pale and ashen, murmured something inaudible under his breath. I did not possess a driver's license at the time.

The drive to Nyeri, much smoother than my earlier escapade, crossed the hilly terrain of the scenic Great Rift Valley. The car did well on flat roads but struggled uphill. There was a one-mile stretch called the Pole Pole Hill (slow slow hill). With a head start at 50 mph, which is the maximum this car would go, and no passengers, I could just barely crest the top. If there were passengers, they had to disembark and walk up a short distance. The police did not stop me. They knew I was a doctor.

A year later, when my assignment was complete, I arrived at the police station and requested a driving test. The officer rolled his eyes in mock outrage, repeatedly exclaiming "dactari, dactari" (doctor, doctor). Then he handed me the new license...without a test.

****

Kenya had six provincial government run hospitals scattered throughout the country. Nairobi's Kenyatta Hospital served as the hub. These were the only medical facilities for miles.

The 300-bed Nyeri Provincial hospital was too small for the vast number of patients who needed care. Many slept on the floors. As many as four babies slept sideways in each cot. Thus, every baby with measles or chickenpox efficiently transmitted its disease to others. This was nature's way of universal vaccination. Unfortunately, the infections killed many. There were no isolation facilities. The only time we used gloves, gowns, or masks was in the operating room.

One surgeon, Dr. Joel R. Wambwa, a highly capable and distinguished man and a rare African surgeon, was assigned to all six regional hospitals in Kenya. He was available in Nyeri just one day each week. On the very first day, he informed us that we were to send "tough" surgical cases to Nairobi by ambulance if we thought they could survive the trip 100 miles south. He did not define "tough." We would know, he said. We were to manage routine things such as Caesarian sections and fractures locally. It was the "teach one" and "do many" system.

The Dutch internist, Dr. Hendrick Vandraager, a smaller version of Gregory Peck, was serious and stern, as though he might be suppressing some internal fury. Etched on his face were the worries of all of Holland. On a three-year assignment, he spoke immaculate English in a soft voice with pursed lips (like Mr. D. N. Khanna, my English teacher), choosing each word deliberately, a cigarette dangling permanently from the corner of his mouth. Perhaps he feared the cigarette would fall if he opened his mouth too wide. It was said that his wife hated being in Africa, even though they lived in a lovely bungalow with servants to cater to all their needs.

Dr. Singleton, a tall, bespectacled, hunched, and bald man, looked much older than his age. He had done an internship in Holland and had chosen to learn what he called "bush medicine" for one year. The two Dutch doctors did not like each other, but no one knew why. Singleton was also assigned a bungalow. That raised no questions because he was white. It was not his fault that blacks in independent Kenya still insisted on giving special privileges to whites but not to Asians.

I was to share a two-room apartment with Onaly Kapasi, an Indian-trained Muslim doctor and fellow intern. We were the two workhorses, working from 7:00 AM to 6:00 PM daily. In addition, we worked nights and weekends, essentially 24/7, every other week. Sleep was impossible during the on-call week. When off, we spent the weekends with my parents. The competent African nursing staff was supported by many German nurses, who came for brief stints to explore exotic and exciting Africa.

Asha arrived soon after and announced that she was pregnant. Somehow, she knew it would be a boy. The baby was due in November 1968.

****

Kikuyu women, some with pelvic disproportion, often arrived late in their pregnancy having had no prenatal care whatsoever. African midwives quickly determined whether there was fetal distress or a need for an urgent C-section. Since we had no telephones, an *askari* (guard) was dispatched to our quarters, just a short walk down the hill, to get the intern on call. Over time, we got quite good and were in and out of the belly in 45 minutes or less.

The surgeon had said fixing broken bones was a matter of common sense. The bones should simply be aligned as they were before the injury! The goal was to achieve symmetry. If the bone alignment was poor, we simply removed the plaster and started over again. For fractures of the femur, we inserted pins through the tibia to apply traction for several weeks.

Singleton and I saw a man with immense abdominal distension who had come in vomiting and was writhing in pain. Convinced that the bowel was obstructed, we operated. He was too ill to send to Nairobi. Singleton made the incision and immediately encountered turgid, writhing loops of healthy pink intestine. The slimy, snake-like loops of bowel escaped from the incision into our gloved hands. Calmly, the Dutchman made an incision in one segment of the small intestine. We were shocked when a long pink worm popped its head out, took a peek at us, and crawled out. Roundworms, hundreds of them, had caused the blockage. We pulled these creatures out and dropped them into a bucket, where they wriggled happily, breathing the fresh air of Kenya. The bowel incision was closed. The patient received an anti-parasitic drug and was cured.

I recalled an incident in high school when an ancestor of the worms we had just pulled out had emerged from the bottom of one student's shorts, slid carefully down one chair leg and slithered away leaving a wet, snail-like track. The student who had housed this creature remained oblivious and the class remained eerily silent. The stoic Mr. Khanna pretended he had seen nothing.

There were no neurosurgeons in Kenya. Even India, with over a hundred medical schools, had just a handful. So when an inebriated

Kenyan walked into our hospital from a nearby pub with a rock stuck in his skull, we had to improvise. He reported no pain, had no obvious paralysis, and smiled as he tottered toward us firmly holding on to the craggy surface of the rock. I began nervously by removing pieces of the crumbling rock. Muddy debris was rinsed off with sterile saline. Singleton joined in. Pieces of broken skull bone, including a rather large flap, were discarded since we did not have the skill or means to preserve them for later use. Intermittently, liquefied brain tissue squirted out.

We were somehow able to approximate the skin over the jagged hole in his mangled skull. The terrible cosmetic results notwithstanding, he thanked us, and walked away a few days later with just mild paralysis of one side. While we had learned that most African patients were strong and stoic, their ability to withstand such pain without narcotics was astonishing.

Kikuyu women, but not the men, often developed calluses and large fluid-filled sacs called bursae on their back, because they most often carried firewood and other heavy loads. Removing the bursa was my least favorite surgery since it was so messy and bloody.

When a man with a large, hard, and tender liver was thought to have end-stage cancer, Dr. Vandraager, a cigarette dangling from his lip, suggested a trial of an antibiotic for a parasitic infection, just in case our hunch about cancer was wrong.

He said, "We don't have facilities for a liver biopsy or pathology. Giving him an antibiotic (Flagyl) for possible amebiasis won't hurt."

Miraculously, the mass shrank rapidly. In America, he would have had a CT scan followed by drainage, a biopsy, or both. Flagyl, in this case, was the poor man's CT scan and surgeon. Little would have been lost if the diagnosis had been incorrect. Embarrassed by our adulation, Vandraager allowed himself a rare smile.

****

One morning, after a particularly difficult night, a nurse called me. When I arrived, I found a distraught mother holding the body of a limp child. The glassy eyes, the dry skin, and the rattle in each shallow breath told me it was too late. I cradled the baby's listless head in my arms and gently placed the boy in a crib. In a desperate attempt to rescue him, I inserted an IV into the scalp using a butterfly needle and injected an antidote for possible insecticide poisoning, but it made no difference.

The child gasped, his rib cage rising and retracting, in a futile effort to satiate its air hunger. Then he was still. This was not the first baby who had died in my hands. The loss was unbearable. Physically and emotionally exhausted, I was angry at a God who treated His creatures this way.

What I did next was unforgivable. In my frustration, I berated the mother in Swahili for not bringing the baby in sooner. This was uncharacteristic behavior, and I was immediately sorry. She looked down at the cold concrete floor, her eyes brimming with tears. She gently picked up her dead child and, despite her terrible loss and my cruelty, found the grace to whisper, "Asante" (thank you).

As her silhouette receded, I felt like an extremely inferior being. She had expressed gratitude, dignity, and class. That memory remains vivid and deeply painful. I dishonored myself and my profession that day.

The soul is numbed when babies die. The daily quota of death had hardened us. We had become robots, working day and night, devoid of emotion. The line of sick, starving, and suffering humanity was endless. Medical assistants did an admirable job of prioritizing the care of the sickest waiting in line, doing blood smears and urine analyses, and checking for diabetes. We learned that anytime someone said, "kichua, kifua, tumbo na uma sana" (head, chest, and stomach are hurting a lot), malaria was likely. Blood in the urine suggested schistosomiasis, a parasitic infection common in Africa. Pallor of the skin and eyes, blood in the stool, and spoon-shaped nails suggested an iron deficiency due to hookworms or a dietary deficiency.

Then there was the 15-year-old boy who came in with jaundice, fever, and excruciating pain all over. His malaria smear was negative. His blood pressure was low. I did not know why he was so ill. I had no time or the means to do blood cultures or blood counts. He was sweating, begging for something for pain. We had no narcotics or injections for pain. His father, who had practically carried him to the clinic, looked on helplessly. I placed the young man on a stretcher with his father's help, started an IV, and rapidly infused saline. I gave him an oral antibiotic, but he threw up.

Chastened by my cruelty to the mother whose baby had died in my arms, I lied and assured the boy and his father that he would be well soon. He said, "Asante sana, dactari" in a feeble voice, attempting to smile. Then the boy's eyes rolled deep in their sunken sockets. He stopped breathing and became limp. His father looked away. He was expecting this. Not willing to accept defeat, I performed CPR until I was exhausted. The father placed a hand on my shoulder. His grief-stricken eyes expressed deep gratitude and sorrow. I hugged him as we both cried. Never before in my 25 years had I seen an Asian hug an African. Why had this boy died? What had I missed? Had deformed red cells clogged his airways and starved his brain of oxygen? Had God's defense system against malaria, sickle-cell anemia, caused this young man's death?

We often saw young children with enormous jaw swellings. This tumor was first described by the British surgeon Denis Burkitt in Uganda and was named to honor him. He had surmised that it was related to mosquito bites, but it was in fact a lymphoma related to the Epstein–Barr virus. These children were sent to Nairobi in an ambulance once a week for further care. I never knew what happened to them once they got there.

Burkitt, not a trained scientist, but a man with exceptional observational skills despite one glass eye, became famous for his theory that lack of roughage in the stool caused severe constipation, which led to straining and increased intra-abdominal pressure, and caused hernias and created pouches in the colon. During a talk at the University of Illinois in the early 1970s, he showed pictures of fresh English, Asian, and African stool and compared it to that of goats, dogs, cows, and elephants respectively. He noted that European stool was small and dry "like goat pellets." The addition of fiber to cereal packages owes much to Burkitt.

The clinic closed at sunset. Those who could not be seen camped out on the cold grounds until the next day. Those who were extremely ill or needed surgery were seen by the intern on call, often all night long.

****

We settled down in our quarters, just 500 feet from the hospital. Asha and I dug up a small patch to grow vegetables. The fertile soil produced the most delicious eggplants, peppers, and coriander we had ever tasted. We raised hens, which supplied a steady supply of eggs. One day, a particularly handsome white rooster with a red plume disappeared. We suspected that our servant was pilfering things from the kitchen and the garden. Another time, my gold cufflinks, a gift from my mother, went missing. Again we had our suspicions, but no proof. Because he made fabulous Indian dishes including *paratha* and curries, we decided to lock things up rather than fire him.

Our plan to take Asha to Nairobi for the delivery hit a snag when our son decided to make an early entry on October 4, 1968, a full month before his expected arrival. Lacking a telephone, Asha was unable to reach me, although I was not too far! Dr. Patel, the only obstetrician in town, somehow got word and took Asha to Nyeri Hospital which, in the past, had catered only to the white and wealthy. An *askari* was finally sent to find me.

The delivery was quick. The boy weighed just 4 pounds. The tall, thin, and very fair fellow entered the world with a reassuring and surprisingly robust cry. We took him to our quarters and placed him in a crib with a bare electric bulb overhead, just beyond his reach, to keep him warm. There was no fuss or panic. We called our son Sandeep, or "bright, good light." My parents arrived soon after.

To protect my premature son from infections, everyone was asked to wear a mask. After considerable thought and superb logic my father asked, "Would it not be simpler to just place a mask on him?"

I had huge plans for this newly born Kenyan, my son.

****

In February 1969, I gave my fellow intern Onaly Kapasi a ride. It had been raining heavily and the mud roads, covered by a canopy of tall trees, were slippery. The car, my mother's Fiat 500, slid and spun around in a full circle, smashing against a massive tree trunk. Smoke belched from under the hood. Onaly was ejected from the passenger window and landed in the mud. Dazed, he got up, checking to see if he was still alive. I remained in the driver's seat. I had just destroyed my mother's favorite car.

We were able to purchase a used Volkswagen from an Indian microbiologist, a teetotaler who was leaving Kenya to go to Milwaukee to brew beer.

I was about to complete my internship. My application for further training at Kenyatta Hospital in Nairobi was rejected again. I could not afford to set up a private practice, and the few remaining Indian doctors in town did not need a partner. Someone advised me to apply for the medical officer position in one of several outpatient clinics run by the government of Kenya. I was to start work at the Rhodes Avenue Clinic in Nairobi in May 1969.

Kapasi and I, never particularly close for unclear reasons, met once in Nairobi and then lost touch. Our coolness to each other had nothing to do with our religion.

I knew that he went to Boston, became an orthopedic surgeon, retired, did charitable work, and published a collection of lovely poems called *In My Mind's Eye* in 2014.

RHODES AVENUE CLINIC

The Rhodes Avenue Clinic, a government dispensary in the heart of Nairobi, was one in a chain of several clinics scattered over the city. I was hired as a medical officer at a salary of 1400 shillings per month (equivalent to $21 at the current exchange rate). Almost all of the patients were Africans.

The Chief Officer, Dr. Gupta, an Indian trained in Ireland; Dr. Oluoch, a Luo doctor; and four medical assistants rounded off the team. We had a small lab to identify malaria, gonorrhea, TB, and parasites. Hundreds of men from the city lined up with the women and children, who came from nearby villages. They waited patiently on wooden benches for hours. Mothers sang softly to their ill babies.

Each of the seven tiny exam rooms contained a cot, a small table, and a chair. No curtains, no privacy. We yelled "Next!" whenever we were free. The next patient in line walked through a common corridor to find the available clinician. The medical record was a 3 x 5 card, on which we wrote the date, the symptoms, the presumed diagnosis, and the treatment all on one line. The patients brought this card whenever they needed care. The visit cost one shilling.

The team saw around 800–1,200 patients each day. There was no shoving, pushing, shouting, or elbowing. The average visit time was 3–5 minutes. The half-hour lunch break was never taken. We just kept going.

Every hour, I walked out to bring in the sickest patients ahead of the line. No one minded. Babies close to death, delirious men, or women bent over in agony were brought in first. Emaciated patients with a chronic cough were sent to the adjacent Chest Clinic for a miniature chest x-ray. If the x-ray suggested TB, we referred the positive cases to experienced African medical assistants in a separate area. This clinic was a research center, supported by the British Research Council, to study protocols for the treatment of tuberculosis. Similar studies were being conducted in Hong Kong.

The lonely men in the city were vulnerable to sexually transmitted diseases. We saw numerous patients with gonorrhea or syphilis. Malaria, pneumonia, measles, and mumps were common.

A toxic African employee of the school where my mother taught came in for deep jaundice, fever, and body aches. We confirmed malaria. He preferred to take pills at home rather than go to the hospital, and I obliged. Worried about him, I asked him to return the next morning, but he did not. He was not at the school either. He had started vomiting, his friend said, and could not keep the tablets down. He was going to tell me about it the next morning, but the man had died that night. Why had I not sent him to Kenyatta Hospital? Why had I not predicted that he might vomit?

I was adding a considerable number of deaths to my résumé. I saw all of them as personal failures. My colleagues reassured me that we were doing the best we could under the circumstances. The work was repetitious, tedious, and exhausting. For the most part, we were patient and kind. But I was getting irritable.

One day a very ill child — limp, listless, and dehydrated — was brought in. He had measles and pneumonia. The mother, a large Somali woman with the traditional Muslim *abayah* (full-length cloak), was grinning. Perhaps it was a nervous smile, but I found it very odd. How could a mother smile when her child was so ill? I asked her why she was "ncheka kama nugu" (laughing like a monkey).

Her smile disappeared. She stood up, her face contorted. Angrily, she informed me that I had no right to speak to her that way. She said her husband was a big shot in the Somali community and that I was going to hear more about this. I was already sorry that I had said it. I was afraid, too. I had visions of being fired and having no means of making a living.

With genuine regret, concern about my future, and my desire to care for the child, I pleaded with her to allow me to start over. She relented and sat down. I examined the child, gave her instructions, and asked her to return the next day. She followed all instructions regarding hydration and taking the antibiotics. The child looked perkier the next morning, and her fever had subsided. I was pleased and relieved that the woman did not broach the subject of my improper behavior. I repeated my apology.

She lived in Eastleigh, near the same mudhole where I had nearly drowned decades earlier. Although it was a predominantly Asian area, there was a scattering of Somalis there. I wondered if they had been allowed in because of their lighter skin color, straight noses, and thin lips. Today the area is called "Little Mogadishu." There are fears that the Somali Al-Shabaaz terror group, responsible for the bombing at the West Gate shopping center, has infiltrated the population. Most of the Asians who lived in Eastleigh had already migrated overseas or moved to more secure areas in Nairobi, where they lived in heavily fortified homes with high walls, sentries, security systems, and watchdogs.

A young white woman, clearly out of place in this sea of black, became my first American patient. With due deference to her race and how ill she looked, someone had escorted her to the front of the line. She had come to "find herself" in Africa. I imagined hippies looked like her. She was no more than my age, wore dirty clothes, and was exhausted. Her skin was hot and she was sweating profusely. While hitchhiking, she had started to feel chilly and then had developed a high fever. She had no money and had not eaten for two days. Her malaria smear was negative. A miniature x-ray showed pneumonia. She appeared so vulnerable. I prescribed an antibiotic and asked her to return the next day.

This was the first white patient I had ever touched in my life! Why had she come to Africa? What had she lacked in America to want to come here and wander aimlessly through a somewhat unsafe country? I never saw her again.

It was a relatively slow day, and I was looking out my office window. A tall, Asian man walked briskly toward the clinic, followed by a child between 8 and 10 years old. Upon arrival, the man informed me in Urdu that he was having chest pain, then started sweating profusely, rolled his eyes, and had a major seizure. He lost his pulse and had no measurable blood pressure. The young boy, in a panic, screamed "Abba, Abba!" and held my hand tightly for assurance. We tried CPR for a few minutes, but I knew it was too late. The dead and dying were sent to Kenyatta Hospital. The ambulance sped off, sirens blaring, carrying the motionless man. I caught a brief glimpse of the boy's face in the rear window as he accompanied his father's corpse to a hospital morgue. His *Abba* was dead because I could do nothing for him. Why were dead people so heavy?

In 1968, the pharmaceutical giant Burroughs Wellcome marketed a new drug called Septrin. The young, British salesperson offered us free boxes containing thousands of these white pills to treat respiratory infections. We prescribed the new drug to patients with bronchitis, bronchopneumonia, and pneumonia. Nearly 200 patients were entered into this trial within a few weeks. This extraordinary feat would have been unimaginable in any other place on the planet. There were no hindrances such as a need to sign consent forms, to obtain approval from institutional review boards, or to keep records.

Most patients, pleased to be receiving the most modern antibiotic in the world, returned for follow-up visits. The results were wonderful. After my departure from Kenya in 1971, I received a copy of a paper published in the *East African Medical Journal* describing the outstanding results from a Septrin study in a Nairobi clinic. I had contributed not a single line and had never seen this paper before. My co-authors were doctors from the Rhodes Avenue Clinic, Dr. Gupta and Dr. Oluoch. The Burroughs Wellcome salesman had written the paper. It was my first publication!

Years later, Roche produced the same pill in a bright yellow-gold color and oblong shape and called it Bactrim. Sales of the yellow pill were far superior to the white pill, although the ingredients were exactly the same. The change in color was a stroke of genius. Color had a deep meaning, affecting human behavior, even in the pharmaceutical business. This pill would save thousands of men and women from infections related to the acquired immune deficiency syndrome (AIDS) when the epidemic hit the world a decade later.

Peter, a distant nephew of Jomo Kenyatta, had joined our staff in 1970. He was an affable young man trained in Britain. Our subsequent friendship led to a dinner invitation from his parents, high-ranking officials in Kenya. The ambassador from Yugoslavia was there too. This was the first time my wife and I had eaten a meal together in a multiracial setting.

We were unprepared. The parents, westernized and elegant, lived in a large mansion. I had never seen such a "rich" home. The European food was alien to me. Asha and I held glasses of water for the toast, while they sipped wine. The Yugoslav ambassador's wife, sitting next to me, pretended not to notice that I was holding her water glass. Fortunately, we knew how to use a fork and knife. I do not remember saying anything important. They tolerated the misfits with great kindness and generosity. We were not invited again, but were in no position to reciprocate anyway. Peter left soon after for Kenyatta Hospital.

The dinner gave me hope that we could be welcome and safe in Kenya, and that the prevailing rhetoric was simply words. But the facts suggested otherwise. The Mzungu were still welcome in Kenya, despite the history of segregation, excesses of British fusiliers, the *kipande*, the slums, and the theft of the best agricultural land. Rules for work permits were apparently more flexible for whites. The Asians, feeling unwelcome and insecure, were trying to leave as soon as they could.

****

I continued the drudgery of work at the clinic. It helped that a new doctor arrived from India. Rumor had it that Dr. A was schizophrenic. His intense demeanor and piercing gaze alarmed me. He preferred to be left alone. Patients who had seen him before avoided him when they could by adjusting their position in the queue.

"Anand, did you know Indians are starving in Nairobi?" he asked and walked away before I could respond. The next day he insisted that I accompany him during his daily evening rounds to ask wealthy Indians for monetary donations, food, and clothing to distribute to needy and jobless Indians without work permits.

We were welcomed with genuine warmth by the predominantly Gujarati business families. Donations and promises of support poured in. A retired schoolteacher, Mrs. Desai, coordinated the entire program (which consisted of Dr. A, myself, and Mrs. Desai) and did the bookkeeping. A sophisticated and striking woman, she was highly regarded in the community. Weeks passed.

"Where is the money going?" some asked.

Others advised us to keep "clean" records to allay concerns about any misappropriation of funds.

"The British should do something. They created this mess."

The whites were referred to as *sala dholia*, a derogatory term.

My family did not understand my preoccupation with this matter, since they had not seen or met any starving Indians in Kenya.

They wanted me to spend more time at home. Mrs. Desai's involvement did not impress them. They were also worried about my security at night.

Compassion fatigue soon set in. It manifested itself first by how long it took donors to open the door, the insincere offer of tea and snacks, and finally an outright refusal to donate. The message was clear: do not return! Now, more often than not, we came back empty-handed. Money and donations ultimately dried up, and I dropped out.

Dr. A remained unflappable and carried on alone.

Some months later we received word that he would not return to work. Had he been locked up in a mental asylum? Had he committed suicide? Had he gone abroad?

On April 20, 1968, British Parliament member Enoch Powell opposed a proposed law that would have made it illegal to refuse employment or public housing to immigrants and to create a race relations board. A member of the conservative party under Edward Heath, he reflected a sentiment commonly expressed by many Britons. In his long speech in Midlands, he said:

Like the Roman, I seem to see "the River Tiber foaming with much blood."

...In this country, in 15 or 20 years' time, the black man will have the whip hand over the white man.

He freely used the word *negro* in this speech, but his ire was directed toward all colored people. This speech received wide attention locally and internationally. The reverberations reached Nairobi. It all started with a nasty letter from a British expatriate to the editor of the *East African Standard*. A few others followed, bemoaning the much-feared Asian exodus to London. The tone became harsher and, frankly, racist. A rare letter begged for more understanding and compassion.

Powell's speech and these letters incensed me. I responded to the correspondence by stating that those rivers would have British blood within them too. I spoke of the enormous sacrifices made by Indians to develop British colonies and to fight their wars, of the deliberate starvation of Indians — under Churchill's watch — so the British could feed their armies during World War II. How their prosperity was built on the backs of their colored citizens. That Kohinoor, the diamond stolen from India, still sat in Britain. This back and forth went on for months. The editor closed the correspondence when the heat became unbearable. Remarkably, I was the only Indian voice in this exchange. The silence of the Asian community was deafening. Some said people feared possible repercussions from the British Embassy and the Kenyan government.

A friend warned me that, as a British citizen, I could be deported for writing such things. I asked "Where would they deport someone who is essentially stateless?" I had written nothing negative about Africans or the Kenyan government. I continued to fight back with my pen.

About this time, the well-known Madhvani family from Uganda shut down some of its operations in Kenya, and my father lost his job at the glass factory they owned. He complained that he was losing new job opportunities with European employers who thought he was writing the anti-British letters. His argument had merit but I felt the need to fight bigots. It led to one heated argument at home.

****

Someone had suggested that I take an American exam called the ECFMG (Educational Commission for Foreign Medical Graduates) while I was still in Nyeri. The multiple-choice format of the exam was alien to me, the failure rate was high, and I had no time to study. I weighed my options. Staying in Kenya was dicey, and my parents would most likely lose their work permits soon. My income could not sustain all of us. The British government, concerned about large scale immigration and the rhetoric coming from pundits, politicians, and priests, stamped the passports of overseas citizens, who were not born or domiciled in Britain, with a "D," which to us stood for "denied." So, it was bizarre to read the following words in our passports:

Her Britannic Majesty's Principal Secretary of State for Foreign Commonwealth Affairs requests and requires in the name of Her Majesty all those, to whom it may concern, to allow the bearer to pass freely without let or hindrance and to afford the bearer such assistance and protection as may be necessary.

I took the exam and passed, but barely. I stared at the ECFMG certificate, the number 1152254 and the date, September 11, 1968, for a long time. Two mail deliveries had changed the course of my life. The first time when a 3 x 5 postcard confirmed my admission to CMC and now this certificate from America.

I went to the US Embassy around May 1969 to apply for the green card. The Civil Rights Act, passed by the Lyndon Johnson administration in 1964, had removed the color bar for immigration to the US. Embassy officials said the ECFMG certificate was most helpful, but a job offer from America would speed up the process.

I was astonished to learn that the most powerful, prosperous, and dynamic nation on the planet had a severe shortage of doctors, at a time when they could not find jobs in India.

****

Perhaps annoyed by my letters or the loss of his job, my father had started drinking again. We smelled the alcohol on his breath but remained quiet, hoping this phase would pass. One evening, he tottered into the common courtyard that led to our apartment. I rushed out to give him a hand so he would not fall onto the concrete floor. From the corner of my eye, I saw three women in the Gujarati owner's kitchen pointing and giggling. They found this very amusing. I gave them a sharp look, and they quickly turned away from the window.

Upon entering, his first words were always addressed to Sandeep, who adored his grandfather. The little boy was allowed to touch my father's Parker pens, typewriter, magazines, and papers and to jump on his bed without any reprimand. Picking him up, my father started spinning around in circles saying, "bala bala" (child, child) while his grandson squealed in delight asking for "ankhin, ankhin" (more, more). Defying the laws of equilibrium, they managed to stay upright.

"Fast, fast!" said Sandeep, thrilled to be on this roller coaster. His squeals got louder.

Apprehensive, I asked Baba to stop. He did not hear me. They continued twirling, swaying…round and round and round.

I grabbed my son, just as they were about to fall. My father somehow held on to the bed railing. I was livid. I had just been humiliated by the neighbors, and now my son's safety had been endangered. I turned to face my father. His response—that same silly smile I had seen before when my mother had aimed a steel plate at his head—angered me further. I shoved him. He fell to the floor. Shaking in anger, I struck his chest once or twice and walked away. My mother, shocked, stood still in the corner. My father sat up on the floor, speechless, his eyes seeking an explanation.

This was something one never did to any elder. My pent-up anger and bottled up resentment had exploded in a split second, unexpectedly, and I had broken all codes of cultural and societal propriety. An apology could never undo the grievous harm I had caused. Not a word was exchanged.

Sandeep did not comprehend what had happened, but wisely went to Asha. The dinner remained untouched. A few minutes later, my mother approached me.

"It would be best if you went to America." She whispered gently. I saw no reproach or reprimand. I stared at her. A tiny woman, beaten down by time and circumstance, resigned to an uncertain future.

That evening, I decided to pursue an American green card.

Tom Mboya rose to the rank of secretary general of the Kenya African National Union (KANU) in 1960. One year after independence, in 1964, he became the minister for justice and later, the minister for economic planning. His star was rising. Kenyatta appeared to have a soft spot for him despite simmering tensions between the Luo and Kikuyu tribes.

One evening, walking down the stairs from the Kenya Theater where we had just seen a forgettable movie, I saw Mboya waiting for the next show. I nodded politely, awed. He nodded back, expressionless, unsmiling. This man, whom I admired so much, wanted to throw me into the ocean based on the perceived misdeeds of other Indians. This was the man who had once stood on the stage alongside Martin Luther King, Jr. in America, the man who Sharad had once hoped to work for in KANU until he heard Mboya's demand for Asians to leave Kenya.

On July 5, 1969, shots rang out in a pharmacy on Government Road, right in the heart of Nairobi. Mboya, mortally wounded, lay bleeding on the floor and died soon after. Unaware, I was busy seeing patients in our dispensary about a mile away. Suddenly the clinic emptied. Grief-stricken citizens rushed to see their hero. There was speculation that Kikuyu rivals in KANU were behind this murder, or that Jomo Kenyatta felt threatened by this fiery orator and perhaps was complicit in the plan. Adding some credence to the tribal jealousy theory, the predominantly Luo party — the Kenya People's Union, led by Oginga Odinga — was banned.

The *East African Standard* and *The Nation* spoke of Kenya's grief eloquently. For a few days, Africans forgot to bash Indians. About this time, trade unions and their activists launched a rather disorganized movement for workers' rights. Most Indians, even the poorer ones, had servants. The polite term "help" was unknown to us. The realities of supply and demand made it simple to hire blacks at low wages, and prevalent laws did not guarantee a minimum wage. Tom Mboya had told his followers that they had the right to a decent life and respect from others. He had promised that, with independence, the inequities in their lives would disappear. Empowered and emboldened by the speeches, servants joined unions to demand higher wages, better housing, and time off from work.

Ndegwa had served us for many years. He came at sunrise, shined the shoes, mopped the floors, washed the clothes, hung them up to dry in the sun, ironed them, and helped with cooking. He stayed until sundown, when he had to scurry back to the safety of the slum, where he shared a hut with our neighbor's servant. He was expected to wear clean clothes, work quietly, and be seen but not heard. We set aside a generous portion of food for him, unlike other families who gave only leftovers. He was expected to eat quietly, alone, in a corner of the kitchen. Some families provided used clothing. For a servant, it was rare to get a paid vacation or sick time. Ndegwa was expected to work seven days a week. It was a rare progressive employer who allowed his domestic employee to take a few days off, once a year, to meet his wife and children in the village many miles away. For most, the village might as well have been on another continent.

The land available to village women was often a small *shamba*, where they grew cassava or maize. Meat and milk were not affordable, so the staples were beans with *ugari*. Protein malnutrition caused the babies to have swollen bellies and brittle, reddish hair. Parasites in their gut competed for what little nutrition was available.

The families did not know how their fathers toiled and lived. In their rare spare time, the men drank cheap beer and released pent-up sexual energy with prostitutes. These women prowled around the ubiquitous bars, where mournful Swahili songs blared through loudspeakers connected to radios that were never turned off.

It was clear that many Asians did not think their fellow human beings were capable of pain, suffering, high aspirations, or an education. It was said that if we paid them too much, all the others would ask for more. If we provided more food, it might become an expectation. If we gave them time off, how would we manage?

"Don't spoil them. They will sit on your heads."

I had the unconfirmed impression that whites, in spite of the misery they had inflicted on the nation, treated their servants with more thought and dignity.

One Sunday morning, there was a loud knock on the door. Three black men in suits, who said they were labor inspectors but carried no identification, stood on the threshold. One man did all the talking. He spoke fluent English with just a slight African inflection. His bloodshot eyes implied that he drank a lot and slept little. The other two remained silent and sullen. He fired off a litany of demands, concerns about work rights and proper wages. Ndegwa was summoned from the kitchen, where he had been chopping vegetables. Meekly, through onion-inspired tears, he confirmed that he knew the men. The leader placed his foot purposefully on the threshold of our apartment. Seeing that I had not budged, the man withdrew his foot.

We felt betrayed by Ndegwa. He had invited strangers to our home and endangered our family. We would probably have raised his salary if he had asked us. We had overworked him for sure, but always gave him good used clothes and fresh food, and paid him more than the neighbors paid their workers. We gave him paid time off when he asked for it on rare occasions. We gave him toys for his children.

Upset, I shut the door. I gave Ndegwa a month's salary then fired him. He mumbled an apology, but I ushered him out. The men glowered menacingly. With a quivering finger, the man with the bloodshot eyes assured me that the Ministry of Labor would be contacting us. Then the agitated inspectors walked away. Ndegwa, stooped and shocked, followed them out. The neighbors, who had overheard much of the discussion, realized that this door-to-door solicitation by union leaders was a new phenomenon.

Fully aware that an African minister would be unsympathetic to our plight and our foreigner status, and fearing serious repercussions, I asked my friend Dr. Gupta at the Rhodes Avenue Clinic for advice. He was a wise man with connections. A week later, we were in the lobby of the new Hilton Hotel (my first visit to any posh hotel) with the minister and one of his assistants, for drinks. I drank orange juice. Ndegwa's name did not come up. Several hours later, inebriated, they departed, patting Gupta on the back. They had evidently reached an agreement.

Two weeks later, my father and I sat across a large, polished mahogany table facing the man Gupta had bribed. Ndegwa sat alone in a corner, fidgety, his gaze directed downwards. The union men had abandoned him. Upon interrogation, he confirmed that we had treated him well, providing food, clothing, toys, and a salary a bit higher than what the neighbors paid their servants. The case was dismissed.

The minister said that we could, at our discretion, rehire him. Ndegwa, suddenly hopeful, looked up at us. We declined. The minister brushed aside our words of gratitude by saying, "What intervention? I am just doing my job." We were dismissed.

The "victory" felt tainted and hollow, having been achieved by unfair means: influence peddling and bribery. It would have been noble and just to raise his salary and to give him more time off. Instead, we had punished a good man, just for seeking a decent wage and better working conditions. This was not a victory at all; it was a form of slavery. Caught up in our personal lives, we had not considered the needs of others. How were we different than the slave traders we criticized and condemned?

****

Apasaheb Pant, the previous Indian envoy in Nairobi, arrived on a private visit in 1969 "to see old friends" in independent Kenya, but his real mission was to see firsthand what was happening to Asians. He had been recalled by India, under British pressure, for being too close to Kenyatta during the Mau Mau era. Despite that, India chose him as its new ambassador in London.

We invited him to attend a dinner we were hosting for Sandeep's first birthday at the local club. All Maharashtrians in the community attended. He had known me as a scrawny child, and I had occasionally played with his children. A prince in the former kingdom of Aundh, Pant's dignity and class reminded me of Nehru.

Taking me aside, he told me he was aware of my agitation and letters, and that diplomatic efforts were being made to help stateless Indians. I was flattered that he remembered me. I shared what I knew of the desperate plight of Indians in Kenya. I reminded Apasaheb that, as a young boy, I had seen him with Jomo Kenyatta, the current president of Kenya, at the RSS camp in 1951. Could he not leverage that friendship? I saw a flash of anger in his eyes. A big and powerful man, he grabbed my arm, squeezed it firmly and getting closer to me, whispered softly, "These things take time. Be careful."

Sandeep, who I had been carrying, looked up at one of the most respected Indian diplomats in the world. The tension was diffused as Apasaheb patted my son's head, pulled his ears playfully, gave him a broad smile, and walked away.

Friends said and wrote that the quality of American medicine was the best in the world. However, it was impossible for a foreign medical graduate (FMG) from a non-European medical school to get a spot in a university or a large academic center. States with the most fun and sun, California and Florida, had additional requirements for licensure. Many southern states were hostile to people of color.

FMGs were most welcome in inner city medical centers, where the poor and dispossessed lived, or in smaller hospitals that did not attract enough American graduates. The higher the crime rate and squalor, the better our chances of acceptance. I was advised that these were the parameters for a fruitful job search. So the doctor shortages appeared to exist in the most undesirable areas in America.

I found a directory of residency positions in a US library. Augustana Hospital in Chicago did not quite fit the profile listed, but the glossy brochure caught my attention. The annual salary of $6,000 was higher than that offered by hospitals in Flint, Michigan, or Hackensack, New Jersey. There were photographs of beautiful white technicians next to gleaming modern machines, distinguished white men in long white coats teaching eager students of all colors, residents and nurses in their starched glory tenderly tending to the sick in this highly livable community near Lincoln Park. When converted to Kenya shillings or the Indian rupee, this was more money than I had ever dreamt of earning. The brochure had a paragraph about faculty from a well-known university nearby.

Hospital officials responded quickly to my handwritten letter. They used fine stationery. Their string of degrees and titles was impressive. To sweeten the deal, they offered an allowance for one air ticket. Lodging was not included. I signed immediately, grateful that a teaching hospital wanted me and fearful that the offer might be withdrawn. Had they overlooked the fact that I was a brown doctor trained in India?

My friends advised against accepting a job in a "such a dangerous city." They reminded me that Chicago had more gangsters than the entire Indian subcontinent and Africa combined. They said it was so cold in the Windy City that "your balls will freeze." It was a city of vice and violence, crime and Capone, of drugs and dealers, of seedy streets and syphilis, where blacks lived in ghettos and the homeless lay in gutters under bridges. It was no place for a Hindu–Brahmin family.

Some suggested we go to a town with lots of Indians, where we would be safer and have access to Indian groceries.

"Go to the UK. No guns or gangsters. More civilized. Your uncles are there and can help you settle down."

"In *Amrika*, brown people go to black bathrooms."

"My relative got shot and killed by *kalias* (blacks) in Chicago. All over a can of beer."

I was always surprised that people who had been victims of the color bar used such racial slurs — *kalia* for blacks and *dholia* or *chitta* for whites — in their daily conversations.

"That happens here, too." I said.

"But not every day."

"Asha will have to do all the housework. No Ndegwa there."

"They throw their elders in nursing homes."

They were unanimous about this point, although I would later learn that this was not true. There was no dearth of advice or advisors.

Sudhir Chitnis and his wife, Chitra, who had visited family members in California, had a more positive view. "America is indeed a land of milk and honey and the people are great. Everything is cheap and many things are free. Every time we needed to call someone, for example, we simply dialed the phone and said 'Collect' and it was free!"

Since I had no savings, we would have to accumulate the funds over the next few months while we waited for our visas to freedom, away from the daily tyranny of Africans calling me an exploiter, a traitor, or worse. And away from the oppressive silence that had become the norm in our home.

****

Months passed with no word from the US Embassy.

The verbal abuse against Asians became more strident and vicious. Emboldened, petty thieves began to snatch necklaces from Indian women as their cars approached stop signs. Home robberies increased, but the police did not arrive. When called, they simply laughed. The pervasive lawlessness and insecurity became a daily fact of life.

One time, as I was about to pull into a vacant parking spot in downtown Nairobi, an irate African woman rammed her jeep — with government license plates — repeatedly into my newly acquired, used Toyota Corona, cursing and screaming in English. Apparently, she had been waiting for the spot to open up. Frightened, my family urged me to leave quickly before a crowd gathered. I knew we would be hurt by a partisan crowd if this obviously important black woman raised a ruckus in now-independent Kenya. This was my first personal encounter of this sort in all my years in Kenya. We were left shaken. The dents on the car suggested that our days were numbered. As I drove away, tires screeching, I saw in my rearview mirror a crowd waving fists and shouting obscenities. The Indian restaurant owner, whose *samosas* we had hoped to buy, shook his head and looked away.

Some years later, I became aware of the African fable noted below. It aptly describes the deadly dance between the hunter and the hunted.

Every morning in Africa, a gazelle wakes up.

It knows it must run faster than the fastest lion or it will get killed.

Every morning, a lion wakes up.

It knows it must outrun the slowest gazelle or it will starve to death.

It doesn't matter whether you are a lion or a gazelle.

When the sun comes up, you better start running.

Unnerved by all this, I decided to send Asha to India with Sandeep, on a tourist visa valid for four months. She was quite homesick anyway. Aji saw her great grandson, Sandeep, for the first time. He was most thrilled by things that Indians took for granted: cows and goats on the streets and elephants in the park.

My parents and I had no option but to stay. I now drove my father to his newest job each morning and brought him back. This kept him away from bars. Sobriety had now been forced upon him. I wonder why I had not thought of this earlier. Neither of us spoke during these drives.

He never mentioned my unforgivable behavior, when I had shoved him to the ground and pounded on his chest.

THE US EMBASSY

The wait for our visas ended abruptly in December 1970, when I received a letter from the US Embassy to report for an interview. The letter stated that everyone getting a green card needed to be present. I sent a telegram to Asha: "Return to Nairobi immediately to collect US visa." Her planned four-month trip was cut short. We once again depleted our funds, paying for Asha's flights to India and back.

We arrived at the embassy far too early. Mrs. Billingsley, a short, smart, and sprightly woman, walked out of her office briskly at the appointed time. I thought she might be 70, but I was not good at judging the ages of white people. She immediately put us at ease, with a kind smile that lit up the whole room. She offered us seats and got down to business immediately.

"Living in America comes with responsibilities," she said. "You have to sign up for the selective service draft."

Seeing a puzzled look on my face, she explained the country was at war with Vietnam, and able-bodied men had to sign up to serve in the armed forces. Green card holders were not exempt, even though they were ineligible for citizenship for five more years. We knew that thousands of Americans had died, or lay wounded, in an unpopular war that seemed to have no end. I figured that as a doctor, I would place bandages on wounds, not pull triggers, so I did not ask for further clarification.

With mischief in her eyes, she also said we would now have the "pleasure of paying taxes" in America. We had never made enough money in Kenya to pay any. My parents and I had regular jobs, but none paid well enough to force us into a significant tax bracket. I wondered if all Americans were as warm and kind as Mrs. Billingsley. Asha and I took the English test and the oath as Sandeep looked on. In our confusion and anxiety, we put our hands on the Bible and swore allegiance to the United States of America. I did not know that I could simply have raised my right hand or asked for the *Gita,* which they had likely never heard of.

Three Alien Resident cards were presented to us. She congratulated us warmly.

Ecstatic, we bolted out of the office before they changed their minds. I was ready to leave the land of my birth, a country that I loved but whose people had rejected me. It was our fate.

We were required to move to the United States before the end of April 1971.

****

I had loved the land where my son and I were born. The bitter reality of a permanent break with Kenya now cast a dark shadow in my life. We were heading to the most powerful and technologically advanced nation on Earth. I felt unprepared. I did not even know how to make a call from a telephone booth! I feared that my medical training might not be rigorous enough. That Americans might ridicule me. They might notice I was ill at ease with white people. The only white patient I had ever treated was the hippie woman who had wandered into my clinic. Would the patients accept me, or ask for a white doctor? How would other doctors interact with me? What would happen to my parents? They still had jobs, but were unsafe. Where would they go if they had to leave in a hurry? If they left Kenya, how would I support them with my meager salary? They had no pension plans and no savings.

Fortunately, India relaxed its ban on the entry of British citizens of Indian origin. It did not abandon its people, who were in dire straits. My parents, always thoughtful and generous, urged us not to worry. They would get shelter in India with Dinkar Kaka in Bombay, or with Subhash and Mai in Baroda. They would go to India as tourists and stay on. No one would question them. Once there, they would change their legal status. They expressed relief that we were heading for a safer place. They smiled and helped us pack, but I could see their hearts were broken.

Shashikant Shah, my dear friend since the fifth grade, who had trained in Britain and joined me in Rhodes Avenue Clinic for a while, promised he would check in on my parents. He assured me that most of the people in the West were fair and just. The occasional bigot had to be tolerated.

A CANNIBAL IN KAMPALA

Events in Uganda convinced us that we had made the right decision.

Idi Amin, a confidant of the Ugandan president, Milton Obote, staged a coup in January 1971, while his boss was in Singapore attending a commonwealth meeting. Amin, an illiterate boxing champion, had earned notoriety for ruthlessly fighting Mau Mau in Kenya as a member of the British King's African Rifles.

What followed was the beginning of one of the darkest periods in Ugandan history. Amin was an animal. There were rumors that he enjoyed the taste of human flesh. He apparently took a fancy to the beautiful widow of the affluent Indian industrialist, Jayant Madhvani, whose sugar plantations, processing plants, cotton mills, and glass container factories were the lifeblood of Uganda, accounting for 12% of the nation's gross domestic product. The glass factory in Nairobi where my father worked was owned by this family as well. The widow rebuffed Amin. In 1972, perhaps in retaliation, he expelled 60,000 Indians from Uganda. They were given 90 days to pack up and leave. The Madhvanis escaped to Britain, where they already had substantial holdings. They left behind mansions and factories, which lay in ruin for years thereafter.

Panicked families drove to the Entebbe Airport or to the Kenyan border, leaving all their belongings behind. Many were shot and killed. Those who made it to the airport clambered onto the first flight out of the country with nothing but the clothes on their backs. Their properties were confiscated. Those who'd had a premonition of such dangers had transferred funds overseas ahead of these events. Some had bought furnished apartments in India.

The community that had built the railroad into Uganda, built its cities and businesses, and staffed its schools and universities was evicted simply because of the color of its people's skin, for economic envy, and because a beautiful Indian widow had rebuffed the advances of an uncouth beast. Thousands of Africans were slaughtered as well. Uganda degenerated into a state of lawlessness. Its entire infrastructure collapsed, as trade and tourism came to a screeching halt. Fear and foreboding filled the lives of those who remained.

Britain was forced to accept the defenseless refugees under international pressure. This decision would pay dividends years later, when these men and women made enormous contributions to the British economy through sheer hard work.

India, too, opened its doors to the refugees. The cities of Baroda and Ahmedabad prospered with the arrival of entrepreneurs with business savvy, unhindered by colonial oppression or racial divide. Gujarat became a shining diamond in India's economy, in no small measure because of Indians from East Africa.

Canada welcomed the refugees with open arms, because they knew these were hardworking people with skills the country needed. Aga Khan, the spiritual leader of the Ismailia community, played a major role in ensuring the safe transfer and settlement of his community overseas.

Amin would provoke international outrage in 1976, when he collaborated with Arab terrorists, who hijacked a French plane at Entebbe Airport. In a brilliantly orchestrated rescue, Israeli commandos -led by Benjamin Netanyahu's elder brother- flew hundreds of miles to the airport to rescue the Jewish hostages. It was a slap in the face of the buffoon who said he could become the King of Scotland, if offered the job. Netanyahu's brother died in that effort.

In a foolish career-ending move in 1979, Amin invaded Tanzania, which had given refuge to Obote. Julius Nyerere, a peaceful man, struck back. His armed forces overwhelmed the Ugandans. Amin was forced to flee to Libya. His crimes against humanity and Islam notwithstanding, the Saudi government gave him asylum, providing luxurious accommodations for him and his large family. The man, who should have been executed for his crimes, died in comfort. He never expressed any regret for the murders, ethnic cleansing, or genocide. He was a disgrace to mankind as were his hosts.

Obote returned to power in Kampala and, in an ironic twist, made a plea to Indians, especially the Madhvanis, to return to Uganda to rebuild the country, which lay in ruins.

****

We knew we would never return to Africa. My parents, who had not seen most of the world-famous tourist spots themselves, suggested Asha and I do so, and volunteered to look after Sandeep.

We saw wild animals at the salt lick at Treetops and flamingos that turned lakes pink. A few weeks later, we drove toward the foothills of Mount Kilimanjaro, where Doctor Kaka had practiced medicine. We heard thousands of wildebeest thundering across the plains and watched rhinoceros, gazelles, antelopes, cheetahs, and lions coexisting within Ngorongoro Crater. Nearby, tree-climbing lions rested on branches of acacia trees.

At Tsavo National Park, where lions had devoured Indian railway workers almost eight decades earlier, we suffered the harsh conditions that the railway coolies had faced in that arid part of Kenya. The relentless heat had forced the animals to find shade and shelter. The huge herds of elephants we had hoped to see did not emerge. A frightened snake slithered across the hot dirt road, barely escaping the wheels of my Toyota.

During these travels, I felt guilty that my parents had not been able to visit the wonderful places we had seen. Despite their labors over four decades, they had not traveled for fun or taken any vacations. Their bank balance was zero. They had nothing to show for their efforts except for my education. Their love and sacrifices had been unconditional.

The beneficiary of their largesse, their only child, had not been a perfect son, but they had forgiven his transgressions. They now wished him and his young family well as they embarked on a new and uncertain life in a new nation.

I sold my last possession, the red Toyota Corona, to pay for airline tickets for Asha and Sandeep.

TRIPOLI, Libya

There were the obligatory farewell dinners with tearful friends. In March 1971, we got cheap tickets on a charter flight and boarded a plane bound for London, with a refueling stop in Tripoli, Libya. We planned to visit my three maternal uncles — Bhau, Sharad, and Anil — in the UK before heading out to America.

All those aboard were Indians. They were leaving Kenya permanently. Many had never been on a plane or traveled overseas. Most carried little money and just one suitcase. Some had savings overseas. Others, like me, were essentially penniless but for the small amount of foreign exchange we were allowed to carry. We were apprehensive, uncertain, and heartbroken.

There was silence as the plane flew over the endless Sahara Desert. Intermittently, the gentle voice of an airline hostess would awaken us from our slumber to offer us food and beverages. It was close to midnight when the captain announced our arrival in Tripoli, overlooking the Mediterranean Sea.

Vehicles of different shapes and sizes, ghostly shadows in the sickly yellow light, advanced rapidly toward the plane. We did not have permission to disembark.

Loud Arab voices awakened the sleepy passengers suddenly and rudely. Four tall, thin, brown men, some with traditional headgear and caftans, entered the cabin noisily. They spoke in a guttural tone, each word rapidly expelled from their mouth like spit laden with desert sand. Methodically, they sprayed an insecticide, first under each seat and then directly over us. Noxious fumes filled the cabin and people began to cough and retch. Children, their eyes smarting, started crying. The men laughed and left as quickly as they had entered, still shouting, spitting, and spraying. Through the haze of the dirty windows, we saw them gesticulating wildly as they gave the go-ahead signal to the pilot.

Their yellow caftans blended perfectly with the sickly hue enveloping the aircraft.

The fumigated and infuriated passengers, wheezing and weeping, let loose a cacophony of profanities in a variety of Indian languages.

"Haramzade, spraying us like *machars* (mosquitoes). May you and your children rot in Hell!"

The plane took off. We were now en route to a more civilized place. As the spasms of cough abated, we went back to a troubled sleep. It was too dark, and we were too high, to see the Mediterranean Sea or the coastline of Europe.

We were out of Africa.

From then on, we would see mostly white faces. I dozed off. In a disturbing dream, I saw a white man standing by the banks of a crimson red river, staring intently as a lifeless body floated by. He was laughing.

LONDON, United Kingdom

I lugged our three suitcases, all our worldly belongings, toward the customs area at Heathrow Airport. I was pleasantly surprised that we were not grilled by the customs officials as many Indians are before entry. The three green cards were apparently ample proof that we were not crashing into the UK to live off their dole. We were foreigners in Britain, even though we carried British passports.

Bhau, who had left his Nairobi University teaching post for a job at the London Polytechnic in 1965, was waving to us. He had developed a little paunch, but still had the same warm smile and the dimple in his cheek. He now waddled trying to maintain his center of gravity.

Our bags barely fit into the trunk of his old car. We made our way to their townhome. Nalutai had not aged one bit and cherished having her own home and the freedom to do as she pleased, and cooking for only her immediate family. She adjusted to English life and blended in easily with her British neighbors. Tall and stately, she was fair and freckled, like many English women. Her heavenly cooking was a draw for neighbors. They had three rather good-looking children.

Asha, now a young woman, was dating a Welshman, John, who resembled Jesus Christ and spoke a version of the English language that none of us understood.

Varsha told me that her best friend was the granddaughter of Dr. L. M. Dickson, who had taught me anatomy from my hospital bed in Ludhiana. She dragged me by my hand to visit the professor, just a few homes away. When I asked Dr. Dickson if she remembered the anatomy lessons she gave me in 1962, she responded with a twinkle in her eyes, "How could one forget a brown-skinned student with yellow eyes and a name like Panwalker, who pretended he loved reading *Gray's Anatomy?*"

I expressed my gratitude for her extraordinary generosity in teaching me when I had been ill. It had been a surprise when she retired, and we wondered if our harsh slogans about foreigners had stung. It was ironic given that similar words from Kenyans had made me leave that country.

Prakash, the youngest and now six years old, was too young to remember that he had walked the seven circles around a fire with me when Asha and I got married in 1967.

Their home was modest and happy. A fire crackled without warming the room. A cold English draft found its way in. I reflected on the disintegration of our joint family, which had once lived in two rooms in Nairobi, its members now dispersed on different continents. This breakup was necessary and inevitable. It allowed each family unit to develop its own personality and passions. It made me feel sad and nostalgic nonetheless.

Anil had lived with Bhau and his family for a while until he could settle down. He got a job with Xerox and made a name for himself in musical circles, including cutting a record with the Beatles. Anil tells the story.

A call came from Angadi asking me if I would play tabla for George. I didn't know who George was! My first question was, "How much do I get paid?" It was £35, which was the biggest fee I had ever been paid, so I immediately agreed. When a white Rolls Royce came to take me to the studio, I was told by the driver that the car belonged to George Harrison, the Beatle. That is when I started sweating!

Harrison had been taught sitar by Ravi Shankar, and they cut the song titled "Love You To" on the album *Revolver*.

Sharad lived in Essex and was training to be a lawyer. To support him, his wife, Sudha, found a job as a secretary. The two daughters, Smita and Nina, were outstanding scholars and were to make a name for themselves. Sudha developed kidney failure years later. When she received a kidney transplant from a Scottish man who had died in an accident, all her former prejudice against whites disappeared, for now — although she was Indian at heart — her urine was Scottish!

Sudha, my mother's younger sister, had married, and both left Mombasa as victims of Africanization. They had reached London, where they had struggled, but then had moved on to Ottawa, Canada, before our visit.

East African Asians in Britain did rather well for themselves. They bought small businesses, which they kept open for long hours. While the English were enjoying their afternoon tea, the Indian "refugees" were toiling to rebuild a new future. They excelled in schools and in trade. They also did jobs no one else wanted to do: cleaners at airports, waiters, dishwashers, and street sweepers. They kept striving for a better life. As they had in Nairobi, they once again built huge temples, mosques, and *gurudwaras*. They packed stadiums when Indian sports teams visited, cheering the visitors, much to the chagrin of locals. The Indian flag was raised, along with the Union Jack, on August 15 for the Indian Independence Day. They sang "Vande Mataram" (I praise thee, Mother). Little India sprang up in Whitehall and Wembley.

The memories of colonial rule and apartheid made assimilation difficult but, over time, an equilibrium was reached. Indians began to eat and sell fish and chips. The English declared the Indian curry their favorite dish. Indians had won the hearts, and palates, of many who had oppressed them, denied entry to them, and segregated them based on their skin color for centuries.

Bigots remained bigots. More open-minded Britons recognized the basic goodness of these new arrivals. They opened their arms and homes to many. Intermarriages were signs of tolerance and acceptance based on individual values and virtues rather than caste, color, or creed.

My parents, meanwhile, remained unsafe and vulnerable, the only family members to remain in Kenya. Frightening changes in Africa were making their stay increasingly perilous. I needed to get them out of danger as soon as possible.

BOOK FOUR:
The Land of the Brave

After three weeks of sightseeing and visiting friends, I concluded that the British were not too bad after all. They did appear a bit stiff and awkward. I noticed that for some of them, a daily bath was optional. Asha and I did not understand what Bhau described as the dry humor of the British. While others laughed their heads off, we mulled over how dry humor differed from the wet type.

I truly believe my relatives thought we were daft, the British word for stupid. I preferred to watch the Asian channel on BBC (British Broadcasting Corporation), where Anil and his band performed each week.

It was time to leave.

We made our rounds saying goodbye and were dropped off at the airport, arriving at John F. Kennedy Airport in New York on April 16, 1971. Overwhelmed by its size and the cacophony of international voices, we approached the bearded white immigration officer with great trepidation. What would he ask?

After a cursory glance at the papers he said, "Welcome home!"

With a smile, he pointed us toward the gate. I have never forgotten those magical words. I could have hugged the man. Escapees from Kenya, shunned by Britain, we were welcomed by a white stranger in a totally foreign land.

I loved the way Americans spoke English. Their diction was crisp, clean, and clear with each word spoken the way it should be. No mumbling or dry humor.

My childhood friend, Mohan, was waiting for us. He and his wife, Karuna, had left Kenya in 1968 and now lived in Hartford, Connecticut. He whisked us away to his home in a rather large car. Impressed, I asked if he owned it. We would have been utterly lost without them, since we knew no one in New York. The often-repeated saga of the Indian immigrant arriving with just a suitcase and $8, the amount permitted under foreign exchange laws, often omits the generosity of friends and family.

Mohan's home in Hartford was bigger than anything I had imagined. It occurred to me that he had become very rich in just two years. Unable to afford college, he had done clerical jobs in Kenya, even sold tires, and had supported his mother and two siblings throughout his life. Each evening, he took insurance courses, and he worked for the Life Insurance Company of India for a while. That helped him land a job with The Hartford insurance company. Mohan and his new Indian friends gave us useful survival tips for living in America.

After several days of generous hospitality, we flew to meet Mira and her husband, also named Subhash, in St. Paul, Minnesota. We shared their small apartment. As children, Mira and I had fought pitched battles. Now I was so happy to see her. I felt welcome and secure in their home. Their tight budget did not limit their hospitality. Their young son, also named Sandeep, was good company for our son. They graciously asked Asha and Sandeep to stay on longer while I traveled to Chicago to begin my internship on May 1, 1971.

We were accumulating many debts of gratitude.

The Greyhound bus reached downtown Chicago at 6:00 AM. A cab driver overheard me asking about a YMCA located near the Augustana Hospital and offered to take me there. A short ride later, the driver announced, "This is as far as I go," and dropped me off about two blocks from the entrance to a brick building.

The area was deserted and eerily quiet. Piles of trash lay on both sides of the street. The dilapidated homes rose like pimples on diseased skin. Occasionally, a curtain opened just slightly, and inscrutable black faces peered at me through the dirty panes. A dog barked halfheartedly. I felt terribly out of place.

I entered the foyer of the YMCA. The person at the broken desk, a sleepy, disheveled man, seemed surprised to see this Asian in a dark suit carrying two suitcases and speaking the King's English. He asked for a $5 deposit, the first night's rent, and gave me the key to a room on the second floor. I saw no one as I found a tiny room with naked metal pipes clanging over the bed. The ceiling had brown stains from leaking water. A small, broken window, which would neither open nor close fully, faced an elevated railway track. Its glass panes, held together by dried, cracked, and disintegrated caulk, quivered each time a train passed by. The misaligned door latch kept the door ajar, occasionally swaying and groaning as though in great pain. An unfamiliar acrid smell rose from the gaps in the floor. Was it marijuana? There was just enough room for the two suitcases.

I stepped out into a dimly lit, dank corridor looking for a restroom and stumbled over an object, which woke up and glared at me with bloodshot eyes. After my profuse and sincere apology, he withdrew the stare and allowed me to proceed. Another man stood near a commode and, missing his aim, stood in a large puddle of his own urine. He stumbled out, his wet shoes squeaking in protest. He did not look at me, but muttered something under his breath as he left the large communal bathroom. I tiptoed back, carefully to avoid the human form I had annoyed. I tried to take a nap, but it was too noisy and smelly. The stained and dirty mattress, hair trapped within its seams, reeked of sweat and urine.

It was an awfully long day and night. I could not sleep and dared not step out to look for food. At around 5:00 AM the next morning, making sure there was no one in the bathroom, I shaved, washed my face, brushed my teeth, picked up my two bags, and escaped from the YMCA. Not a soul stirred. The streets were empty. As I walked north, the landscape and the people seemed less scary. I was amazed that there was such a huge difference between the YMCA environment and what I saw as I crossed Fullerton Avenue and approached the hospital.

Exhausted and relieved, I arrived at the front desk in my crumpled suit with my two bags and announced, "I am Dr. Panwalker and I am the new intern."

The receptionist offered me a seat while she went looking for the hospital director. He was visibly alarmed when I told him where I had spent the night. He informed me that I had walked through perhaps the most notorious and dangerous black ghetto, known for grinding poverty, crime, killings, and drug addicts. It was an island of great destitution in the midst of the genteel white neighborhoods in Lincoln Park.

After some pleasantries, he offered me a dorm room with amenities for just a few days until a new batch of student nurses occupied them. Wishing me luck, he handed me a copy of the *Chicago Tribune* classified ads page. I was to share the dorm room with Dr. Rudiger Andrasch, who was expected to arrive soon from Germany. Four other interns—three from South Korea and one from Thailand— had found housing elsewhere.

My work at the hospital, just across the street, began the next morning. There was no orientation. I was to perform histories and physical examinations (H&Ps) for the patients of private doctors. The to-do list was placed in a box with our names on it every day. We did the H&Ps, answered calls—mostly requests for laxatives and sleeping pills from elderly women—and got to sleep much of the night.

Sometimes, patients were managed quite inappropriately, but I dared not question the absent senior doctors. My co-interns from Korea and Thailand remained mute much of the time. The nurses were kind and friendly, unlike the "sisters" in India, but hardly ever asked us any medical questions. I got the distinct impression that they did not think we knew much. This impression – mostly correct- has survived intact to present-day internships.

Rudi was fearless. I was fascinated by his German accent. The only time I had ever heard English spoken this way was when we had met a German on Kilimanjaro, who had worn shorts as though he had been on an evening stroll. He was halfway down the mountain when we were still gasping upward. If there were German hippies, Rudi was a prime example. He had long, unkempt blond hair, piercing blue eyes, and loose-fitting clothes. He was restless and daring, constantly questioning the care American attending physicians suggested. He would say, "In Germany, we would do it this way." I could not very well argue that in India or Kenya we would do it this way or that way, since everyone assumed that non-European schools and doctors were inferior. The Asian interns were silenced by the reputation that preceded them.

Our "teachers" were content, in this teaching program, to have us do the thankless and dirty work. Most of the senior doctors barely glanced at us, even though we did several H&Ps for them each day. They were happiest if we left them alone and simply responded to pleas for relief from their constipated patrons. We were not to make any important clinical decisions. The nurses had been well trained to direct those questions to the real doctors. A senior surgeon from South Africa was the only person who took the time to teach, and even invited us to his condo overlooking Lake Michigan for a meal. I was quite surprised that apartheid had not affected his ability to treat all people with respect.

There was no training program, no teaching rounds or lectures. We were simply slave labor. Our efforts saved them time so they could make money and do other things, such as playing golf or sleeping.

Exaggerating his workload, Rudi successfully pleaded that he had been so busy that he'd had little time to look for apartments, and could we just stay in the nurses' dorm a little longer? Some student nurses had already arrived. I had never seen so many beautiful white women in one place at one time. Rudi got to know each one within days. One or two occasionally joined us to eat the sandwiches he made using a liver-like paste with a German name. I hated this meal as much as he hated the Indian-style tea I prepared for him. It struck me as odd that a white German and a brown Indian, coming from our unique historical backgrounds of racial hatred, were happily sharing a room in America. Getting to know him taught me not to pre-judge individuals based on their color or national history.

America changed everything. Instead of Indian tea and *paratha*, I was now ordering steak, eggs, and coffee for breakfast at the corner café. This became my only meal for the day, and it cost just $1.50.

Each evening for three weeks, I trudged through the neighborhood to look for an apartment. Oddly, every advertised apartment had already been rented. They had simply "forgotten" to remove the signs, yet those signs were still present the next day. My shoes now had holes in them. I felt intimidated by phone booths. The machines in the public booths scared me, demanding coins at unexpected times and talking back to me from within their metallic bowels. I tried calling collect, but most people hung up on me. Perhaps the friends in Nairobi who had given us that tip had found more generous people in California!

One time I stated my name, "Panwalker." But the person on the other end heard "Dan Walker" and immediately responded, "And I'm Rocky Marciano," and hung up. I suspect he thought it was a crank call. (Dan Walker was the Governor of Illinois.)

Exhausted by the search, I settled for a room in a nearby hotel. It was a high-rise with security and a park nearby. The monthly rent was $275. Asha and Sandeep arrived from Minnesota. On the bus ride to Chicago, a slightly deranged woman decided that my son's hair was unkempt, pulled out a comb, and started working on it. Sandeep sat still, frozen with fear. Asha diplomatically exchanged seats. After a brief conversation, the woman walked away in a huff toward another victim.

After a few weeks in this tiny hotel room, we felt the need for more space. We found a dilapidated one-bedroom apartment in an old converted hotel at 525 Arlington Place. It had a large foyer and musty carpets. The tenants were elderly widows, who wore heavy makeup and fake fur coats. There was a little area outside with a bench and a patch of grass. The location was great since it was in Lincoln Park, walking distance from the hospital, and close to shops and the zoo.

The bed had to be pulled down from the wall each night. The kitchen was barely 6 x 6 feet. An east-facing window in the bedroom had broken sills and rotting wood, but a sliver of blue water was just visible.

I wrote to my parents describing "our lakefront condo off Lake Michigan"! They bragged to others that we had achieved this within two months of our arrival in the US. Definitely a land of milk and honey, everyone said.

The rent consumed much of my $500 monthly salary. Aetna Bank rewarded us with a set of dinner plates and a tropical plant for opening a new account. We deposited $100, but balances rarely exceeded $10.

As May became June, a sense of disquiet and frustration took over. The work was boring and there was no learning. We were not involved in any way with the healing process. The patients, kind and courteous, knew who their real doctors were. I was nobody at this mediocre facility. I had expected some curiosity about my background, but no one seemed to care. All they wanted us to do was prescribe Milk of Magnesia. Rudi and I felt cheated, but any protest might leave us jobless and homeless. We had signed one-year contracts, and they had paid my airfare. So I remained quiet and miserable.

One June morning, with no warning, Rudi dragged me to the director's office to protest our working conditions. He produced the glossy printed brochures they had mailed to entice us to join. I was alarmed as the German, frustrated by his limited vocabulary, stuttered with increasing agitation.

The executive showed no irritation, did not interrupt, and listened to Rudi's litany of complaints patiently. He then turned and asked me if I felt the same way. I nodded yes. I also blurted out that I needed his permission to breach the contract and begged him to help me pay our way back to Kenya. I had no money and no way to borrow any. Left unstated was my belief that I had practiced better medicine in the unsophisticated clinics in Nairobi and the provincial hospital in Kenya. We waited anxiously.

He sighed. Tapping his fingers on the shiny table, he asked for time to think about it. We were dismissed. I wished that I had never listened to this German hippie. I was terrified that the director might hold us to our contract — or worse, agree to pay my way back to Kenya. Both would be disastrous. I had a sleepless night. Rudi slept soundly.

****

The next day, the director called both of us to his office and informed us that the University of Illinois was seeking doctors for their internship class. He had spoken to someone there, and we were to go to the university campus the next day for interviews.

We deeply appreciated his effort. He acknowledged that we had been given an unfair deal and his conscience did not allow him to hold us to the contract. He knew we were right about the lack of a teaching program and knew that we had been recruited so the real doctors — the teachers and professors — could get uninterrupted sleep. I was amazed at his honesty, but I repeatedly saw examples of such justice during my career in America. I admired such men and their values.

That offer was not extended to the Thai and Korean interns. They remained detached from us for the most part, worked hard, obeyed all rules, and never complained. I wondered if they were victims of our meek Asian culture. Why was Rudi able to state so unambiguously how he felt, while we Asians suppressed our sorrows and suffered silently?

Churchill had contemptuously called Gandhi "the naked *fakir*." Was it possible that westerners equated politeness, silence, and non-confrontation as signs of weakness? Would Rudi have said what he had if he had been Indian, Thai, or Korean?

We took a bus to the University of Illinois campus on a beautiful morning. We were met by Mark Richards, who was the chief resident in medicine. He did not waste time with niceties nor did he offer us a seat.

After a quick look to size us up, he asked, "Are you interested in medicine, surgery, or pediatrics?"

The question stunned us. We had expected a tough interview followed by a rejection, since FMGs were generally unwelcome at universities. We mumbled something about medicine. That decision was made in less than 15 seconds! There was no formal interview. To this day, I am not sure why I chose medicine. I knew nothing about the institution or their teaching program.

We learned soon after that it was not our looks, language, or talent that had precipitated the offer. It was Vietnam. Young doctors were being drafted in huge numbers. Some Americans had crossed the border into Canada to escape the draft. Others were conscientious objectors who faced jail time if their appeals failed. I was aware of foreign students who became "perpetual students," acquiring an impressive list of degrees rather than becoming legal immigrants or citizens, in order to evade the draft.

We were hired by the Department of Medicine for the three-year medicine program. There was no orientation. There were no piles of papers to sign or visas to check. Little did we know that only 4 of the 40 intern slots had been filled. Rudi and I were numbers 5 and 6. Just 6 of us were going to do the work of 40 interns. This had never happened before. A few more stragglers came in. I was astonished to see Vinod Patel, a dear friend from Nairobi, on the roster of new interns. What a small world!

But I was ecstatic, not nervous, and we began our work with no fanfare on June 23. I was assigned to the emergency department (ED). My very first patient had a urethral discharge. A formidable, bearded attending physician named Larry asked me to do a Gram's stain (a way of identifying the type of bacteria by putting stain on a slide) of the purulent material in the ED. I had a vague memory of a microbiology demonstration in medical school. Larry quickly realized that I had never done one. Despite his outwardly stern appearance, he taught me patiently. The patient was diagnosed with gonorrhea.

The work was enjoyable and exciting, and the teachers were patient and learned. Life became fun again, even though we spent long hours at work.

Sandeep, now three years old, sometimes asked Asha, "Where does Anand live?" He had not learned to call me Dad or to speak English.

I took a bus to work. My first application for a credit card was turned down since I had no credit history. The trick, we learned, was to buy something small with borrowed money, then pay the bill on time. Paying with cash did not count. Bus travel in summer was fine. In winter, however, our frozen eyebrows thawed on the bus and left a puddle on the floor. They would refreeze after we disembarked. The bus windows were misty, and the overpowering scent of perfume and body odor gave me headaches. This became a daily routine for a year.

We were on call every third night. At that time, the concept of physician fatigue and its effect on safety was largely unknown. Our batch of six interns swelled over the year with a few physicians who had completed their tours of duty in Vietnam. I had imagined they would be rugged, tired, cynical young men embittered by the war. Instead, they turned out to be "regular" men who were just glad to come back alive. I wondered if they had killed anyone.

I had been told by Mrs. Billingsley in the US Embassy in Nairobi that I could be drafted, but I did not know I was supposed to carry a selective service card and inform authorities about any change in address. I had moved from the hospital to two hotels, but had not forwarded the information to anyone. One day, an irate man called to ask me why I had not signed up. He implied that I was trying to evade the draft. I explained, apologized, and gave him my new address. A colleague informed me that being married with a young family, I would be lower in the "lottery."

I had an even greater fright in 1972, when the Internal Revenue Service audited my tax return, which had been completed by an elderly woman at a kiosk. A young man looked at my return, asked a few questions, decided that I owed nothing, and apologized for the inconvenience. He wondered why a doctor needed tax help for such a low income!

****

It was September, but there was a chill in the air. With $200 in savings, we tried on some winter clothes at Macy's in downtown Chicago. At the counter, Asha realized her purse was open and the money was gone. We left the clothes on the counter, apologized to customers behind us, and walked away. We had let our guard down because we thought petty thefts would be unlikely in this land of plenty. Feeling the loss acutely, we got on a bus with just enough fare for the ride home. My application for a credit card was denied again. I delayed our small monthly remittances to my parents in Nairobi and to Aji in Bombay to purchase cheap outerwear some weeks later.

Mr. Nagy, a Chicago-born American, and his French wife, our young next-door neighbors in this hotel for transients and widows, informed us that they were moving to France permanently. Would we like to have their two cane chairs, two beautiful table lamps, a few side tables, and some tools, including a hammer? We accepted gratefully. They said they could no longer live in a country that waged war against innocent civilians in some remote godforsaken corner of Asia. Mrs. Nagy, upon learning how we could not find an apartment to rent, accompanied Asha in our ongoing search.

Dorothy Ranft and her husband, Max, a fine artist and a good man, whom we met by chance on Clark Street, took us under their wings. They were warm, loving, and generous. They helped us understand American customs and slang. Their daughter, Katie, encouraged Sandeep to get on a bicycle without fear. Dorothy, incensed by the racially motivated rejection by landlords, also accompanied Asha, who had taken over our search for better housing. It was an odd couple — a Polish woman escorting an Indian woman in a sari — but they saw no contradiction in this.

In 2014, we looked them up in Chicago. Dorothy was bent over and had aged significantly. But her cake tasted just as delicious. Max, who had lost his memory, gently rebuked his wife for not allowing him to drive anymore. He could not understand why, and complained that she made up new reasons every time he asked. He was baffled as to why his children, Katie and little Max, now far away and settled in their own lives, agreed with their mother. Although his memory had failed him and he would sometimes forget his wife's name, he said he loved her just as he always had. She said it was just a ploy to get another piece of her delicious cake. We took the customary photographs and departed with a heavy heart. The pictures showed two decent human beings who had worked hard and given us constant love and support when we had needed it the most. All we could offer was friendship and gratitude.

Asha and I had begun to understand the basic decency of Americans even when an occasional individual hurt us based on our skin color. The friendly smiles and their sense of justice, fairness, and dignity inspired us.

The hammer given to us by the Nagys is still in use, and reminds me of the extraordinary generosity of total strangers.

****

A department chair — I will call him Dr. X — often proclaimed that our university was a fine place for healing, and it offended him that our employees would go elsewhere for their care.

One day, just four months into my internship, he developed pain radiating down one leg and, true to his philosophy, chose to become a patient at our hospital. The conventional therapy in those days was bed rest and traction. Since I was on call, he became my patient. This state-financed hospital had no private physicians or private patients. The majority of patients were poor blacks from the surrounding neighborhoods on the west side of Chicago. We made a concession and found a single room for him instead of placing him in a general ward. He did not protest.

The University of Illinois Research and Education Hospital (as it was called in those days) had lured Dr. X away from a famous university to become the chair of a large department. He had replaced a legendary and nationally known individual. Dr. X's forthright manner, reflective nature, bedside manner, and desire for excellence inspired house officers. He believed and taught that the mind plays tricks with the body, something he called the psychosomatic effect. He recruited promising investigators from across the nation. They called themselves "Young Turks," even though none of them were Turkish.

Dr. X emphasized the importance of a complete exam, which included a rectal exam, a urine analysis, and Gram's stains when indicated, and he did not tolerate any shortcuts. One of the leaders of the Young Turk pack, fresh from a stint in the army, asked me with a straight face if I had done the rectal exam on Dr. X yet. It did not occur to me that he was teasing. I asked my supervising resident for advice. He said it was the intern's job.

"But shouldn't a department chair have a more experienced person do it?" I protested.

The answer was no. I struggled with my options. One was to skip the rectal check and be criticized for an incomplete exam. The other was to simply go ahead and honor the principle that all patients should get the same care and face his wrath or refusal. I chose the second one. Two days into the admission, already late with my complete exam, I gathered enough courage to remind him that I needed to perform a rectal exam.

"You are kidding, right?"

Noting my resolve, he turned on his left side, gave me a second look, a mixture of surprise, mirth, and a plea, and flexed his right hip and knee. The exam was normal as expected. What had been recorded as "deferred" was now duly recorded as done. I pulled the curtain open and saw a small crowd discreetly applauding me with silent glee. Word had gotten around that this was THE big day. I was, they said, the first intern on the planet to have done a rectal exam on a sitting chairman of a major department of a university that produced more doctors each year than any other.

The next day during my morning rounds, I discovered that the bird had flown the coop. The weights, unattached to any human leg, sat limply on the bed. He had slipped out without permission. I called his home number rather than security, but neither he nor his wife answered. The following morning, he was in his bed, pretending he had been there all along. He had the look of a child caught stealing cookies. Emboldened, I chastised him with as much authority as I could muster, for breaking the rules. He provided a weak apology, mumbling something about leaking pipes at home.

Miraculously, he also claimed that his back and leg pain had resolved and that he was ready to rest at home for a few days. Weeks later, we discovered that he had gone elsewhere for back surgery!

A CIVIL WAR

In December 1971, Indians switched their attention to dramatic events unfolding in the subcontinent. We did not own a TV, so all the news came from portable radios and the BBC. Asha's brother, Vijay, and three of his college friends from Ohio State University were visiting us in our tiny apartment. All of us remained glued to the radio, and I was unable to focus on my work.

The British, in their infinite wisdom, had created two wings of Pakistan. One in the west with Punjabi-, Pashto-, or Urdu-speaking Muslims and the other in the east, where the people were predominantly Bengali-speaking Muslims. The seat of presidential and military power had always resided in the western segment. Western Pakistanis — generally tall, fair, and strong — dominated all sectors of the economy. The Bengalis, often shorter and darker, suffered from extreme poverty, floods, cyclones, and starvation.

The color bar existed here too. Bengalis, underrepresented in government, were looked down upon by their fairer countrymen in the western half of Pakistan.

When the Awami Party, led by Sheikh Mujibur Rahman of East Pakistan, won the election with enough seats to rule both wings, the ruling leaders of the western wing, led by Yayha Khan, balked. Talks for power sharing were unsuccessful. Pakistan's ruling military leaders arrested the Sheikh on March 26, 1971. Protests swelled. Sheikh Mujibur uttered the following words, which lit a fire of in the hearts of Bengalis:

> Ebarer Shongram Amader Muktir Shongram, Ebarer Shongram Shadhinotar Shongram. (Our struggle this time is a struggle for our freedom, our struggle this time is a struggle for our independence.)

Small Bengali militias became a formidable force called Mukti Bahini. Thousands of soldiers were flown from West Pakistan to suppress the insurgency. Thus began a campaign of terror, looting, rape, and mass killings perpetrated by Pakistani soldiers. No one knows how many died, but it was in the hundreds of thousands. During this civil war, almost 10 million refugees, mostly Hindus, poured into India seeking shelter.

East Pakistan was in flames. India, concerned about the treatment of civilians and the Hindu minorities, gave material support to the Mukti Bahini and appealed to the world to stop the carnage. The pleas fell on deaf ears. In a highly provocative and ultimately idiotic move, Pakistan's air force bombed military camps in North India, thus declaring war. The Indian Army and Air Force retaliated by opening two fronts: one in the west, where considerable territory was captured, including the area around Kargil; and the other in East Pakistan, where over 90,000 Pakistani soldiers surrendered, the largest surrender of an army since World War II. A new nation called Bangladesh was born. Pakistan's decision not to honor the people's vote had resulted in its dismemberment. India treated the prisoners of war with the respect they had not earned and did not deserve.

During the conflict, in spite of the genocide being committed against Hindu and Muslim Bengalis, and the loss of thousands of lives, Nixon and Kissinger sided with Pakistan and dispatched the *USS Enterprise* to the Bay of Bengal. So much for democracy! China, which was also being wooed by America with "ping-pong" diplomacy, gave verbal support to its strategic ally, Pakistan. Russia, to support India, sent a warship to counter the threat by the American Navy. The rest of the world remained silent.

Indians were incensed by the American tilt toward Pakistan. Relations between Nixon and Indira Gandhi, the prime minister of India and daughter of Nehru, became frosty. The goodwill created by Jackie Kennedy evaporated.

****

We feared the morning report at the affiliated West Side Veterans Administration (VA) hospital. Clifford Pilz, a great teacher and chair of the Department of Medicine, would unleash a stream of invectives when upset. His fury and intemperate language became shriller during morbidity and mortality conferences, where his preferred victims were established senior physicians. Short and obese, he had a volatile temper. He had a habit of pacing on the stage, like a predator stalking its prey before the kill. Breaking cadence, he would suddenly dash toward his chosen victim and ask a question, which typically had to do with the history of medicine, a question no one could answer. He was genuinely upset if someone got the answer right. Residents were always on pins and needles.

Nonetheless, he was highly regarded for his dedication to education and patient care. Many thought his exterior hid a kind and gentle man who cared deeply about his students, residents, and the poor veterans who sought care here. People flocked to his conferences. He spared no one, student or attending. He was sure to catch those who sat in the back row. Attendance was mandatory. He was the hunter and we the hunted. His harsh tongue never failed to cut and hurt. But we recognized his passion for medicine, his great love for its history, and his legendary status as an educator. People left licking their emotional wounds even as they thanked him for inflicting them!

At one morning report, he lunged up to me, addressing me as "Panwalker" — for he never used first names — and asked me a question. I did not know the answer, but found the courage to request that he not get mad or use foul language. He stopped in his tracks, pondered his options, and decided to walk on. I was petrified, and was sure I would pay for this later.

Two years passed quickly in this wonderful place of learning with great teachers and scholars. At no time did I feel discriminated against or looked down upon. In 1973, Dr. Bogdonoff, the Chairman of the Department of Medicine and the Editor of the Archives of Internal Medicine, asked me to become his chief resident in medicine. I was deeply flattered. I would become responsible for dozens of interns, residents, and fellows in internal medicine for the entire university program. The job had been offered initially to a senior resident, who had turned it down because he was heading to Vietnam.

Sometimes I gave Dr. Bogdonoff a ride, when his wife needed his car. We generally talked about departmental business. One day, he asked me about rumors that I was moonlighting at other hospitals, something prohibited by our rules. For some reason, I felt compelled to share my background, my father's addiction, and our continued financial woes. I trusted him and saw him as a mentor, friend, and father figure. My words came effortlessly, without embarrassment or regret. I acknowledged the sacrifices my parents had made for me. He listened thoughtfully. He had a unique habit of letting his eyebrows speak for him, and they did so eloquently. He said he understood why I needed to make extra money by working my off weekends in the emergency departments of seedy run-down hospitals in poor black neighborhoods, where giant rats stared at night through broken baseboards.

About the time I was appointed as the Chief Resident, Dr. Pilz called to say he wanted to see me. I was quite certain he had not forgotten the incident when I had asked him not to abuse me if I did not know the answer to a question from two years prior. Now he was going to tear me apart.

"Would you like a cup of coffee?" he asked.

"No, sir. Thank you."

He said he wanted to congratulate me and, because he could not stand Dr. Bogdonoff, asked whether I could become the intermediary between the two chiefs!

It was now the spring of 1973.

A stateless British citizen who could not enter Britain, I could not remain in Kenya or compete in India, but I had become the chief resident at one of the largest medical schools in the nation, and would work for two of the greatest teachers I had ever known. And I was just an FMG.

****

I met two remarkable survivors of the holocaust during my internship. Both Jewish men had been left for dead in pits, after their friends and family members had been shot by Nazi execution squads. They had crawled out across the heap of bodies, under cover of darkness, and somehow found their way through Europe and to Chicago.

Dr. Max Samter was recruited by Clifford Pilz and was told he would be the allergist and immunologist, at a time when these specialties did not exist. He went on to write a two-volume textbook on immunology. His constant smile and amiable manner hid the deep despair he felt within.

I once asked him how he defined asthma.

His response, "I am still trying to understand the disease."

His humility drove us nuts. As an attending, he was charming and completely unaware of things beyond immunology. However, he had a heart of gold. At his invitation, I went to his home in Evanston to discuss a new initiative: a series of lectures on ethics and morality. As he spoke, the gentle waves of Lake Michigan stroked the stone steps that led from the beach to his sunroom. He appeared to be lost in reverie, staring at the layer of foam and froth the blue water left behind. I admired this man who had suffered deeply this unspoken loss.

Paul Heller, a brilliant hematologist, also arrived around that time. He had a deep voice and an unmistakable German accent. He gave no hint that he'd had such a tragic past. I recalled vaguely that he had described an abnormal hemoglobin. A master storyteller, he never spoke about Germany or the Nazis.

I looked for numbers tattooed on their arms, but they were always covered.

I was curious what my blond, blue-eyed German co-interns and residents — who now included Rudiger Andrasch and three others — felt about the two professors. Had they inherited a collective national guilt for what their forefathers had done?

Then it struck me.

This was a nation where new beginnings were possible. There was something noble about America. It allowed former enemies to break bread together and leave the rancor of old history behind them. In these United States, many Hindus and Muslims, Indians and Pakistanis, Germans and Jews, the Brahmins and untouchables were able to shed some of the old baggage imported from other continents and to establish new relationships based on mutual respect.

****

The year passed quickly. I managed the call and vacation schedules, made rounds with interns and helped them get settled, taught students, became a liaison between the faculty and residents, listened to gripes, helped people mend fences, held patients' hands, and was always available to help with crises. One such instance occurred when a bruised and battered woman came to my office begging for protection from her husband, a newly hired intern, who was later diagnosed to be a paranoid schizophrenic.

I arranged grand rounds (a weekly guest lecture) every week with increasing confidence and had the immense privilege of meeting famous physicians and public figures, and sometimes taking them on short tours. It was an extraordinary experience to stand among these giants and revel in their shadows.

There were ethical challenges as well. As American graduates returned from Vietnam, FMGs became dispensable. I was a member of the house staff selection committee and repeatedly saw two piles of papers. The first heap included graduates of American, British, European, or Canadian schools; the résumés of Asian graduates sat untouched in the second pile. I rarely saw applications from South America or Africa. The candidates in the second group had been rejected already, but some obscure legal issue had resulted in some of them receiving interview invitations anyway. This troubled me greatly.

I informed the committee that these men (for there were hardly any women coming in from Asia in those days) had very little money, and it was unfair to give them false hope. In the end, a decision was made to stop that practice of sham interviews and instead to reject them outright. I firmly believed that Indian doctors, given the opportunity, could compete with the best anywhere in the world, although I also understood the need to give priority to graduates trained in the US. But I could not accept skin color and country of origin as the basis for denying taxpaying legal immigrants who could be asked to die in Vietnam.

The call schedule kept me away from home much of the time. Sandeep thought I lived somewhere else! I relished the little time we had together when he clung to me and jumbled his letters so I became "Andan." He had not yet learned English, since we spoke Marathi at home. And he sang old Hindi songs. He was cute and cuddly. I proudly told others that my son, born premature, was destined to follow the path of famous premature babies like Isaac Newton and Alfred Einstein. I decided he would never undergo the hardships I had suffered. My son would have all the opportunities available in America. He would be brought up with everlasting love and sheltered from all harm.

One evening, I was more exhausted than usual, trying to catch up on mail, meals, and sleep. He cuddled as usual, happy and excited, hoping for my undivided attention, our little games and songs. He sang:

Sone ka Hindustan hai mera, Sone ka Hindustan (My Hindustan [India] is golden.)

Jaha me sub se pyara he mera Hindustan (My Hindustan is dearer than the rest of the world.)

One song followed another. And another, until I felt exhausted and needed to be alone for a while. I gently told him that was it for today.

"Nahi," he yelled. No.

Snatching papers from my hand, he tore one. He screamed, again and again. I picked him up and sat him on a ledge. My tone was now gruff. I asked him to please sit still for a few minutes. He came down, pushed me in protest, and sulked. I had never provoked such feelings in him before. I had rebuffed him when he was simply expressing his affection. Like a puppy who has been yelled at, his eyes revealed his hurt.

He relished walks in the nearby parks and trips to the zoo. Asha enrolled him in a kindergarten, which we could barely afford, for three hours each weekday. He refused to take his jacket or hood off, but the teacher said it was okay. It was his security blanket. Was it the foreign-looking children, his lack of English skills, or shyness? He remained ill at ease and unassimilated after several weeks. Over time, his English vocabulary and reading skills progressed rapidly without a TV or *Sesame Street*. In 1974, we decided the suburbs would be a safer and happier place for Sandeep.

We rented an apartment on Dunlop Street in Forest Park, a little subdivision just south of Oak Park. Sandeep walked to the Field Stevenson School, eight blocks away.

Figure 16: Contemplation with Sandeep

Sandeep blossomed in the third grade. Unlike the previous two years, he woke up without fuss, got ready quickly, and looked forward to school. He smiled a lot and occasionally requested food items that we rarely consumed at home. He had fallen under the spell of a new teacher, Ms. Armstrong, who played the guitar, sang songs, and cheered students on to sing and laugh louder and louder still. His grades improved dramatically. He had adjusted nicely to a new school, neighbors, and country. Sandeep also requested that we get him a toy called Stretch Armstrong because he had the same last name! He joined music classes, learned to pay the trombone, and even won a contest. He played Harry Belafonte's song "Jamaica Farewell" on the harmonica for a talent show.

The next year, when Sandeep realized that Ms. Armstrong would not be his teacher and would be moving to another city, his world collapsed and his performance deteriorated.

The fourth-grade teacher complained that he did not listen. She criticized his attention span and how he "tuned her out." Impatient and irritable, she complained that "his eyes become glassy" when she tried to talk to him. He simply looked down. He defied her instructions by not completing the assigned homework and refusing to answer when she asked, "Why not?" It was a disastrous start. She was shrill and unkind at parent–teacher meetings. We promised to talk to him and supervise his work. He somehow managed to get through the year. The next year was uneventful. Things had settled down.

One evening, on my way home, I saw him surrounded by three bigger boys. He kept his eyes to the ground. There was something menacing in the way they bent over him and got close to his face. I stopped the car and got out, and they scattered. Sandeep refused to tell me what they were after. The bullying stopped when the older boy realized I knew his father.

Meanwhile, Asha got restless. She had been a brilliant student in school and college, a gold medalist for academic excellence from a prestigious Indian university. But her qualifications were not recognized in the US. To get a job, she would have to start from scratch. She enrolled in the University of Illinois' nutrition program. Sandeep would now be alone at home for extended periods of time.

Asha was now doing double duty with home and school responsibilities, but found the coursework easy and graduated with high honors. She and a girl named Carol, who became her lifelong friend, were the only two to do so well. Soon after, Asha found work at the Cook County Hospital in Chicago. We were immensely grateful every day for the great teachers we had and the beautiful country that had accepted us. We developed great friendships with fellow immigrants like Gurinder and Narinder Grewal, Omesh and Gita Chopra, Vijay and Kumud Kumar. Their families became our own. My fellows at work, (particularly Jim Malow, Wes White, Claudio Ramirez) and our microbiologists (Vita Zimelis and Pat Porembski) became my delightful colleagues.

****

Immersed in my day-to-day duties, I had given little thought to the future. I had heard that chief residents from university programs often got prestigious fellowships and went on to academic medicine, but I had concerns that other programs might reject me for being an FMG. The corrosive effect of the discriminatory selection system and my lack of self-confidence made it difficult to dream big. I still suffered the same inhibitions that had made me choose an inferior hospital in Chicago for my first internship. Besides, I did not know what fellowship I wanted to pursue.

In May 1974, I had a rude awakening when Dr. Bogdonoff asked me what I planned to do in the future. I had submitted no applications, sought no advice from anyone, and had precisely four weeks to decide.

I stammered, "I don't know, and do not know how to decide."

He asked if I would be interested in endocrinology, his specialty, and my emphatic answer was, "No!"

I was not interested in a specialty based on abnormal physiologic values. He shrugged in mock amusement. Before he could ask, I added, "Nephrology tuned me off the day I heard a lecture on turtle bladders!" I also had no interest in fields with a narrow focus on invasive procedures.

He sighed. "In that case, you should find the best teacher in a cognitive field."

That was the best advice I ever received.

That is how George G. Jackson (GGJ) entered my life. He was head of the Infectious Disease (ID) department, the president of the Infectious Diseases Society of America, and soon-to-be editor of the premier *Journal of Infectious Diseases*. He struck me as an excellent teacher with great values and a gentle manner. He had been trained by Max Finland, the "little giant" from Boston's Harvard Medical School and founder of the field of infectious diseases in America.

I was awed by Jackson's towering personality and teaching rounds. I knew I could learn a lot from him. I was curious about his Mormon religion, who called themselves "Latter Day Saints," did not drink tea, coffee, or alcohol, did not smoke, did missionary service, and gave a portion of their income to charity. A noble tribe, I thought. Like the Indians in Africa, they too had been chased from a little town in Illinois to find sanctuary in remote Utah.

Figure 17: With George Jackson (beloved professor and mentor)

I approached him about a fellowship at this 11th hour. He appeared pleased, but said all 12 positions had been filled (8 Americans and 4 special international positions). But he promised to speak to "Mort" Bogdonoff. They struck a deal to create an extra position through a "creative transfer" of funds. I became a fellow in July 1974 at one of the most prestigious and desirable ID programs in the country, without filing a single application. I felt especially lucky and proud.

Just around this time, simmering tensions about Dr. Bogdonoff's management style came to a head and he resigned. He had alienated the faculty with his autocratic style. In a particularly low moment, he misdirected his anger at me by uttering "FMG" as we passed each other in a corridor. Unsmiling, he walked on. Why would he say such a thing? I did not understand. It was unprovoked and unfair.

It was ironic that the offspring of a persecuted Russian Jew, an immigrant's son, would address another immigrant with such contempt.

Similar comments by others over the years suggested that this xenophobia remained embedded in the DNA of some white doctors. In later years I wrote strong notes of protest to colleagues who disparaged FMGs and received apologies from both. They explained there was a perception that teaching hospitals with "too many" foreign-trained doctors make the programs less attractive to white American doctors. This was despite the reality that most medical schools have a sizable number of highly qualified FMGs on their faculties, and data that suggests fewer Medicare patients die when international graduates take care of them as opposed to those trained in the US.

At a dinner at the Drake Hotel in Chicago in 1974, Dr. Bogdonoff gave me a silver letter opener from Tiffany's engraved with the words *In high regard: MDB to AP*. Still in use today, it reminds me every day of a fine teacher and mentor who, in a moment of frustration, forgot his humanity and called me the insulting term FMG, a label I would always carry and have to live with. It had hurt deeply. But I owed much to him and quickly forgave him.

He became a dean at Cornell University and kept winning teaching awards until the ripe old age of 90. Intermittently, he and I exchanged letters, and one time even planned to meet. My last letter to him went unanswered. An online search revealed he had passed away in March 2015.

BACK TO THE BEGINNING

Meanwhile, the situation in Nairobi remained fragile. My parents, with a little financial help from me, returned to India, the land of their birth. They had gone to Africa penniless almost 35 years earlier, and left with nothing to show for their toil. They were at the mercy of others for the basic necessities of life. A rental apartment in any India major city was extremely expensive and required a large non-refundable deposit called *paghdi,* which we could not afford.

Mai, my grandmother, and Subhash generously offered to share their small home in Baroda with my parents, who were treated well and were comfortable. Yet it was an awkward arrangement. Subhash had married Aruna, a gentle young woman, and as the family expanded, the space got tight. A few years later my parents decided to move to Pune. Their initial residence was an old friend's rat-infested garage. This infuriated me, because the owner had frequently enjoyed my father's hospitality and generosity in Nairobi when we were wealthy. I felt my parents should have been invited into the home as honored guests.

A few months later, they were able to first rent and then buy a one-bedroom flat at a busy junction. Nalutai's father had owned this property and that surely made the transaction easier and more affordable. Once again, she and Bhau had come to our rescue.

Thousands of vehicles, people, and carts passed by the second-story flat at all hours of the day and night. The cacophony of noises was both fascinating and irritating. On this street, cattle competed with cars, cops, and cobblers for the right of way.

Idleness irked my father. His restless mind gave birth to an idea. He got someone to print a huge sign on canvas that read "Panwalker's English Conversational Classes." He nailed this sign onto a wooden board and hung it up outside the balcony so it would be visible to thousands of commuters.

People trickled in to inquire. College students bound for Britain or America; well-groomed wives who wanted to be more proficient in English so they did not embarrass their highly placed executive husbands during overseas trips; budding actors from the famous Film Institute of India nearby; foreign students, especially from Thailand and Burma, who came to Indian universities; and ordinary housewives who simply had a burning desire to learn the *lingua franca* of the world.

As the demand increased, my mother joined in. They held several hourly sessions, six days a week. The students mingled and bonded easily. Grammar was less important than the conversation. The fear of ridicule was quickly replaced by a confidence they never knew they possessed. Snacks and beverages, although not part of the package, were served at no extra charge, to reflect the famous Panwalker hospitality. Over the years, my father wanted to expand the business, so when the adjoining apartment became available, he asked my mother to write to me for a "loan." His pride did not permit him to ask me directly. He planned to break down some walls, add another two tables, and have as many as 30 students an hour. My mother, concerned about further expansion and our own needs, forwarded his request, but suggested discreetly that I plead for time in order to accumulate the needed funds. The opportunity to buy was quickly lost.

My mother, always gregarious and cheerful, started a *bhajan* group who sang devotional songs, planned picnics, and went for movies, meals, and shows with her friends. They were now able to afford a more middle-class life. Once again, the home bustled with frenetic activity. I was proud of their accomplishments and entrepreneurial spirit. They did not mope, moan, or behave like most Indian retirees, who did essentially nothing useful. The sign outside the balcony became frayed and tattered, but the business thrived. Soon they were earning enough to visit Singapore and Bangkok.

At a time when my parents were starting all over again, others were forced into mandatory retirement at age 55. Asha's father was given three extra years to serve before he too had to stop working. He subsequently built a stone mansion in Pune, a few miles from the flat my parents owned. They met occasionally and were cordial, but there was a formality and distance in the relationship.

We had moved to Forest Park, a suburb outside Chicago, in search of suburban tranquility, safety, better schools, and open spaces. A year later, we found a larger, somewhat run-down, two-bedroom apartment. Our apartment, on the ground floor, lay underneath a smaller one upstairs. A few months later, we purchased the building. Our mortgage would be no more than the rent we were paying, and the income from the upstairs apartment would help with the maintenance. We now owned a dilapidated piece of America and were landlords.

The tenant upstairs, a quiet Cuban and his wife, had escaped Castro's regime. Over the years, he had dumped a lot of junk in the basement and into the two stand-alone garages several feet away from the home.

I began to scrub, scrape, spackle, sand, and paint in my spare time. The home, built perhaps 60 years earlier, had 64 wooden windows and plenty of sunshine. I cleaned out the basement after the upstairs tenant repeatedly ignored my pleas to remove his stuff. The junk was replaced with a ping-pong table. I learned to do simple electrical repairs, placed a new floor and wall tiles in the kitchen, removed and replaced rotted wood, seeded and mowed the lawn, and planted bushes. My efforts at plumbing were miserable failures.

One afternoon, I asked the Cuban if he would help me to clear out his stuff in the garage. His demeanor changed and, with a flushed face, he snarled, "Don't be a Jew."

A Batista follower and now a refugee from Castro's Cuba, he was an anti-Semitic bigot who believed my request was about money. I had had no intention of raising his rent. I just wanted quiet, clean, and thoughtful tenants. When he left soon after, I discovered that he had dismantled all the electrical ceiling fixtures and left bare wires. After fixing up the mess, we rented the place to an Indian engineer, who had found life in Iran uncomfortable. The property now looked clean, green, and well maintained.

However, the village of Forest Park disagreed. The building inspector left a note telling us that one of the garages needed to be demolished. He also wanted new siding installed on the entire home. The contractors would have to be approved by his office. I was surprised, unaware of any code violations. It took many phone calls to get an appointment with him. A neighbor, worried about his own property, wondered if the inspector wanted a bribe to make the problem go away.

Asha and I were ushered into a large room with modest furniture and a dark interior. A short, obese and deeply tanned man arrived several minutes later. He made no eye contact, sat down without a word, crossed his legs, clasped his two chubby hands together, then slowly looked up at us. His glasses hung precariously from the tip of his ample bulbous nose, which indicated a devotion to wine and liquor. One of his bushy eyebrows rose, and he asked us what we wanted. I explained that I did not understand the need for new siding or demolition of one garage when both garages were identical. The building was structurally strong, the colors of the current siding were not garish and matched the neighborhood, and there had been no previous concerns about the property.

A man of few words, he said something about his plans to beautify the neighborhood, to restore pride in the community, and to enforce "rules," which he could not define. It became apparent that further discussion would be futile when he finally put his palm up, effectively telling us to stop talking. He rose and walked out without a word. We were left with no choice but to demolish the garage and get a contractor of his choice to place the new siding.

A worker arrived with his tools the next day and, within an hour, broke his hand trying to demolish the sturdy garage. Screaming in pain, he vanished and was replaced. The inspector came again, sniffed around for a few minutes and said he was satisfied. We never saw him again. He had just forced us to demolish a perfectly good garage and waste $1500 on siding that was not needed. I suspected that the workers were his friends or family members.

****

The division of Infectious Diseases, highly regarded nationally and internationally, recruited 12 fellows each year. Applicants included highly recommended residents from American universities, international doctors, epidemiologists trained by the CDC (Centers for Disease Control and Prevention), aspiring academicians, and researchers. Jackson had influenced, inspired, or trained many of the world's top infectious disease specialists. Many went on to become chairs of departments or deans at universities in the US or overseas.

GGJ took me under his wings.

My "office" was a little closet situated next to the incubators, where machines washed the glassware. The odors unique to a microbiology lab permeated our nostrils all day long. People moved in and out to check a plate or two for bacterial growth. The elderly black dishwasher who sat four feet away from me regaled me with stories about her life in the west side of Chicago while puffing on cheap cigarettes. I learned that this area had a connection to the Black Panther movement.

Several Latvian and Lithuanian immigrants taught me bacteriology, virology, and research methods. Pipettes, plates, and pungent smells became constant companions as we measured drug levels, performed in vitro studies, and diluted powders. We began to understand the intricacies of microbiology.

The master clinicians put on a show during rounds. The city-wide conferences, especially with participants from the Cook County Hospital, were phenomenal educational activities. I was appointed chief fellow in the second year, and two happy years passed quickly.

I wrote a few letters to universities, asking for interviews for an infectious disease faculty position, but no one responded. My white colleagues had little trouble finding such posts. I placed an ad in the *New England Journal of Medicine*. There was one response from a place I did not wish to go to. I suspected that my FMG status was once again interfering with my future. I gave up on the job search when Herb Bessinger, the Chief of Medicine at Weiss Memorial Hospital asked me to join his teaching faculty as the ID expert. I knew him from my weekends moonlighting there. In June 1976, nearly done with my fellowship, I asked GGJ for a letter of recommendation, but instead he shook his head and walked away.

I was puzzled. He had never been so abrupt with me before. Perhaps I had misjudged his affection for me. So it came as a huge surprise the next day when he invited me to join the faculty as an Assistant Professor of Medicine. Apparently, he had planned it all along, but needed approval from the new chair of medicine. Herb congratulated me and graciously released me from the verbal commitment.

My parents arrived in Chicago on tourist visas at a time when the nation was celebrating 200 years of independence. They were impressed. We took them to the John Hancock Tower, Lake Michigan, the planetarium, the Baha'i Temple in Wilmette, and the Field Museum (which housed the now embalmed man-eaters of Tsavo). In Canada, we went to Niagara Falls and to Ottawa to meet Sudha, my mother's younger sister, and then continued to Minnesota in my brand-new, orange Chevy Nova to see Mira and her husband, Subhash.

Dr. Jackson invited my overwhelmed and speechless parents to his home during their first trip to America. They asked, "Why would such an important man invite us?" Amy Jackson had made a delicious soufflé and fussed that it was getting cold while we chatted.

American pride at its bicentennial was palpable. The nation, inhabited by good, kind, and generous people, was stronger than any other, confident of its values, purpose, and destiny, and stood as a beacon of hope for the oppressed and dispossessed all over the world. Americans stood proudly as the tall ships sailed by to celebrate our achievements in sports and science, and as saviors of mankind.

Awed by the energy and dynamism of the people, in love with America, we became US citizens in 1976. It was a proud moment to hold the documents of a country which allowed me to feel free and welcome.

Bill O'Neill, a friend and previous chief resident, gave me a gift before he left Chicago to attend Wake Forest University. It was a biography, *Markings* by Dag Hammarskjold, who had died in a plane crash in Rhodesia while on a peace mission to the Congo as the secretary general of the United Nations. An inscription in the book read: *To Anand Panwalker: A credit to his profession and country on its bicentennial.*

****

As a young faculty member, I thought I might get a new office, but space was limited and I stayed in the same closet next to the incubators. During the first year, we investigated new yet-to-be-licensed antibiotics to see if they were safe and effective. A cadre of fellows joined me, not because of any special expertise, but because we had good chemistry and became friends for life. We continued to learn from Vita Zimelis, the microbiologist who had published more papers than most fellows.

The next year, I was provided a large laboratory space and a new office, and had enough pharmaceutical company grants for research and salaries. I knew the grants were a result of GGJ's reputation, not mine. My lab stood next to that of Dr. Ananda Chakrabarty, who had discovered "oil-eating" bacteria of the *Pseudomonas* species and was the first man ever to obtain a patent on genetically modified living organisms in June 1980.

As the coordinator for education in infectious diseases, I inaugurated a two-month training course for medical students with a $0 budget. Faculty from nearby medical schools volunteered their time and expertise to lecture for the Practice Procedures course. Nearly 120 lectures spread out over one month were followed by a 4-week clinical rotation at the university or nearby teaching institutions. Approximately 200 students enrolled each year. My star was rising and I was content.

However, this peace and happiness did not last long. GGJ was often away. Murmurs of discontent were heard when he took a two-year sabbatical in London with Professor Williams and then at the Max Planck Institute in Germany. In Dr. Jackson's absence, I ran the fellowship program by default, since no one seemed to be in charge. Newly recruited fellows felt deceived to learn that GGJ would be away.

One fellow expressed his great upset. A bright and ambitious young man, he had just completed training at the CDC. I had known Paul since our residency days, when he had called me to help care for his dog, which had cut his paw on a glass shard. We had held the yelping animal firmly as we stitched him back to health. The landlord was not happy about the pet or the blood-stained carpets. I told Paul I would explain things to Dr. Jackson if he chose to leave the program and go elsewhere. He did transfer to the University of Chicago and later became the head of their ID department.

Faculty members, some jealous of GGJ's fame, others angered by his prolonged absence, began to clamor for his dismissal. Others began to plant the seed of discontent in the minds of newly recruited young fellows. The rumblings ceased when GGJ returned, but the damage had been done.

I too began to tire of the mechanical nature of lab research. I had too much free time, since most of the lab work was done by fellows and technicians. Frankly, I was bored. I often told my fellows that I could train a chimpanzee to do the work we were doing. They thought I was joking. We published papers and abstracts and traveled all over the country. Pharmaceutical companies subsidized our travel and meals and put us up in posh hotels where kings and queens were said to have rested. We felt like prostitutes hired by drug companies to advertise their products. The tensions around research integrity, the source of funding, and the pressures of publication were intense.

It also became apparent that academic advancement was difficult unless one performed the "sexier" molecular research, for which I had neither the training nor the aptitude. That is what geniuses did, not simple clinicians like me.

I recall going to London as a fellow in 1975 with GGJ, to present a paper on a new antibiotic for urinary infections. There was nothing earth-shattering about it, except we were the first to do the work. The company was keen to advertise its upcoming product. They paid our way to London to the International Congress of Pyelonephritis (kidney infections). My presentation was brief and, as expected, brought no rave reviews. However, throughout the day, I got to sit between GGJ, my mentor, and Max Finland, the legend who was considered to be the father of the field of Infectious Diseases in America. This "little giant" put his head on my shoulder and slept like a child throughout the meeting, waking only to use the restroom. On one bathroom break, he stared at me intently for a few seconds and asked if we had met before.

The hold that pharmaceutical companies have on investigators became obvious during a study we conducted with a new and exciting antibiotic. It was possibly less toxic to the patients' ears and kidneys compared to older drugs. We, however, found subtle abnormalities of liver function tests in 40% of the patients and submitted a journal article reporting this. We had asked the company officials if others had noticed this. They said no. A courtesy copy was sent to the company. The monitors at the company tried to have us modify the language and suppress some data, but we refused. The CEO called Dr. Jackson, but we did not budge. That enterprise never gave us a grant again.

On another occasion, a new and powerful antibiotic—unique because of its activity against a common bacterium—caused severe bleeding, diarrhea, and sometimes super infections in a majority of our trial patients. The drug had such huge promise that it had been sent to Yugoslavia to treat Marshall Tito as he lay dying of pneumonia. However, our attempts to obtain raw data from the sponsors failed. The company, perhaps inadvertently, had misled us into believing that our experience was unique. We wanted the medical community to know this, and therefore published a brief report in the *Journal of Infectious Diseases*. Others reported similar problems soon after. A few weeks later, the drug was withdrawn from the market. We did not receive another grant for future studies from this company either.

The work became deeply dissatisfying, yet was so essential. Without effective antibiotics, patients died terrible deaths. It was essential to continue to test new chemicals in the lab and clinic. However, I preferred to see patients and teach students.

My students awarded me with a Golden Apple for teaching in my first year as a faculty member. Three years later, I was awarded the Clifford Pilz Best Teacher of the Year award. I was baffled, because there were so many great teachers at this university. People told me I would soon have "an orchard full of apples" and would need more walls on which to hang the plaques.

While this brought great joy, there was still something missing. I realized that my best work would come at the bedside, teaching students, as we healed patients together. With our faculty so large, I could teach only two months each year. I was supposed to do research, lecture, and travel the rest of the year.

Dr. Jackson, somewhat prematurely, forwarded a proposal for my promotion to associate professor. I did not really think I was ready, but he believed that my clinical work was superb and my research commendable. Flattered but anxious, I consented. I had published half a dozen papers by then with my fellows, and had abstracts at the annual Infectious Disease and Inter science Conference on Antimicrobial Agents and Chemotherapy meetings each year. Perhaps that would be enough to move my application forward. I worried that one of his rivals was the chair of the promotions committee.

The denial came swiftly. They stated that I was young and did not yet have significant bench research or publications. The committee deeply valued my clinical and teaching skills and saw a bright career ahead for me. They explained that basic bench research was preferable to the type of work I was doing.

I did not disagree with the decision nor was I terribly disappointed. My being an FMG or Jackson's rival being the chair of the committee had nothing to do with the verdict.

In a brief moment of paranoia, I wondered if the new department chair, of Portuguese origin, resented me because Indians had forcibly taken over the Portuguese colonies of Goa, Daman, and Diu in 1961 after a brief skirmish. A western power had been deeply humiliated. I was particularly thrilled then because one of the Indian navy commanders during that brief battle was a man whose family we knew and who would later marry my favorite cousin, Surekha Badve.

The denial of this promotion affected Dr. Jackson deeply. He felt the message was clear. Antimicrobial research, which I was involved with (and bored by) was not highly valued, and the rules for promotion had been rewritten.

This was the kick in the butt I needed to take charge of my own future. I did not think their decision was wrong, but it gave me a reason to pause and re-examine my goals for the future.

Around this time, an African–American couple bought a home in Forest Park. Two weeks later, someone doused a woodpile near their garage with gasoline and put a match to it. The charred garage door smoldered but did not burn. Stunned, the family moved out and never returned. They had had no time to make any friends in the neighborhood. Whether it was bigotry, racism, or some neighborhood kids vandalizing property was unknown. Neighbors did not express outrage. I wondered why we had been spared. Perhaps the neighbors had tolerated us as "less black." Now I understood why the black intern at the University of Illinois had worn a pin-striped suit to impress a landlord in segregated Chicago.

Other than some housing hassles, our family had had no experience with xenophobia in America. That changed in 1979, when Asha's brother, Vijay, then an assistant professor at the Harvard Business School, and his wife, Shanu, came to see us and we decided to visit a nearby park. Sandeep walked toward the swings and was accosted immediately by 6 white boys, ranging in age from about 6 to 12. They were clearly up to no good. Sandeep froze. I could not hear what they said. I rushed over and asked what they wanted. They growled and said something about reserved swings. A bunch of older boys joined the group. Sandeep tried to walk toward me, but they cut off his path. Forcing my way through the ring, I pulled my son away and we started walking toward the car. The mob followed menacingly, then began pounding on the car with their fists.

One boy, with an oily puff of black hair on his pimpled forehead and the hatred of centuries etched in his dark eyes, yelled, "Go back to Iran!"

"We are going nowhere. YOU go back to Europe!" I retorted. They glared.

Echoes of Tom Mboya again. Except now it was white children telling us to leave the country.

My family and guests, wary of the escalating situation and the futility of argument, frantically urged me to just leave. I saw the wisdom in that, but did not like the idea that we had to surrender to a bunch of bigots.

Preparing to drive off, I shouted, "This is so stupid!"

The chief brat's young blue eyes hardened and he said, "Who you calling stupid, mister?"

Just like I had seen and heard in old gangster movies. We were at a standstill.

The mob now stood still, blocking our path. I honked to draw attention, shouted, and drove toward them, careful not to hit anyone. Unsure of my intent, they dispersed, shaking their fists and shouting obscenities. These children were perhaps unaware that each wave of immigrants, including their own parents, had probably escaped poverty, famine, war, or worse in their lifetime, before and after their arrival in America. They had ruined our stroll in the park. In matters of bigotry, they had proven that age did not matter. They made us feel vulnerable once again.

When we returned home, no one said a word. This was a silent acceptance of the immigrant experience. I now worried they might pick on my son as he walked to school. What if they also attended the Field Stevenson School? Should we arrange an escort for Sandeep?

We did not reveal to our visitors that an Indian neighbor, a distinguished professor of microbiology, had returned home one evening to find his frightened wife cowering with her children in the bedroom. The home had been pelted (yet again) with raw eggs, and newly planted roses had been uprooted and thrown onto the sidewalk. Worried about retaliation, they had not dared to call the police, but instead chose to move away. Their home, just across the park where we had met the punks, had become their prison.

Nor did I tell anyone, including my own family, that the neighborhood Italian barber, whose shop was open and empty, refused to give me a haircut, choosing to ignore my presence and my questions.

He simply shook his head and stared out his window, a clear hint that I should leave. Asha, at my request, purchased a home kit and became my barber. This was better than facing the humiliation again. Ever since, I have been leery about entering barber shops where I see many whites present.

Once, as an intern, I had been denied an apartment by a landlord in Oak Park, supposedly a bastion of progressive, multicultural, and liberal beliefs. That incident too is seared in my memory. A friend and fellow resident in the department was leaving for Vietnam, and had spoken to the landlord about subletting the place to me. Oddly, the apartment became "unavailable" as soon as the landlord saw us. Hearing this, Rudi Andrasch, my German co intern, called the landlord pretending he needed a place to stay. Upon receipt of the keys, Rudi unleashed a barrage of unprintable invectives and threats upon the cowering landlord, who then not only offered to rent the apartment to me but also to lower the rent. But I was too wounded to accept this hollow "victory." I did appreciate, however, that a blond, blue-eyed physician from Hitler's Germany had come to the defense of a brown family in the Land of Lincoln!

Innocent questions from whites such as "Where are you from?" put us on guard. The answer "Forest Park" was insufficient. Our color and appearance led to an expectation that we would tell them which country we came from. The questions were not malicious, but we were suspicious of their motive. Sometimes someone asked, "Will you be going back to India?" whereupon I would confuse them further by saying I was from Kenya. Whites, who always "belong," and blacks, descendants of slaves from yesteryears, were not asked such questions.

It was so difficult to feel a sense of belonging. The truth was that we, as new immigrants, were deeply grateful to be allowed to live here, to become citizens, and to unleash our pent-up energy and enormous potential to create a happy, healthy, and successful future for our families and for the nation we had come to love. Very few of us would ever return to our countries of origin. We were just too comfortable and happy here. We resented the questions.

Forest Park now became an intimidating place. We wondered what our white neighbors, who rarely spoke to us, really felt about us. I remembered the signs in Kenya warning Indians and dogs to stay out and the ban on "lower castes" entering temples in India. No one, and no place, seemed immune to the pull or push of bigotry.

Maya Angelou wrote: "I've learned that people will forget what you said, people will forget what you did, but people will never forget how you made them feel."

Asha's sister, Kumutai, arrived in Forest Park for her first visit to the US. Gentle, charming, and kind, she had considerable artistic talent and a college degree and believed that she could speak to her ancestors through a Ouija board, which she called a *planchet*. At her request, I obtained a piece of cardboard, writing the letters of the alphabet in one arc at the top and numbers from 1-10 in another arc at the bottom.

We placed our fingers lightly on the board. Sensing that I was skeptical, she requested that there be no laughter or mockery. Once there was pin-drop silence, she invited her deceased grandfather, the judge from Lahore, to "talk" to her. I was expecting nothing to happen, so I was astonished when Asha's fingers moved in what seemed like a random involuntarily manner, to the letter *W*, then *I*, then *L*, and finally to *M* and stopped. I saw no sleight of hand. The letters *WILM* meant nothing to us.

But Kumutai was sure it meant something important, and asked us to focus and try to remember. We came up blank. Asha also had great faith in the supernatural and the omnipotence of God, and highly respected her grandfather, a self-made man who had found his way out of poverty to glory as a distinguished scholar and judge. He could not be wrong.

I secretly concluded that while the finger movement remained perplexing, this board exercise was a ridiculous waste of time. We would not realize until much later that I was wrong.

I had now been on the faculty for four years, doing research I did not enjoy, and was unable to get more teaching time. I loved Chicago, the university, and the training I had received. Several on the faculty had a national reputation. I admired them, had been deferential and respectful, but I was excluded from conversations about GGJ since they knew I was loyal to him. My initial faculty appointment perhaps riled them because I had declared my interest in teaching and patient care rather than "fancy research."

In an effort to see what my worth might be outside the university, I responded to several advertised faculty positions elsewhere, but got no responses. I placed an ad in the *New England Journal of Medicine* and received one response from a remote place. I thought I had a decent résumé, with a Golden Apple (Best Teacher of the Year award), many publications, and national recognition for antibiotic research. I had been the chief resident in medicine, the chief fellow and director of a well-known student teaching program, and a sought-after lecturer in the city. In 1979, I had been elected a fellow of the American College of Physicians and the Infectious Diseases Society of America.

Was my being an FMG a factor? Did they have stronger candidates? Demoralized by the futile search, I decided to aim lower. Perhaps a job in a mediocre place with mediocre doctors. I did not ask GGJ to place any calls on my behalf, fearful that he might talk me out of it. I responded to an ad for an academic infectious disease physician at the Veterans Administration hospital in Delaware. Jefferson Medical College, due to its large class size, was seeking an affiliation with this VA medical center. Within three days, I received an invitation for an interview.

The shuttle ride from Philadelphia Airport on January 15, 1980, a balmy 55-degree day, was a welcome surprise after the bitter cold and dirty snow of Chicago. The gentle rolling hills and the tree-lined streets were lovely. I was received warmly by Brajesh Agarwal, an Indian nephrologist, who had previously worked at the Philadelphia VA Hospital (affiliated with the University of Pennsylvania) and was now the Chief of Medicine in Elsmere at the Delaware VA. His task was to recruit core teaching faculty.

The 300-bed hospital with a brown brick exterior stood tall on a hill. Familiar with the workings of the VA system because I had trained partly at the Westside VA in Chicago, I was pleased with the facility and the people I met. They made sure I understood that a job offer was contingent upon approval by the Department of Medicine at Jefferson Medical College. My salary would be higher than it had been in Chicago.

Dr. Agarwal drove me to Jefferson, wished me luck, and promised to be in touch. Frank Gray, the Chairman of Medicine at Jefferson, upon learning about my life in Nairobi, shared stories of his own safari in "beautiful" Kenya. He voiced no objection to my becoming the Chief of Infectious Diseases at the Elsmere VA location. As the only ID specialist to be hired, I would be both the chief and the Indian!

I did ask, as a condition of acceptance, that I be promoted to the associate professor level. He approved. What the Abraham Lincoln School of Medicine at the University of Illinois had denied was granted rather easily by Thomas Jefferson Medical College and University. Sheila Murphey, a brilliant clinician and head of the ID section at Jefferson, was extremely cordial and supportive.

I accepted the position. I was to start on July 1, 1980.

GGJ returned from his sabbatical and was quite unhappy. He cautioned that I was going into an "academic wilderness" and should rethink the plan. He was particularly upset that I had not shared my plans with him. Sulking, he mentioned to another faculty member that if I was so keen to leave, why wait six months? I brushed that comment aside. I needed six months to wind things up, sell my home in Forest Park, and search for a new home in Delaware. I knew he liked me and that his outburst was an expression of sadness that the university had not tried to retain me. Proof of his true feelings came when he arranged a farewell party at his home and invited the entire ID faculty and fellows. That was the first time he had hosted such a dinner.

I felt great sadness at leaving these good people.

I suddenly understood what *WILM* referred to. Elsmere was simply a suburb of Wilmington! The Ouija board prediction had come true.

It was a terrible time to sell or buy a home. Jimmy Carter, a president I admired and voted for, was a decent man but left a legacy of a faltering economy, high inflation, mortgage rates of 17%, the Iran hostage crisis, and the Panama Canal "giveaway," all of which hurt the real estate market. It was too late, however, for us to change our plans.

My neighbor in Forest Park, whose name I never knew, had occasionally waved to me halfheartedly during our five-year stay there. Neither he nor his wife had ever spoken to us. One evening, as I was pulling weeds, he leaned over the fence and asked for a word with me. I hoped he was going to tell me how sorry he was to lose such good neighbors. I waited.

Finally, he blurted the words out. "This is a nice neighborhood and we would like to keep it that way. I hope you will sell it to the right people. You know what I mean?" His wife, he said, had seen a black couple entering our home with our real estate agent the day before. The words seared through my brain and left both of us uncomfortable. Smiling nervously, uncertain whether his message had resonated, he gave me a conspiratorial look, grabbed my hand with both his hands, squeezing it in a display of fake friendship and shuffled away. My outrage remained silent.

The real estate agent called. She thought the couple was interested and would make a reasonable offer in spite of the high interest rates and faltering economy. I stood to make a decent profit and needed the money. Agonizing over the right thing to do, Asha and I decided to call the potential buyers. We felt compelled to share what the neighbor had said, the stories about the burned garage door, the eggs thrown at the windows of an Indian professor, of prejudice in the park and my suspicion that my son was being bullied by white boys. The couple, both pharmacists, listened carefully, perhaps uncertain whether I was a bigot or an angel trying to protect them from racists.

After a pause, they said it was "noble" of me to warn them. They withdrew their offer.

More than a hundred years after the end of the American Civil War, there remained a darkness within some white hearts. Our home remained unsold for two years, but the rents kept us solvent. Our next home in Delaware would have to be far less expensive than we had planned.

Many years later, Dr. Joan Delfattore, a professor of English and Legal Studies at the University of Delaware, reminded me of a poem titled "The Incident" by Countee Cullen.

Once riding in old Baltimore,
Heart-filled, head-filled with glee,
I saw a Baltimorean
Keep looking straight at me.

Now I was eight and very small,
And he was no whit bigger,
And so I smiled, but he poked out
His tongue, and called me, 'Nigger.

I saw the whole of Baltimore
From May until December;
Of all the things that happened there
That's all that I remember.

A SMALL WONDER

I drove to Delaware in April 1980 to transport our plants, some books, and one car to the home of Avijit Banerjee, a professor at the University of Delaware who happened to be Vijay's friend. Amused drivers stared as I drove this veritable botanical garden from Chicago to Newark, Delaware.

It was a beautiful spring day with a splash of blooming flowers. I was struck once again by how pretty the state was. Everywhere I looked, there were open green spaces and forests. The sky reminded me of Nairobi. People smiled and appeared unhurried. I thought we would be happy here.

A month later, Asha, Sandeep, and I made a trip together to find a house. Luckily, we loved the only home we could afford. We were elated when our realtor was able to negotiate the mortgage rate down to 15%!

Figure 18: With Asha and Sandeep

We moved in May 1980. The agent treated us to a seafood platter in a pub and watched in awe as Sandeep, a scrawny little fellow, now 12, polished off everything on his plate. As a two-year-old, he had been fussy and uninterested in food, and we worried about his nutrition. One day, after a discussion, Asha and I had decided to save his uneaten food. He quickly realized that food not eaten at one meal would return to the table as the next meal. He looked in surprise at Asha then at me, to appeal an egregious harm. Seeing no response, he picked at the food, waiting for us to relent. But we put the uneaten meal back in the refrigerator and offered it to him for dinner. It is amazing what hunger can do to a person's resolve!

Girija Parameswaran, who lived just a few doors down, excitedly ran over even before the furniture was unloaded, with a glass of milk for Sandeep. She was thrilled to have an Indian family on the same street. Her husband, Param, worked for DuPont, a chemical giant that had a huge presence in the state. Our families were destined to share many joys and sorrows together.

All 600 Indians in the state knew each other, even though there was no central meeting location, club, or organization. Our white neighbors were polite, warm, and friendly. We learned that Delaware was the corporate headquarters for numerous Fortune 500 companies, the first place in the US to manufacture gun powder commercially, where nylon was invented, and the state with more PhDs per capita than any other in the country and perhaps the world. It had also been the first to ratify the constitution. The University of Delaware, with its lovely campus, was internationally praised for its chemical engineering programs and affordable tuition.

They called it "The Diamond State," the "Small Wonder," and the "First State." This is where Swedes had settled 400 hundred years earlier and where William Penn had first landed. Harriet Tubman had rescued southern slaves here. It was a shopping mecca with no sales tax. The weather was mild, the landscape pretty, the streets tree-lined, and the state had more open spaces and parks than we had seen anywhere. A short car drive away from major cities, yet insulated from the madness of those urban areas. If you were not paying attention driving westward, you would enter Maryland before you knew it, and if you drove too far east, you would reach the Delaware River, which flowed toward the Delaware Bay, the Atlantic Ocean, and Rehoboth Beach, the playground of senators. We fell in love with Delaware. Here one could meet the governor or the senator in public places even when elections were far away.

Like most places in the US, Wilmington had a history of segregation, race riots, and ghettos. Violence was generally at a low level, until several decades later when the city acquired the dubious distinction of being the "Murder Capital of the US" among midsized towns.

We still loved the place and were happy we had made the decision to move.

****

In March 1980, Dr. Agarwal had called to say that he did not yet have the required number of specialists, and the residency program at the VA would be delayed by one year. He would understand if I were to cancel my contract. But it was too late.

My work at the Elsmere VA began on July 1, 1980.

The general internists on staff had little academic experience. As FMGs, they had received their training at one of the numerous mediocre hospitals in the US. A few consultants from a nearby medical center came infrequently, though they generally gave unhelpful advice and were often condescending or pompous. They rarely examined the patients, as though it might taint them to touch veterans.

An exception was the world-renowned expert on the disease sarcoidosis, Harold Israel, who came once a month from Jefferson to check on a few patients. The discoverer of hormone called erythropoietin, Dr. Erslev, sometimes gave a lecture. Besides me, there were just two specialists: one for cardiology and one for nephrology. As GGJ had said, this VA was truly an academic desert with substandard doctors and poor care. Transforming this place was going to be a very steep challenge. The ENT (ear, nose, and throat) and orthopedic programs ran well, but the general surgery section was awful. It was a common practice to dump desperately ill patients into the Philadelphia VA, especially on Friday evenings. As a result, the big-city folks had justified contempt for our VA. We often fielded irate calls from them. It was quite embarrassing.

I introduced myself to William Holloway, the head of the Infectious Disease section at the Medical Center of Delaware, where he did consultations. Bill welcomed me as warmly as Sheila Murphey had. This connection was to serve me well later.

All 300 beds in the VA hospital were occupied by patients in varying degrees of clinical need. A flood of consults for FUO (fever of unknown origin) greeted me immediately. The reasons for the "unknown" were laziness and a lack of basic efforts to make the diagnosis. They had simply been undiagnosed or misdiagnosed. The blissful ignorance and lack of urgency astounded me.

I was shocked that my very first patient, who had mitral valve endocarditis, a fatal disease if left untreated, had been labeled as an FUO for four weeks. Every one of his blood cultures had been positive, but incredibly, they were all labeled as "contaminants," both by the laboratory and the internists. The fever, the heart murmur, and the cultures—all ignored—were all classic features of endocarditis, a heart valve infection. There were other classic signs that no remotely competent physician should have missed. This was poor care by incompetent and lazy doctors. The patient had been wasting away, waiting to die. Imagine his joy when he was told that we could cure the infection. He improved rapidly and was discharged soon after. Interestingly, gentamicin, an extremely effective antibiotic, had never been used in this hospital. Dr. Jackson, then one of the world's experts on this drug, had taught us how to use it safely.

The microbiology lab was terrible. The American pathologist, a rather nasty man who viewed his FMG colleagues with great contempt, regarded me with suspicion and disdain. He was combative every time an improvement was suggested for "his" laboratory.

One surgeon, a peanut-eating FMG, used the most interesting and unusual antibiotic combinations I had ever seen. My suggestions to shorten the prolonged courses of treatment were rejected. To bully me, he lodged a harassment complaint with the university. He was deeply angered when I stood my ground and prevailed.

I learned that the VA system was used by a small minority of veterans who were poor or had significant social issues. The Elsmere patients rarely complained. Many of them had few choices and accepted any care they could get from the disinterested, poorly trained doctors, who lacked motivation and had lost much of their self-esteem.

The doctors had fallen into the trap of poor residency training at inept institutions and suffered from a lack of accountability. The news media ran sensational stories about poor VA care. The generalizations failed to separate the outstanding VA hospitals from the substandard ones. Indeed, the Elsmere VA was vastly inferior to the West Side VA, where Clifford Pilz ran a tight ship, and the clinicians gave kind and brilliant care with some of the finest faculty members in the nation.

Non-physician directors assigned to these hospitals were some of the worst administrators in the country. A malaise lingered over anything they touched. The media picked up on the scandals within the VA quickly, while ignoring the poor care at numerous private institutions.

Vietnam veterans, who had been shunned and spat upon when they had returned from a lost war, battled their own personal demons and had no appetite or resources to take on the large bureaucracy. Many veterans did not know how poor their care really was, or were forced to accept it because of poverty, drug addiction, or homelessness.

I began to have second thoughts. Should I swallow my pride, call Dr. Jackson, and beg to be hired again at the University of Illinois? Perhaps Clifford Pilz could arrange a VA to VA transfer? Surely they would welcome me back, especially after a member of the board of directors, Earl Porter, had sent me a thank-you note upon discovering that I was leaving. I had treated him for a postoperative infection after the resection of a kidney tumor. Dr. Lloyd Nyhus, the world-renowned abdominal surgeon, had called me for the consultation even before I had entered the ID fellowship.

If we returned to Chicago, we would have to sell our Delaware home, wait for the Forest Park rental leases to expire, and buy or rent a new place somewhere. In the end, swayed by memories of brutal Chicago winters, the bigotry we had suffered in Forest Park, and the professional reasons that had led to my move in the first place, we decided to tough it out.

I did not want my family to be uprooted again, so I convinced myself that this was a huge opportunity to make the place better. If Israel could create a garden out of a desert, why could we not transform the Elsmere VA into a safe place for healing, caring, and learning? I wanted to be part of a system where patients and families could walk in without fear in their hearts, or any doubts in their minds, that they would receive excellent and safe care.

Fortunately, we were able to hire specialists fairly quickly.

Dr. Brajesh Agarwal, a Hindu from North India, had trained at the University of Pennsylvania. A brilliant man and chair of the department, he was the nephrologist and managed all the consultations and dialysis.

Dr. Ehsan Rahman, the cardiologist, and a Sunni Muslim, was already there. He had trained in Dacca, Bangladesh, and then at the University of Miami. He had moved to the private sector a year later and established an outstanding clinical and teaching reputation at the private hospital in Delaware. They named the teaching award at Christiana Care Hospital after him.

Dr. Husein Campwala, the sole hematologist and oncologist, had been at the top of his class at a prestigious medical school in Bombay, and had found a residency at a New York hospital on Coney Island. He had impressed his supervisors enough to get a fellowship with one of the world's foremost hematologists, Dr. Jane Desforges. He and his wife, Shamima, Gujarati-speaking Shia Muslims, became our dear friends.

Dr. Vijay Babu arrived from Kansas as an interventional pulmonologist. Quiet and introspective, he was a man of few words, but did his work diligently. He had a comical appearance with a dark face, a huge black moustache, and afro-style hair so he would look as tall as his pretty, fair-skinned wife, who had a PhD in respiratory physiology. No one minded his thick Indian accent, because the pearls of wisdom he shared were eagerly anticipated. A South Indian, he came from a staunch and aristocratic orthodox Hindu–Brahmin family. Sadly, both were killed in a vehicle crash 30 years later.

Dr. Virinder Reddy, a Hindu cardiologist who we dubbed "the walking encyclopedia," transferred from another VA. His favorite pastime was reading. Upon marriage, his only lament was that he could no longer read as much! He was known to have contacted the distinguished author of a cardiology textbook in South Africa to point out errors on some EKG readings. That had led them to meet and collaborate on a paper on right ventricular infarction.

Remarkably, responses to our advertisements were answered mostly by Indian FMGs with specialty training in the US. Apparently, it was easier for them to get certain fellowships than internships. They had trained in good Indian schools and represented the diversity of India. I believe they drew comfort in knowing that the Chief of Medicine was an Indian who might look upon their foreign degree with less scorn. Now we had a core group of specialists who were highly trained. The newly recruited specialists began to question and challenge the status quo. We destroyed the existing comfort zone and created a new paradigm shift to embrace quality and excellence.

This academic desert would bloom under the guidance of FMGs, who had often been turned down for residency training by academic centers. Now these previous discards were going to train residents of the Jefferson University program!

All of us were, at times, victims of deliberate discrimination based on our countries of origin and the color of our skin. All were legal taxpaying citizens, eligible for the selective service draft. We, the Indian FMGs, called ourselves the "Hind Clinic," Hind or Hindustan being another name for India.

We were determined to bring this place to life by establishing benchmarks, adhering to guidelines, creating high expectations, improving systems of accountability, and developing superior teaching programs. It was our conscious plan to make the Elsmere VA a shining jewel in Jefferson's crown. Even better, we wanted to outshine the university so that residents would clamor to come to us for their rotations.

We were raring to go!

We received word that two teams of residents and students from Jefferson Medical College would begin their work at our VA in July 1981.

CANCER

When I heard my mother's voice on the phone in September 1980, I knew something was terribly wrong. She rarely called, because it was very expensive. Calmly, she informed me that my father had discovered a swelling in his neck in September, and that a biopsy had confirmed cancer. He had been advised to get radiation treatment. She did not know what to do next. Unstated was her worry about the cost of care.

Dr. Agarwal, without a word, approved an advanced leave of absence for four weeks so I could travel to Bombay. I was forever grateful. The British Airways flight via London was followed by a three-hour cab ride to Pune through the western Ghats.

Dr. S, the surgeon who had performed the biopsy, did not apologize for the infection he had caused at the biopsy site. Wanting my father to get the best care possible, I turned to my childhood friend and cousin, Surekha (Sulu) Badve.

She and I had grown up together in Kenya. She had gone to the UK, received a degree in mathematics and statistics, and married Anand Badve, a flamboyant commander in the Indian Navy, who was studying at the Imperial College in London. Anand had grown up in Dar es Salam and studied in India before joining the navy. He had served in Goa during the 1961 ouster of the Portuguese, and told stories about how the Portuguese soldiers kept shooting because no one told them that their commanders had surrendered after receiving instructions from Lisbon. Sulu and Anand had returned to India and built several businesses together in Bombay and Hyderabad.

Sulu was able to arrange a consultation with a prominent US-trained oncologist, Dr. Praful Desai, who was the director of what was then known as the Tata Cancer Institute in Bombay. A kind and thoughtful man who had treated presidents, politicians, and prime ministers, he referred us to the radiation unit. Surgery, he said, was not an option. The prognosis was poor.

Figure 19: With my cousin Surekha Badve

We walked past a number of poor families waiting in line, often sitting on bare concrete floors, for the free care they needed. They did not express any resentment at the preferential treatment we had received.

My father moaned in pain as the rough technician and officious radiologist forcibly extended his extremely tender neck, shoving, shouting, pressing, and pushing. After a few moments of this rough treatment, I approached the doctor—who had thus far ignored my presence—and suggested politely that they use a pillow. He did not respond, and they continued their quest for proper positioning. My father looked at me, a plea in his eyes for mercy. I stepped forward and told his tormentors that I was a physician, a friend of their director (which was not entirely true), and I was upset by the way they manhandled my father. Worried that he might have heard bad things about the VA system, I told the doctor that I was a university professor (which was true). Advertising my title and status in this pretentious manner was uncharacteristic behavior for me, but it did have the intended effect. The radiologist's demeanor changed quickly. He offered me a seat, asked a few questions about my work in the US, and ordered the technician to get a clean pillow. My father's skin was marked for future radiation.

We returned to Pune to follow up at a local radiation facility.

My grandmother from Baroda, Mai, arrived to help out. She and my father, even during the years we had been separated from my father, had developed a special affinity and understanding. I think my father saw kindness and understanding in this woman and therefore was always respectful to her, as he would be to his own sister.

One evening, the now macerated boil burst through the taut skin, instantly relieving the pain and the low-grade fever. After checking with numerous pharmacies, walking from door to door, I was able to find imported tablets of an appropriate antibiotic in a refrigerator, using up hundreds of now scarce rupees. It was October 1981.

Hoping to get my father to the US for further care as soon as possible, I went to the US Embassy in Bombay to apply for green cards for my parents. As the dependents of a US citizen, my parents were eligible. I stood in line for quite a while. The gruff and impatient Indian staff handed me some forms, asking me to fill them out and to mail them back. They shooed me away when I tried to speak about the urgency of cancer care. I searched through the consulate to find a white American official who might help a fellow citizen. A polite young man basically told me the same thing about "established channels."

Back in the US, I filled out more forms, mailed notarized affidavits, and wrote letters to the US Consulate in Bombay, but heard nothing back from them. I called the office of our senator, Joseph Biden, later to become the Vice President of the US. He was known to be very responsive to the needs of Delawareans. His office promised to look into it, and may have sent a letter, but nothing happened. Months passed.

The radiation therapy did shrink the tumor a bit, and my parents reopened the English Tuition Classes. In May 1981, Surekha Badve called to say she had learned about my green card applications through the grapevine and that her husband, Anand, had spoken to an official he knew at the US Consulate. My parents needed to go to Bombay immediately to sign some papers.

Immensely relieved and grateful, I wondered why an Indian citizen was so influential when I, an American citizen, had failed to expedite this process.

My parents flew to Philadelphia via London in May 1981, and we drove 35 miles to our home in Delaware.

To my huge surprise, I discovered that Yogish Patel, who had been my classmate in Nairobi when we attended grade school, was a highly-regarded oncologist in the state. He remembered me, but not the bullock cart rides we had sometimes taken together nor the loquats we had stolen from fenced yards.

A short course of chemotherapy resulted in further shrinkage of the tumor. Despite what I read, hope rose again that my father might recover.

When his voice became hoarse, I took him to an ENT surgeon. Assuming my father spoke no English, he informed me, in front of my father, that there was grape-like tumor surrounding the larynx and that he could do nothing about it. He said it was far advanced. Shrugging his shoulders, he walked away. No charge.

I now knew my father would die soon. But my mother had great faith in the American medical system, had seen the tumor shrink, and was so optimistic that I just could not break the bad news to her. Hope had found a new home in her heart.

Asha's father, Kaka, had also arrived in Boston, to get hip replacement surgery for terrible stiffness and pain in both hips. During my trip to India in 1980, I had gone with him to the home of an orthopedic surgeon in Pune to review the x-rays. Vijay and I later went to the Massachusetts General Hospital in Boston to discuss our options. A decision was made to have Dr. Clement Sledge do both hip operations at the same time. Asha joined her family in Boston for his postoperative recovery. Sandeep and I drove up there one weekend for a courtesy visit.

Most evenings, I took my parents to the nearby Del Castle Park. They enjoyed the short walks and the fresh air. One such evening, I walked ahead with Sandeep and, looking back, noticed that my father had interrupted his walk and now sat on a bench clutching his chest. My mother rushed over. He was somewhat short of breath and sweaty. After a few minutes, not given to theatrics, he asked to go home, insisting he was fine. I took Mom aside.

"I think he is having a heart attack. Should I call an ambulance? I can go to the nearby shopping center and call 911."

She deferred to me. This forced me to blurt out the two most difficult sentences I had ever spoken in my life.

"He might survive the heart attack, but his cancer is very advanced and he might require intensive care, tubes, and machines. He will not survive more than 2–3 months, even with aggressive treatment."

I omitted the part about the potential of choking to death when his airway became totally obstructed with the tumor. She listened quietly. With a look of resignation, she walked back to Baba and spoke to him.

We went home. I gave him an aspirin and his symptoms subsided. He ate supper and went to bed. When I left for work the next morning, he was dressed, said he'd had a good night and felt well.

That evening, Sandeep and I went out to the home of our friends Rajesh and Alka for dinner. My parents did not wish to come. Asha was still in Boston. Midway through the dinner, my mother called and asked me to come home immediately. When I arrived, she was sitting by my father's side, holding his cold hand in hers, a tear in each eye, memories of 39 years of a tumultuous marriage flooding her senses.

My father had asked for a glass of water, taken a sip, and passed away. Mom said Hindus believe that asking for and taking a sip of water before death is a good omen. It seemed to me that, water or not, he was still dead. I did not see any deep meaning in this. There were no tears in my eyes, but there was a deep ache in my heart. I was conflicted about this man. He had been a hardworking and good man with qualities I wished I had: generosity and gentleness. He was naive and noble, with the courage to explore and experiment. Men like him went to Heaven, if there was such a thing, despite their weaknesses and excesses.

Yogish signed the death certificate, which omitted any mention of an enlarged liver, previous stroke, or severe vascular disease. The date on the death certificate was July 11, 1981. Asha returned from Boston where she had been for two months and broke down when she saw his body in the morgue. Sandeep said nothing. Perhaps 30 people from different religions said goodbye to a man who had gone to Africa in 1938, had squandered a fortune, and had lived a miserable life with a fractured family, before returning to India and coming to America to die. Other than the apartment they lived in, he had owned close to nothing.

Only a few of the many people who had benefited from his benevolence took the time to grieve with us or to send a note. But Younus Masih, my classmate from CMC Ludhiana, who had never met my dad, left a busy practice and flew in from Hartford, Connecticut the same night to be with me. I was deeply touched. Unable to find a Hindu priest, I asked a Christian pastor to say a brief generic prayer. Hindu and Muslim attendees as well as a few closet atheists raised their eyebrows. I imagined my father would go to a Heaven where there was just one religion called Goodness, the one he practiced. We could not afford a casket. It is not a Hindu custom anyway. The remains of a good and kind but imperfect man, who had harmed not a soul except himself and his own family, were cremated after his only son pulled the switch.

A moonlighting Indian priest, employed by the Indian Consulate in New York, arrived on the 13th day for a ceremony. He knew the things that Brahmins are supposed to know and say at such events. He lit a fire in our den, embers from which ignited a silk scarf given to us by Avijit's wife, Ratula Banerjee. Before it could burn our home down, the scarf was doused with "holy water," which actually came from the Artesian Water Company to our kitchen faucet.

Mourners in the room, a dozen or so of them—Christians, Muslims, and Hindus—said the ceremony, translated from Sanskrit to English, reminded them of their own rites. The priest changed into western clothes and was disappointed to learn that we had no whiskey.

He said it was not necessary to take the ashes to the Ganges in India, since all bodies of water are destined to meet somewhere, sometime. Uncertain as to whether it was legal, I quickly scattered my father's ashes in the Delaware River.

His elderly mother in Bombay grieved for her son, the apple of her eye, who had left so suddenly one day for Africa and was now cremated among strangers in a foreign land. She waited for the ashes to wash up on the shores of India.

With 1.3 billion Indians on the planet, one would think there would be a slender chance that two families would bump into each other in remote cities or states overseas. It was therefore astonishing that this happened to us repeatedly.

Vinod Patel and Yogish Patel, both classmates from Nairobi, my co-intern in Chicago and my father's oncologist in Delaware respectively, were such examples. I did not even know they were in America.

A year later, the Campwala family came over for dinner. Husein's father, with his flowing white beard and long white robe befitting an Islamic scholar, and my father-in-law, in his western attire, both visiting their children in the US, exchanged greetings, stared at each other intently for a few seconds, then pointed excitedly and broke into wide grins. They had gone to school together in Bombay 50 years earlier! Here we were in tiny Delaware, a state unknown to most in the world, breaking bread together. We joked that if we discussed this any longer, we might find that we were all cousins. It would have been extremely unlikely that these men, one Hindu and one Muslim, would have dined together in secular India. When the elder Campwala passed away some years later from widespread cancer, I was given the trust and honor of driving the mourning Muslim womenfolk to the funeral services in New Jersey.

At another dinner event, my father-in-law stared at the pretty hostess for what seemed an inappropriate period of time. A question lingered on his lips. Finally, throwing caution to the wind, he smiled and asked Bharati Ogale, "Is your mother's name...?"

With considerable astonishment, she said, "Yes!"

"Well," my father-in-law announced triumphantly, "your mother and I were students together in London in 1934. You are an exact replica of your mother." Kaka had never met Bharati before.

Shortly thereafter, we were invited to the home of Pradip and Shaila Khaladkar, folks we had just met. Asha's mother, the daughter of the judge from Lahore, was introduced to the elderly mother of the hostess. After some hesitation, they exclaimed in sync that they had been classmates decades earlier in Pune. Daughters of distinguished men, one an esteemed judge named Justice Bhide and the other one of India's greatest classical vocalists, Pandit Bakhle, they were destined to meet unexpectedly in little Delaware. The two women then retreated to another room to recall stories of the pranks they had played in class! With Indians, it is said, there are only two degrees of separation.

Figure 20: Asha's parents

****

Delaware had no Indian stores, restaurants, or social clubs in 1980. Instead, time was spent with other families to meet, greet, eat, sing, or pray. A few entrepreneurs became rich when they opened grocery stores or rented and sold terrible copies of pirated Indian music or movies.

The paucity of accomplished Indian musicians led to the formation of the tax-exempt Jhankar Group, dedicated to bringing famous artists to Delaware. A small group of volunteers, led by Pradip Khaldkar, did most of the work. A hundred members signed up. The State of Delaware gave a small grant, and the first concert sold out in minutes. On different occasions, we heard musicians such as Hariprasad Chorasia, India's greatest flute player; and Ustad Zakir Hussain, the world's most exciting tabla player, the razzle and dazzle of whose hands, his huge stage presence, and his showmanship were legendary. He had starred with Julie Christie in the movie *Heat and Dust*, was a music director for motion pictures, and had performed for monarchs, prime ministers, and presidents. He also taught at the School of Music in San Rafael near San Francisco when he was not away performing across the globe. I hoped one day to learn to play tabla from him.

One time, he and his father Ustad Alla Rakha were both in Delaware for a three-day music festival, where some of India's greatest musicians had assembled. The story goes that the Ustad and his two sons, Zakir and Faizal, practiced so much that their mother used to tell them to "stop the din."

I went to pay my respects to the elder Ustad. He was in a bad mood.

I heard him ask, "Kahan hei wo haramzada?" (Where is that no good son of mine?). Apparently, Zakir had slipped away to meet friends in Philadelphia without telling his dad! The father accepted my hero worship and then shooed me away before I could tell him that, as a high-school senior, for the final Senior Cambridge examination, I had made up an essay about him and Pandit Ravi Shankar performing in a concert that I had created in my mind.

Another year, the Jhankar committee asked me to pick up Ustad Zakir Hussain from the John F. Kennedy (JFK) Airport and bring him to Delaware for a concert the next day. He was to stay at our home. That is how we kept costs down. When I reached JFK, he said he not been informed about this plan and was booked to go to Washington, DC, in an hour. He apologized sincerely and left. I was shattered. I had rehearsed all the things I would ask him about tabla, Indian music, and his life story. Additionally, Asha had made a great meal in anticipation of his visit. Then my feelings turned to anger. I was upset with the folks who had made these arrangements. I had driven to and from New York City to meet my hero, and now I was coming back alone, feeling like an idiot. Someone was going to hear about this.

The next day, just before the concert, my hero sought me out, had pictures taken with me and my family, and apologized for my inconvenience. Two oceans away, my mother, who had returned to

India after my father's death, kept a copy of this photograph in her showcase and told everyone that I was a disciple of Ustad Zakir Hussain! Everyone thus assumed I was a great tabla player. That belief came crashing down several years later when I accompanied a *bhajan* group in India. They now knew the photograph was authentic, but the talent was not. It was written off as a mother's love.

These brilliant artistes made me feel worthless. Asha suggested a different perspective. She asked "Do you know of any other infectious disease doctor and professor in the world who can play tabla?"

Figure 21: With Ustad Zakir Hussain

I did become the tabla player for Pradip, a brilliant DuPont engineer and a flute player. During his business trips, he annoyed countless people all over the world as he practiced his craft in foreign hotel rooms. We performed for local charities, on social occasions, and at India Fest for a few years.

I started teaching young children the basics of tabla so they would have a glimpse into their music and culture. Although two of the six students became fairly proficient and were always grateful, the others had no interest or aptitude for this music. They had been forced to attend while their parents went shopping. Asha wisely said that people have no value for things unless a fee is charged.

Over time, Jhankar lost steam, crumbled, and closed. It had been a great ride. The Who's Who of Indian classical music had come to this little state, broken bread with us, and regaled us with stories of their rise to the top. We had put Delaware on the map for Indian classical music.

Over time, people clamored for a temple where there would be no meat or alcohol. A fierce debate broke out about whether a community hall, secular by design to reflect India, was a better deal. The Sikhs wanted a *gurudwara*, the Muslims, a mosque. In the end, while the majority quarreled about everything, a small and tenacious group succeeded in raising funds to buy land and bring in craftsmen from India to build a Hindu temple.

North Indians grumbled that only South Indian deities resided in this place but, lacking any alternatives, they attended as well. Priests and pundits were followed by cooks, for no worship is complete without food.

Christians — including Syrian Christians from Kerala — did not need to build anything. They found easy access to churches of many denominations. Indeed, there are five churches of different denominations on the road where we live, making us wonder if there is so much sin in the area. I saw whites in some, Koreans or blacks in others, and sometimes a mixed congregation.

The Indo–American Association was formed due to the hard work and tenacity of Manju and Jitu Asthana and a few others, who kept toiling while the rest provided unsolicited advice and criticism. Thus began an annual India Fest, where thousands came for food, fun, music, and dance and where politicians came for votes.

Indian scientists, doctors, engineers, accountants, teachers, social workers, and nutritionists formed the initial nucleus of migrants from India, followed by builders, contractors, gas station owners, shopkeepers selling Indian groceries and liquor, restaurant and motel owners, and others who purchased franchises for Dunkin Donuts and McDonald's. Indeed, Indians established a monopoly on many of these businesses. Their children went to top colleges and often returned to the state to serve its people.

In time, the community grew from around 600 people to over 15,000- still a tiny fraction of the total Delaware population of a million people. Indians, who had previously happily crossed the street to greet newcomers, began to ignore each other. There were just too many to keep up with.

The community now gathered in groups based on their languages, cuisine, the deities they prayed to, or the places of worship they visited. The Indian community in Delaware became a microcosm of India. Younger members assimilated with greater ease into the fabric of the society.

REBUILDING

The Jefferson teaching program was launched in 1981. It was an inauspicious start. Some Jefferson residents came to the VA with a poor attitude. Perhaps they felt no need to respect these foreign doctors and down-on-their-luck veterans.

My team included a resident, an intern, and two medical students.

On day one, an assertive, white, female resident who was to become a future chief resident looked at the first chart and immediately, in front of the patient, exclaimed, "Why is this man still here? I don't believe it. He is here because he is homeless!"

She established herself as the boss and ignored me. This went on for an hour or so. Other students and interns began to fidget, clearly uncomfortable. My irritation rose and reached a point where I could not bear it. I asked the team to step outside to huddle in a private place. I addressed them politely but firmly in words that went somewhat as follows:

> This is my hospital, these are my patients, and you will respect them. They have shed blood for our country. If you or your colleagues feel that there is not much to learn here, you are free to return to Jefferson. I am embarrassed to be a member of this team. Those of you who feel as I do may continue on rounds with me. The rest should report to Dr. Gray (the chair of the Department of Medicine at Jefferson Medical College) why I will not permit you to remain.

I informed them they might learn a lot about human suffering and our profession if they listened carefully to the stories these men had to tell. I demanded that they treat my patients at the VA just as they would treat their private patients at Jefferson. The female resident was stunned, the rest deeply embarrassed.

The tone on our rounds, which sometimes lasted two to three hours, improved. I grilled them about history taking and physical diagnosis signs, which I had taught to eager students in Chicago on weekends. We wanted them to have autonomy, but peered over their shoulders all the time. They could walk into our offices or call us anytime they had a question. We asked them why they ordered certain tests. We were teaching the concepts of "choosing wisely" and "value." It amused me many years later when serious-looking senior physician executives droned on about these "newly discovered" virtues.

The teaching teams soon expanded to four. The attending MDs spoke fluent English, even though they had unmistakably Indian accents. It became apparent to students that this was not the VA they had heard about. The chastised resident now encouraged others to rotate at this VA, telling them that the doctors were "great" and some spoke "the King's English."

It was remarkable how many Indian doctors there were in the VA, the largest healthcare system in America. It became obvious to me that much like the National Health Service in Britain, the VA would collapse without FMGs. Very few American-trained doctors applied to join the VA. The pay was low, and there was little prestige or glamour in caring for veterans, with their unique problems such as substance abuse and psychosocial issues.

American graduates gravitated toward university programs, where FMGs had few opportunities, or went for procedural specialties, which promised much more money, so they could repay their huge student loans. Indian doctors typically had no debt when they arrived in the US. In the 70s, areas such as pathology, anesthesiology, dermatology, and psychiatry were easy to get into, so FMGs applied in large numbers. To get into the field of internal medicine was a dream for most FMGs. Once in, they could find fellowships, which Americans did not desire.

I had been accepted as an intern only because many American doctors had been drafted to go to Vietnam. In many ways, I owed a debt to the veterans who had served in that theater. I was determined to make my infectious disease program, a one-man show, a force to be reckoned with.

HIV (human immunodeficiency virus) was unknown during my training. In 1979, a new syndrome was recognized on both coasts, mostly affecting gay men. No one knew then that this was the beginning of a massive global epidemic that would kill millions and devastate the economies of many emerging nations. Something was gobbling up certain human cells needed for proper immune function. Among many theories, including mass poisoning by the Russians, were pious proclamations that this was divine retribution for a non-Christian lifestyle. Many conservatives around the world did not really care if these "sinners" died. Indeed, a health minister in India announced that it did not have a problem with HIV because his was a country with "high morals."

Many died of a type of pneumonia first seen in starving infants after major world wars; others became blind, lost their memories, went insane, had terrible diarrhea, developed cancers, could not swallow, developed deep sores on their genitals, buttocks, and groin, or simply wasted away. I began to see emaciated patients with reddish, rough, and brittle hair. We did not know how to address the root cause of the immune defect. Young men in their 20s and 30s, drug addicts, and gay men died terrible deaths, their frightened faces deeply etched in my memory.

I became known as the "AIDS doctor." To be perfectly honest, I would not have chosen infectious disease as a specialty if I had known about the impending epidemic. It was physically and emotionally exhausting to care for young men who invariably died. Over time, it became both a challenge and a calling. I bonded with these unfortunate men, who were often shunned by their own families. Hemophiliacs, homosexuals, and heroin addicts (the feared *H* categories) were among the first groups identified and marginalized. Haitians were also placed in the *H* category, without much scientific proof. In the first few years of the epidemic, all patients with suspected AIDS were isolated. Some children were denied admission to school or were expelled.

The term "innocent victims" was applied to infants of affected mothers, recipients of tainted blood, and women who acquired the disease from errant husbands or partners. The unspoken implication was that all others had brought it on themselves and deserved little pity.

In 1985, a blood test to identify the infection was developed. AZT, an unsuccessful cancer drug, was taken off a dusty shelf in a laboratory in Michigan in 1987 and resurrected as an HIV agent. It caused terrible side effects including anemia and failed to cure AIDS. In many African-Americans, it caused embarrassing blue staining of the nails. I published a brief report about this in the *Annals of Internal Medicine*.

My family worried about possible contagion. I was aware of the occupational risks from having worked in a leprosy camp in Punjab, the TB clinic in Nairobi, and now the AIDS clinic in Delaware. It was a risk we had pledged to accept when we became doctors. I knew my positive test for Hepatitis B was from a forgotten needle stick. A needle stick from an AIDS patient could be a death sentence.

Ignorance and fear, rather than malice, sometimes caused great suffering. One day an aide left a food tray outside the room on a cart for a patient who was forbidden from leaving the room. No one informed him. It was a cardboard tray with paper plates and plastic utensils used for isolation rooms. The gravy had spilled over, soaking through the plate, and lay in a congealed mass on the isolation cart. The slop of meat and potatoes, disgusting and cold, remained there for the entire afternoon. The man imprisoned inside was starving within the four walls of a sanctuary that was supposed to care for him.

On rounds, we asked about his appetite, whether he could swallow, and why he had not touched his food. Frightened and hungry, he meekly responded that he had not received any food for almost 48 hours and was afraid to complain. He had not dared to open the door and peek out. No one had come in to draw blood. Horrified and outraged, we created new rules and expectations. All food had to be served on proper plates, warm, and delivered to the bedside. Isolation signs were to be posted only if recommended by the infection prevention nurse or me. A small rebellion was quelled after a sympathetic director gave me full support. Staff members who defied this new rule were offered two choices: follow the rule or be fired. One chose to resign.

We demanded that reluctant consultants and colleagues help us when requested. They did. The number of patients increased rapidly.

One time, citing budgetary concerns, a new pharmacist simply denied my patient a new HIV drug based on its cost. He did not intend to budge. Whether it was the budget or his possible disdain of those who suffered from AIDS was never clear to me, but I suspected a mixture of the two. I asked why our patients could not get licensed drugs that were available in the private sector and in larger VA hospitals. He believed that such "complicated" patients should go to a larger center, such as the one in Philadelphia.

After much agitation, all licensed HIV agents were placed in our pharmacy. About the same time, Randy Shilts wrote *And the Band Played On*, a severe critique of the Ronald Reagan administration's hands-off policies regarding this epidemic. Activists including ACT UP (AIDS Coalition to Unleash Power) rallied and chained themselves to fences and pillars demanding more attention.

As our understanding of the disease grew and better treatments emerged, I reflected on that era of anguish and discovery. Historians will note that this was the finest hour for infectious disease doctors, scientists, and chemists. They figured out how the virus lives, multiplies, spreads, and kills. In just two decades, HIV became a chronic disease similar to hypertension and diabetes. Nursing homes housing dying AIDS patients emptied. Hospital admissions became less common as we learned how to control the virus and manage the complications more effectively.

To paraphrase Churchill, one could say, "Never had so few done so much for science and humanity."

We had conquered our personal fears and embarked on an exciting journey of discovery. We had controlled a deadly disease. We had a right to be proud. Over time, the clinic became a training ground for a number of future infectious disease doctors and HIV experts.

Intermittently, major medical journals published essays and letters about FMGs. Some were thoughtful and kind, others harsh and even racist. The accents of foreigners and their high exam failure rates were highlighted with a broad brush. A few urged a ban on their entry; many urged strict controls. We were accused of abandoning millions of sick people in dire need, in the nations that had trained us. It was implied that we were greedy and disloyal. The sting of these comments felt, once again, like the chants from African leaders ordering us to "Go back to Bombay."

One day as I rushed past a line of patients waiting to be seen, I overheard someone say, "Why can't they get some American doctors here?"

The underlying tone was "How could a brown doctor possibly be an American?" I walked on, aware that the man who had uttered these words was here to see me. Perhaps he did not realize that he would be shunned, feared, or rejected by most other doctors since he had AIDS and had no insurance. He did not know that this "HIV doctor" was waging a fight on his behalf to make sure nurses did not ignore him, that dietitians did not leave cold food on cardboard trays, or that I had gone to the director and requested strong actions against those who refused to touch patients with HIV. Or how often I had to beg an endoscopist or a surgeon to go ahead and do a procedure, or convince our pharmacy to place needed medications on its formulary.

Most of all, he did not know that I did not wear gloves, masks, or gowns, purposely to diminish the isolation these patients felt, and that I too was afraid of an accidental needle stick that might kill me.

Yet, here I was, listening to a man who wished he could have another doctor who was "American." As a taxpayer who could have been drafted to Vietnam – and perhaps fought with him in that hopeless war – I was deeply hurt.

He was all smiles as he walked in.

"Artificial bastard," I muttered to myself. This Vietnam veteran, spat upon at one time by angry anti-war protestors, now jobless, stealing to buy drugs, and unemployed, was passing judgment on my worth based on the color of my skin. All he had to show for himself was that he was white. I decided I would be purely professional. No smiles, no handshakes, minimal empathy. I was not going to reward his racist comment with compassion.

Over the months, he opened up about his personal life and brought small gifts, which I refused to accept based on VA rules. We arranged for rations, housing, and social work support. The poison in his heart had been diluted by the care we provided.

Once again, the FMGs had to struggle hard before being accepted. I had been the sole person managing HIV patients and my roster had grown to 150 patients with full-blown AIDS. Some years later, the ponderous VA bureaucracy approved an HIV nurse coordinator position to help me. Lisa Nepon, a nurse from New York City, answered my single question (about the interpretation of a skin test for tuberculosis) correctly and was hired. She became the heart and soul of our two-person HIV practice. Tough and kind, she was able to get patients to listen to her when I was unable to convince them about something. We gave them free pill boxes to manage the numerous medications.

I became adept at puncturing a vein in the groin to get blood samples from drug addicts whose arm veins had scarred. The samples were placed in plastic bags to avoid the wrath of the laboratory supervisor. Infectious disease specialists at VA hospitals became the primary care providers for HIV-infected patients instead of just consultants, a much better model than the one prevalent in the private sector.

In addition to caring for patients with HIV/AIDS, I performed consultations, made teaching rounds, supervised ID electives, wrote letters of recommendations for students and residents as they sought to advance their careers, taught physical diagnosis, took calls every day except when on vacation, and gave weekly lectures. We established a system to expedite and coordinate the care of patients suffering from

Hepatitis C, hired a nurse coordinator, and created a new regional registry. Our work came to the attention of the chief medical officer for the VA region 4, and she asked me to coordinate the program for 10 VA hospitals in Pennsylvania, West Virginia, Maryland, and Delaware.

In my spare time, I wrote papers, read journals, and reviewed books for the *Journal of the American Medical Association (JAMA)*, thanks to their book editor, who sent material my way. Stepping out of the shadow of giants who had mentored me in Chicago had been a wise decision. It had allowed me to expand my horizons and become an independent thinker.

Patient care improved. The affiliation was strong. The teaching program became so popular that students and residents chose to drive 40 miles each way from Philadelphia to Elsmere. Jefferson Medical School's Department of Medicine, suddenly unable to attract enough residents for university rotations, decided that five core "electives" including Infectious Diseases would be completed at the University Hospital. This policy severely damaged our programs. We continued to teach the "leftovers."

Overall, my 21 years at this VA were wonderful. Jefferson residents chose me as the "best teacher" 15 times. The class of 1985 inducted me into their honor society, Alpha Omega Alpha ("worthy to serve the suffering").

And several residents chose to train in infectious diseases based on their experience at the Elsmere VA.

A ROUTINE

Asha had graduated with high honors from the nutrition program at the University of Illinois and worked for a while at the Cook County Hospital. In Delaware, she found a job with the Women, Infants, and Children (WIC) program via connections with Indian friends such as Nirmala Abraham, a Syrian Christian from India. This woman with indefatigable energy and her husband had lived in this area for many years and indeed were the leaders of the cultural and social scene that ultimately developed. We would enjoy their generosity and grace for decades.

Sandeep did very well in middle school. He was happy and there was peace at home. He routinely came home with good grades. It had been my belief that children should go to public schools and meet people of different social and economic levels. But we were uncertain about the high school in our district. Worried about drugs, alcohol, and violence, we chose to enroll him in an elite private high school, which had a stiff entrance test and high fees. Sandeep sailed through the test in half the allotted time and was accepted quickly. The admissions officer was quite impressed.

But it was a huge mistake. Sandeep was miserable for the next three years. The curriculum was unorthodox. He did not connect well with the children of the predominantly white, rich, and well-connected professionals, although they were always kind to him. He was not having any fun. I began to get calls from the school about unfinished homework and requests for parent–teacher meetings. A pattern emerged. They were really good at identifying problems, but no had solutions to offer. We did not know how to fix the problem.

I had developed a dislike for the principal, a Harvard-trained teacher, who had only a litany of complaints but no remedies. He had little empathy, but was great about soliciting funds for the school. One thing led to another and, with the help of a kinder and gentler guidance counselor at the school, we transferred Sandeep to another school for his final year. Once again, our son was thrust among strangers.

The class he loved the most was Spanish. Soon he was fluent and thus trilingual. At his high-school graduation, in an act of rebellion, he decided that he would violate the rules and loosen his tie. Asha, my mother, and I watched happily as he crossed the milestone after so much turmoil.

We began a search for colleges. He indicated an interest in a business degree with a focus on marketing. I was not pleased when Asha decided it would be an opportune time to travel to India to meet her parents. Her trip lasted the entire summer. I completed the paperwork, and we drove to several nearby campuses. We finally chose York College, a two-hour drive from our home. Sandeep showed neither joy nor displeasure. It was a small campus with a small class size, and I was sure he would shine. Asha returned from India and had no opinion about the location or choice.

Sandeep, our only son, was going to live by himself in a dorm. He was a handsome young man, about 5' 9", easily mistaken for Italian, Hispanic, or Jewish, with a fair complexion, brown eyes, thick shiny black hair, nice features, and a lovely smile. He was quiet, invariably courteous, and well mannered.

We had fought pitched battles over his homework, but I knew I would miss him dearly.

My eyes teared up as we left him in the dorm room with a new roommate. He was homesick, but never called us, and he was usually unreachable when we called. Every other Friday, I drove 80 miles to York to pick him up and bring him home, then took him back on Sunday evenings. He enjoyed being home, but was tight-lipped about college. The next year, I gave him my Impala so he could drive himself.

One morning, two years later, the phone rang urgently at 4:00 AM. The orthopedic surgeon, Dr. M, said my son had been in an accident. He was seeking my consent to operate. Apparently, the boys had been out late and their van had crashed into a ditch. The driver and a friend had run off leaving my son trapped in the debris until a Good Samaritan called police. They had to use saws to cut him loose.

The surgeon started by saying, "Mr. Panwalker, your son has a broken thigh bone and I need to place a metal rod to stabilize it. Do I have your permission? Do you want us to wait until you get here? He is going to be okay."

After I informed him that I was a physician, he switched to medical jargon. I asked him to wait until we got there.

"My family is out of town, and you and your wife are both welcome to stay with me for a couple of days if you wish. I am rarely home, so you will have the house to yourselves."

I was astonished at the offer, but we graciously declined. This was small-town professional courtesy at its finest!

Sandeep was groggy and frightened. His eyes were bloodshot. Sunk into the stretcher, he appeared small, frail, and very vulnerable. I felt a deep ache within me. Two hours in the OR felt like two decades. The surgery went well. On the third day, in his hospital bed, Sandeep informed us that he would rather go to a local community college. We rather liked that idea.

Asha and I went to the office of one of the deans to arrange a transfer. A tall, bearded, and unfriendly man peered at us, got up, and started to walk out as soon as he was told we were Sandeep's parents. I stood in his way. He refused to speak, simply shaking his head. He did not look at us. His secretary sat still without any expression. Then the dean squeezed past me and walked out. Shocked at the extreme lack of courtesy, we left, not knowing what had led to this behavior. All kinds of wild thoughts crossed my mind. Did the whole campus hold a secret that I did not know about? We never found out why the dean behaved that way.

The driver who had left the scene of the accident came to visit. I restrained the urge to yell at the scrawny, unshaven, acne-riddled kid who was telling us he was so groggy that he did not even know how he got home. But he was "So sorry!" He had not had the courtesy to call 911 or to check if my son was safe. He had left his friend alone on a very cold night, under metal debris, which firemen had to saw through.

Happy to be home, we set up Sandeep in a downstairs room. I shampooed his hair for two days until we realized that there was nothing wrong with his hands. We burst out laughing.

He enrolled in a small, business-oriented community college nearby. They said they would get the transcripts from York College for us. Sandeep assured me he would get a degree in two more years. I could not wait for him to graduate with a business degree. We would help him set up a small business. With his smarts, pleasant personality, and good looks, he would find a great bride — or we would fine one for him. We would celebrate late into the night with song and dance. It would be more lavish than a *Monsoon Wedding* (a Bollywood movie celebrating a typical Indian marriage). The razzle and dazzle of the celebration would be remembered for eons.

However, my fantasies for his future came crashing down when Sandeep indicated he was not having fun in college and would rather find a job. It was obvious that college had been a waste of time and money. He had only been going in order to please me.

Asha stunned me by saying that the *planchet* had predicted this outcome some years ago. I wondered whether that prediction had been responsible for her lack of interest in the college search. We reached an agreement that if Sandeep attended college part-time after work, we would reimburse his fees. It was now his responsibility to find his long-term vocation in life.

One evening, he asked me, "What if I become a truck driver?" Clearly a challenge to my higher aspirations for him.

"Drive carefully, be safe and happy," I replied.

He stared in disbelief. I had to accept the inevitable.

The Ouija board had won. The judge had been right about WILM (Wilmington) and now about college. Omar Khayyam came to mind.

> *The Moving Finger writes; and, having writ,*
> *Moves on: nor all thy Piety nor Wit*
> *Shall lure it back to cancel half a Line,*
> *Nor all thy Tears wash out a Word of it.*

APOCALYPSE

1989 was not a good year for us. That year, during a visit to pay my respects to elders in India, I was thrilled to meet Doctor Kaka, to hug him and also to show off my limited tabla skills. Well into his nineties, his mind was clear, and he was enjoying his well-deserved retirement. Three months later, he was hit by a motorcycle on his way to the *gymkhana* and died instantly. I was devastated.

November 1989 — I do not recall what triggered our quarrel on that fateful Thursday evening. As is true with such events, it started small but escalated. The thunder and rage were replaced by a deep sadness, which descended upon the home like a dark and ominous cloud. Drained of all energy and emotion, Asha and I spent the next three days avoiding each other. The days were marked by averted looks, silence, and the fatigue that follows a protracted battle. The TVs and radios were silent, as were the forks and knives.

I could not wait to get out of the house each morning before Asha left for her job. In the evening, leaving my workplace as late as possible, I retreated to the master bedroom alone, since she had moved into the guest room. The kitchen was silent. No one was hungry. Pride and self-righteousness kept each of us from ending the feud. To bend would be a sign of weakness. Agonizing memories of what we had promised each other when we were married 21 years earlier came back to haunt us.

The house was empty when I returned from work on Monday evening. A note informed me that Asha had gone to Claremont, California, to be with her brother and think things over. The secret departure was well coordinated by both sides. There had been other times she had gone away for a few days, but there was a sense of finality to this episode.

I called but was unable to talk to her. Sandeep was stoic. I called again with no luck. The third day, she picked up the phone but, recognizing my voice, quickly hung up. I stopped calling.

Surrogates intervened to no avail. Anticipating questions from friends and neighbors, I informed our close friends that we'd had a quarrel that had careened out of control and that she wanted to think things over. A mutual friend in Delaware said that he had been told about my father's alcoholism by someone. I made a guess about the probable source and was furious. No one had a right to malign my dead father, who had nothing to do with this. I was infuriated when untrained people suggested counseling for me as the child of an alcoholic. Memories of previous slights and humiliation resurfaced. Now outsiders were digging up my father's past and advertising it widely.

Family friends called and checked often. Without them, I would have been lost. Most were torn by their affection for both of us and had to walk a tight line. After a while, friends got tired of hearing the same old stories and laments. I felt indebted, lonely, and exhausted. I was always grateful to those who never abandoned me during one of the darkest periods in my life.

Over the next four months, I contemplated all kinds of solutions, considered the possibility that a divorce was inevitable, and was resigned to whatever happened. Household chores, newly acquired culinary skills (thanks to recipes from Madhur Jaffrey's cookbook), work at the VA, and attempts to keep Sandeep relatively happy became my primary goals.

Truth be told, I was largely responsible for the situation, which had arisen out of my passion to see my son succeed, but I had used all the wrong tools. My volatile temper made matters worse. I had blamed Asha for not sharing responsibility for the failures or acknowledging my feelings. Asha's family remained silent and distant except for one feeble offer of mediation, which I feared would not be fair or balanced given our history.

My mother, who had returned to India after my father's death, offered to come to the US. Asha sent word to me through a mutual friend that she would not approve of this plan. Why did I need her permission to have my mother visit? But I held off. As things were coming to a head, I asked Sandeep how he wanted me to handle this situation. He replied that he would like to have his mother return to Delaware.

Exhausted by the process, Sandeep and I decided to take a vacation to Hawaii. It was my plan, after our vacation was over, to give the process one more chance. If that failed, I would cut off all communication. Remarkably, that decision made me feel free again.

Asha returned, but only after I agreed to marriage counseling with a psychologist chosen by her. Dr. H was a tall, handsome Irishman with a gentle voice and intelligent eyes. He had neither the beard nor the pin-striped dark suit I associated with those who probed the human mind. We were perched in three corners of a large office, several feet from each other, in an old home that served now as an office building. I looked for the couch but saw none. Dr. H acknowledged that he knew I was unhappy being there and perhaps understood too that I had a fairly negative perception of his profession.

Every word pierced me like a sharp knife. I felt really rotten and small, worthless, an abject failure. My rebuttal unearthed all prior memories of personal humiliation. I left the meetings emotionally exhausted. One day, the counselor asked if he could speak to Sandeep privately. We readily agreed. Knowing Sandeep, he probably minimized his personal feelings of hurt. I hoped he said that he loved me.

This went on for several weeks. I did want to give this process a chance, but the inquisition would have to end soon. There did not appear to be an end point. I felt worse after each session, but it was cathartic for Asha. After six or seven sessions, I told the counselor that I needed to know how much longer this exercise would last. He said attendance was voluntary and the decision was up to me.

At the next session, I informed him that the visit was my last one. I thanked him for his efforts. In a thank-you note, I admitted I had learned some coping skills, such as how to ignore certain things and how to take a time out. I would never raise my voice or hand in anger again. Unconditional love would replace my fury and frustration. He did not respond to my letter. I promised the same to Asha. The episode was so traumatic that I was determined never to go through it again. If she left again, however, I would not make any effort to revive the marriage. I did not want the past to be a heavy anchor that would weigh me down for the rest of my life.

The intervention had been successful. Asha, in hindsight, had been wise and right to take us to the brink. Her actions had saved us from falling off the precipice. I now began a healthier relationship with my family. I understood that my son's happiness did not depend on a degree, titles, or social status. My dreams need not be his dreams.

Figure 22: With Sandeep, Asha and my mother

I sent my mother a ticket to come visit us during the summer. She had stood by me steadfastly when much of the rest of the world, with a few notable exceptions, had abandoned me. Asha continued the therapy sessions with the counselor for a few weeks and returned to her previous job. Three years later, we celebrated our 25th wedding anniversary.

We agreed that Sandeep was old enough to live separately, but some inertia prevented that from happening until 1997.

One weekend, I helped him move to a rental town home we owned nearby. As we drove away, my mother stood outside the garage shedding huge tears and bemoaning the fact that her grandson was being "evicted" by his own father. It broke my heart too, but he needed to learn to stand on his own feet.

Figure 23: 25ᵗʰ Anniversary Celebration

Figure 24: Asha and I

BOOKS, AUTHORS, AND FRIENDS

Harriet Meyer, the book editor at *JAMA*, had an uncanny sense of what I might enjoy reading. She sent me textbooks, medical mysteries, memoirs, or novels to review.

One of the books, *My Own Country: A Doctor's Story* by Abraham Verghese, published in 1994, resonated with me on a personal level. His story was somewhat parallel to mine. His parents had emigrated from India to Ethiopia. A coup against the emperor had interrupted the author's medical school education, which he completed in India. As a foreign medical graduate (FMG) he faced the same struggles I had. Ultimately, he found a residency position in a VA hospital and did a fellowship in infectious diseases in Boston where, ironically, his mentor was Bill McCabe, who had been trained by Dr. George Jackson in Chicago. He was another example of a doctor who, given the opportunity, could become outstanding and a role model.

This book was the first account of the AIDS epidemic from a physician's point of view. Deeply touched by the beauty of his words, I reached out to him after my review was published. In 1999, as a guest speaker at the annual infectious disease seminar, he dedicated the speech to Asha and me. We spoke privately about the Indian immigrant experience and how, in spite of his fame, he continued to feel the jabs of words that marginalized him. This immigrant from Ethiopia, who had worked as an orderly in a nursing home in New York at one time, rose to be one of the most recognized and important educators, writers, and thought leaders in American medicine. President Obama honored him with the National Humanities Medal at the White House in 2016. Abraham sent me a copy of the photograph taken on that occasion. His Indian origin and FMG status were important footnotes for those of us who had undertaken the same journey. The achievements of these men validated the presence of at least some of us in this land. He went on to write other books including "The Tennis Partner" and "Cutting for Stone."

I also had the great pleasure of meeting Dr. William Close, a surgeon, author, father of actress Glenn Close, and a physician to President Joseph Mobutu, the general who had staged a coup in the former Belgian Congo. Bill was trapped and unable to leave and, through a set of wild circumstances, forced to become Mobutu's personal physician. After his return to the US, Bill wrote a marvelous book documenting the first Ebola epidemic and his collaboration with the CDC. He called to thank me for a favorable review in *JAMA*. That was the start of a long friendship, which lasted until his death.

We invited him to speak at our conference in Wilmington. Before the lecture, Bill and I had lunch at the Hotel DuPont. He spoke about Mobutu with sadness, but it was clear that they had bonded in some ways. I told him I had seen white Belgian refugees from Congo at the train station as they passed through Nairobi, victims of the revolution he had witnessed personally in 1960. He heard me in silence. We had a common bond; both of us had been physicians in Africa, were forced out by circumstances beyond our control, and now were eating a meal together in the Green Room of a posh American hotel. Unspoken was the fact that he and I could never have eaten a meal together in Nairobi in the 50s due to the color bar.

He spoke about his family and how proud he was of each one of his four children and his wife, Tine. We joked about boiled rabbits and *Fatal Attraction*. After I introduced him to the audience, Bill insisted I show and describe the first few slides, which he had forwarded to me. One photograph showed him and Mobutu together on a boat, the other with Glenn Close when she visited Congo. A master storyteller, he enchanted the audience. Subsequently, he asked me to review other books he was writing, including *A Doctor's Life* and *Beyond the Storm*. Occasionally he called to ask advice about a patient. He was the only surgeon I knew who was still doing Gram's stains of the sputum or urine.

One day, he called to tell me of his own colon cancer diagnosis, but assured me it had been caught early. He invited Asha and me to visit their ranch in Wyoming. I was devastated when he passed away a few months later, before I could tell him how much I valued his friendship.

My work with *JAMA* ended abruptly after a rather nasty experience.

Germs of War, a work of fiction by Ketan Desai, was about a Pakistani scientist sent to steal biological secrets from the Mayo Clinic at the urging of the ISI (Inter-Services Intelligence), the Pakistani intelligence unit. The ISI was portrayed in an extremely negative manner. There was a mention of slaves and slavery. A group of Pakistani physicians in Michigan reacted angrily to my positive review of the book. Seeing the author's name and mine together, they correctly concluded that we were Hindus of Indian origin and assumed that we had maliciously displayed bias toward Pakistan. They accused me of intentionally praising a book because it fit my preconceived notions of their beloved motherland and its spy agencies.

I had ignited an India–Pakistan war all over again, but this time in America. Clearly the emotions of the Partition of India in 1947 were still raw and the chasms of Hindu–Muslim strife had not been bridged even after immigration to America.

The editor of *JAMA* called me and requested a written response. My rebuttal, which contained no apology, was watered down. I had written that reviewers should not be handcuffed by the fear of censorship or political correctness. The book was a work of fiction, set in the background of great violence fomented by spy agencies and terrorists. I protested that millions do live in slavery all over the world, something my critics thought was untrue. I provided references citing the United Nations and other non-governmental agencies including Pakistani human rights groups. What galled me more was that none of the Pakistanis could have read the book, since it was not yet available in stores.

They had made it a Hindu–Muslim feud when it was just another story. In a pointedly brief response, Desai responded by restating that it was a work of fiction, but that the current state of affairs suggested that he was not far from the truth.

The editor's decision to dilute my response and make it sound like an apology upset me. It suggested that I had backed down. I felt that such censorship was harmful and an abdication of the principles of free expression in a free country. I informed Harriet Meyer, with regret, that I would not review material for *JAMA* in the future.

My relocation to Delaware had allowed me to meet and establish lasting friendships with Bennett Lorber, the distinguished and beloved guitar-playing physician and professor from Temple University; Michael Bach, the electrifying lecturer who had grown up in South Africa and was still writing scientific papers as he lay dying of malignant melanoma in Florida; William Close, the surgeon and author who described the first epidemic of Ebola in Congo; and Abraham Verghese, who inscribed my copy of his book with the following words:

With the feeling that we are kindred souls

With the exception of Bennett, all of them had deep roots in Africa.

Several events led me to reconsider my future. The first one had devastating consequences for some of my patients.

Prior to 1996, and before the advent of powerful AIDS cocktails, I had numerous patients in a variety of HIV drug research studies. I had seen so many young people die that I felt compelled to do something for them. It took a considerable amount of paperwork, filing Food and Drug Administration forms for a compassionate new drug request, and data gathering. At the time, the investigational drugs were a last resort. I had followed the Investigative Research Board (IRB) rules and regulations to the letter. Our clinic nurse, Lisa, and I kept meticulous records of each patient's progress and provided regular reports to the IRB as requested.

An external federal agency surprised us with an unannounced inspection of our research program. The team recommended that the research program be closed immediately. They cited poor recordkeeping by the IRB and research committee, and a lack of timely minutes. They found no fault with my research or the records we kept in the HIV clinic.

I had no responsibility for the inaction or inefficiency of others.

I pleaded with the reviewers, our hospital director, and the chief of HIV programs in Washington, DC, whom I had come to know personally. Everyone ignored my requests. I had to drop out of a RAND corporation study of 16 hospitals randomized to use electronic HIV algorithms to guide care or to serve as a "control" hospital. Wilmington was going to receive an algorithm with reminders about vaccines, prophylaxis, etc. I also wrote to my collaborators for non-HIV research projects developed at the University of Pittsburgh and the University of Pennsylvania, letting them know that I needed to drop out of the studies. It was very awkward and embarrassing.

What caused me greater anguish was the terrible impact of this decision on one particular patient. This man had HIV/AIDS with severe, cholera-like diarrhea due to the parasite *cryptosporidium*. All the previous medications I had tried had no effect on his immune system or the infection. I sought a second opinion from a private MD in town, who said there was not much else that could be done. My patient was dying. Several liters of fluid, given daily by an intravenous route, kept him barely alive.

He had lost an enormous amount of weight. His chubby face had withered and his eyes, lodged between prominent cheekbones, bulged from their sockets. I researched the options and enrolled him in a study of a new investigational drug. The drug had had mixed results in France, where it was already licensed. There was insufficient proof of its efficacy, but I had no choice. After I completed the required paperwork, the manufacturer shipped the drug to us overnight from Florida.

Miraculously, my patient's diarrhea stopped within days. He gained weight and his eyes receded into their prior space, once more surrounded by chubby fat and flesh. I was thrilled; he was ecstatic. He thought I had been sent to Earth by the good Lord Himself to heal him. A devout Christian, this black and gay American ex-soldier hugged a brown, Hindu–Brahmin immigrant physician, while a white Jewish nurse from New York looked on!

However, the inspectors ordered me to remove him from the study immediately. The director from the seventh floor — which we had dubbed the Seventh Heaven because of the comfortable lives the administrators led — stood by, expressionless, while another individual stuttered incoherently as was his habit when he was anxious and uncertain. The external reviewers, one seemingly with a PhD in Cruelty, would not budge. I told them I had detailed records even if the research committee did not. No response. They asked me to send the patient to another hospital, but I could not find any that were doing this study. I begged them to make an exception for this one patient. I pleaded with our hospital director repeatedly. He said he had no power to intervene. The "feds" had spoken. I even sent an appeal to the Washington VA headquarters.

Crestfallen, I informed the patient that I would have to stop his treatment. I promised I would watch him carefully and, if needed, give him IV fluids every day as needed. His diarrhea returned with a vengeance, requiring frequent infusions. He was increasingly withdrawn, depressed, and silent.

When I pressed him, he simply looked up and said, "I am okay."

His eyes betrayed a deep despair. It was obvious that we had shattered his faith in our system. He lost weight again. I wanted to tell him it was not my fault, but kept quiet. I comforted him, as did Lisa. He tried to smile, but his wasted facial muscles would not cooperate. He did not keep his next appointment. We were worried because he had never missed an appointment in over seven years of follow-up. No one answered his phone when we called to check on him. We knew he had become estranged from his conservative black family after he had revealed his homosexuality. They had been unforgiving and cut off all contact with him. He had spoken of a sister who worked in a jewelry store, but we did not have her name or contact information.

Some weeks later, the sister called to tell us that his neighbors had called the police because of a strong odor. The stench overwhelmed them when they smashed the door open. The decomposing body and putrid flesh lay covered with maggots. He had died all alone, ostracized, shunned by society, fighting a disease that could not be cured, even by more powerful "cocktails" that had just been developed. There was no injury on his body. He had simply become dehydrated and starved to death. It occurred to me that in a state of profound hopelessness, he had made that last visit to us to say goodbye. He had no friends on the planet except for his HIV nurse, Lisa, and his helpless VA doctor.

The callous external research review team and our worthless local bureaucrats had killed my patient. The national VA director, responsible for HIV research, never returned my calls or emails pleading on behalf of this patient. When I met him a year later, he acknowledged that he had received my frantic messages, but did not think he could or should intervene. They just did not care. No one shared my anguish.

A senior physician said to me, "We could have saved the research program," but his manner implied "you," not "we." That incensed me because I blamed him for the sloppy oversight of the research program committee and IRB. He was the one who had appointed a nurse practitioner, who had never done any research. She kept poor records of meetings and had no system in place for the follow-up of various projects at the institution.

I began to wonder if this was really the place for me.

My relationship with the senior leader was further damaged by a second event. One time, he fell ill and needed to be away for three months, so he asked me to serve as the acting chief. During his absence, the staff voted unanimously to increase teaching and supervisory rounds to seven days a week instead of five, to ensure better teaching of residents and supervision of the care our veterans received. We had volunteered to work extra days and hours. On his return, he chastised me for not asking his permission. I thought he would be delighted. I informed him that I would not serve as his acting chief in the future. He raised his eyebrow, shrugged, and said, "Fine." He remained curt and formal after that refusal.

It was the third event that forced my decision. My friend and colleague, Len Katz, a wonderful neurologist and a man with great humility and talent, had been the chief of staff. He was the only bright light in this desolate land of administrative misfits. His intense and honest blue eyes, superior intellect, and modesty did not seem like a good fit in this sea of mediocre bureaucrats. However, he brought stability to the VA hospital, and I found him a great ally in our efforts to provide the best care we could.

Having toiled at the job for decades, he decided to retire. He informed me that he would recommend me to succeed him. He was sure I would do a great job. I could not picture myself talking about policies and procedures with administrators I generally disliked, but I thought it might be a way to escape from my current reality. I applied for the job. A telephone interview was held with a team of officials, three internal and three external. I thought it went well, but in my politically incorrect blunt manner, I informed them that my goal was a radical change in how things were done. I wanted more input and output from doctors, more efficiency, lower costs, and greater accountability.

There were other applicants for the job, including a vice admiral of the navy who had a résumé thicker than my thigh. I became slightly paranoid about internal machinations to prevent me from getting the job. The director, the one who had ignored my dying patient, was in no mood for major changes. He wanted to retire in a couple of years. Others, I figured, might not want me to have the job since I would become their boss.

One of the perks, if selected, would be a higher salary and no clinical work. I was getting tired of providing solo HIV care after 23 years. In the end, the job went to the admiral. That was the correct decision since he was a highly-accomplished surgeon trained in a US medical school, a veteran, and an officer with significant administrative experience. Nonetheless, I could not shed some of the conspiracy theories from my mind.

He arrived on the campus, asked to meet me—perhaps to console me, or to size me up—and was very gracious. Perhaps the shortest and fattest admiral in history, he huffed and puffed after each sentence. A cardiovascular collapse seemed imminent. I just hoped he would wait until I left the room. I did not relish the idea of mouth to mouth resuscitation on a massive corpse. He could barely extricate his bottom from the depths of the swiveling chair. However, I congratulated him and promised him my sincere support. I never saw him again. He remained in his swivel chair, unseen, unheard, and ghostlike in his posh office on the seventh floor.

Very few people ever saw him. He did nothing.

Over the course of a few months, he managed to alienate almost everyone by telephone, acquiring a reputation for laziness and pomposity. Our directors, generally older men who had been demoted from another VA, were content to sit in their offices, counting the days until they could retire. Young leaders with promise and energy rarely stayed long enough to have an impact. Our pleas for help usually fell on deaf ears. Now we had two disinterested executives. Not only did they not participate actively in the day-to-day management of the institution, but they also had no dreams or ambitions for improvement.

We had been focusing on the threat of bioterrorism from al-Qaida and I had been tasked to work on that for our VA. Others were assigned to the related chemical and radiation dangers. The superiors held a single meeting with us to ask whether such attacks were possible or likely. Had they forgotten about the terrorist attacks on 9/11? It was disheartening to work for such men.

I began to look at ads for physicians in medical journals. I applied to a VA in California but got no reply. Would anyone really hire a 60-year-old Indian FMG who had worked in a small unknown VA hospital? I saw potential rejection in every advertisement.

I pondered retirement in 2003. I was 60 years old and had been in the medical field for almost 36 years. But I was still very active, had a lot of ambition, and did not want to feel irrelevant. Far too many retired physicians are discarded like old shoes, forgotten and disrespected by younger generations. I would not handle that very well. When my mentor, Dr. Jackson, had turned 94, he had written to me.

"Anand, you are the only advocate I have left in this world. I am just an old man in society and of little value to others." Those words broke my heart.

In many countries, one is forced to retire at age 55, or a little later if they are exceptional at their work. In the old days, everyone was glad to do so because the remaining life span was so short. Indeed, the average life expectancy of an Indian around 1947 was only 43. When someone made it to age 61, there was a huge celebration because it was so uncommon.

With increasing longevity and early retirement, Indian male retirees are now at home for years or even decades. Indian wives probably dread the day their husbands retire. Consider a typical case, where a man would harass his wife by demanding three freshly cooked meals a day, 7 days a week, 365 days a year, unless they could afford "help." After each of the three satiating meals, the gentleman lets out a loud belch, pats his stomach, and reluctantly rises from his armchair to go for a stroll and to talk with fellow retirees on one of the numerous benches placed strategically in a nearby park. In India, he would likely read a newspaper or gossip. In Cuba, he might play chess.

Of course, the walk tires him out. So, he returns home after a few minutes, puts his tired feet up on the coffee table, and demands another hot cup of strong tea as a reward for the exertion. (Why it is called a coffee table is beyond me, for most Indians do not drink coffee.) The wife dutifully makes a cup of tea—silently, sometimes with a genuine smile, but more often sullenly—and then makes a rapid exit to shield herself from additional requests.

The cleanup, dishwashing, laundry, cooking, and shopping are the wife's responsibility, unless they have servants. (The word *help* is not typically used in Indian households). To see an Indian husband get up and wash a dish or clean the floor is a novelty, worth commemorating with a photograph. They will not even carry their own soiled dishes to the sink. The floors are mopped daily if there is help. But when help does not arrive, a barrage of blasphemous words is uttered, and the wife gets to do the job.

A female physician of Indian descent once described her father as a typical, short Indian with a pot belly, adding, "You know how they are." I wondered if her image of Indian men may have subconsciously led to her choice of a non-Indian life partner. Why do so many Indian girls marry non-Indians? Is this because Indian girls, observing their fathers' behaviors and their mothers' silent suffering, want no part of it? Sometimes, I see Indian women marry unattractive, but nice, non Indian Americans. Is it because the men have hearts of gold and do not treat their women as slaves?

Some retired doctors speak of an initial euphoria followed by an empty feeling, a loss of purpose and sense of worth. They no longer know anyone on the medical campus and feel lost and neglected. I remembered that Bill Holloway, after serving the community for 50 years, was essentially unknown to young residents a few years after he retired.

Asha read my inner thoughts. She knew my restless nature. She did not think I would do well smelling the roses or learning to paint. Perhaps I could go away to San Rafael and learn tabla from Ustad Zakir Hussain, as he and I had discussed one time?

We had come to another crossroads.

****

Some months after I left the VA, the new chief of staff was placed under investigation for unclear reasons. The entire system went downhill. A succession of "leaders" came and left, each one damaging the program even further.

A decade later, a program that a few of us had built and were proud of was destroyed by white, American medical-school-trained physicians and administrators. My previous colleagues who remained counted their days to retirement. Instead of a 300-bed teaching hospital, it became a 60-bed hospital that could provide very few services aside from outpatient visits.

Scandals erupted and made headlines in local papers. Incompetent people filled major positions. Jefferson University pulled its residents out. The affiliation died 36 years after we had arrived to build it.

Dr. Agarwal continued to fight to save the programs he had built, but it was too late. He resigned after a gallant fight. The VA system in Delaware, the subject of well-deserved ridicule in the 1970s, once again became the laughingstock of the town.

****

We did not wish to leave Delaware. Many outside Delaware think it is a sleepy, backward, and dull place. But we found it to be vibrant, with nice people, lovely surroundings, and quick access to major cities.

Staying at the VA was not an option. I was burned out and had been scorched by events there. It had become just another job. I was not having any fun. I had alienated some because of my obsession with perfect care and true caring. I had read that Albert Schweitzer, my hero because of his work in Africa, was so consumed by the cause that he was often insensitive to even those he cared about deeply. Personal passion becomes a handicap when imposed on those with different thresholds and benchmarks.

Leaving the state to start a new career elsewhere would pose the same challenges as before. Being an FMG and an Indian, having a dark complexion, and being 60 years old would be major handicaps. Universities might hesitate to hire me, since I had little bench research and clinical skills are greatly undervalued. Indeed, some of the greatest researchers I had met were the worst clinicians I knew.

Bill Holloway, then retired but still active, encouraged me to talk to different local practices. I knew several doctors in this community, and received two job offers simultaneously. They were prepared to take the risk of hiring a 60-year-old FMG. I accepted the second group's offer, even though their compensation package was smaller. It was a better cultural fit for me.

A total of 9 infectious disease consultants in 4 distinct private practices covered 1,100 beds on the campus as well as in their own private offices. Each had been well trained at a major university and was well established in the community. We had more ID consultants than Jefferson University Hospital! I was the only FMG.

Dr. Agarwal got wind of my plans, but made no effort to dissuade me. He wished me luck in the "rat race" I was entering. I resigned in May 2003. The VA pension, although not a hefty one, would support our simple lifestyle if I found private practice too strenuous or stressful. I was making a reverse migration from the VA to a private practice, at an age when most people were thinking of retiring or moving to a VA for the cozier lifestyle and fixed hours.

My VA colleagues were incredulous that I could be so naive and stupid. They reminded me of sleepless nights, the omnipresent pager, the stress, the competition, the burnout, and the high risk of lawsuits.

ALL THE GLITTER

My new colleagues, all white, were outstanding infectious disease experts. Trained in famous universities, they were highly regarded in the community. I felt fortunate that they wanted me aboard. My age, foreign training, race, and religion were never an issue. It was amazing that these things, which had been potential barriers in my path all along, had suddenly dissipated.

The campus, consisting of two large hospitals, was far more complex and capable than the VA facility. The place was so huge that I asked for a map and a tour. The chair of the Department of Medicine at the time warned me that there would be a probation period of one year "even if you walk on water." I told him I could not even swim. He turned to a colleague and they concluded that I had a good sense of humor.

To get a feel for rounds, I walked with one of my three new partners and his entourage of students, residents, and pharmacists. He was scheduled to see 25 patients in one afternoon. Each bedside visit lasted 5–10 minutes. The physical examination was cursory. Charts were old-fashioned folders with handwritten notes. There was a constant battle between nurses, doctors, dietitians, and others to access the massive and macerated chart filled with superficial and often illegible notes. No one sat down eye to eye with a patient. Patients sensed the need to be brief, and squeezed in questions almost like an apology. Discussions with the family, if any, were very brief. Any question unrelated to infectious disease was unceremoniously deferred to "your primary care doctor." Students and residents were not asked to justify the need for, or cost of, a test. There was ample evidence of defensive medicine just to cover one's ass.

Surprisingly, most patients seemed happy and grateful for the care. Almost 20 patients had been seen within three hours. Alarmed, I excused myself, quite disturbed. My style of rounding was quite different. I had never in my career spent so little time with each patient or written such perfunctory notes.

The VA was more advanced than many private hospitals in matters of safety and cost. For one, the electronic medical record at the VA, installed almost two decades earlier, made the records in my new hospital look primitive. Radiology films were available on VA electronic screens, so we did not have to trudge down to the film room and beg a radiologist to pull them up for us. The VA pharmacy menu was simple, alerting us to the many hazards related to doses, drug interactions, allergies, and contraindications. I had rarely seen the medication errors that I was about to witness in this modern medical center. To be fair, the volume of prescriptions was vastly different in the two hospitals.

I was struck by how many people worked here. Outside, the fountains, flowers, green lawns, tall trees, and ponds reminded me of a posh resort. Geese gathered by the big pond each day to honk and hiss together. The parking lot had gleaming, expensive cars. Patients were more affluent and mostly insured, although the campus provided a considerable amount of free care. I never saw patients turned away.

Hundreds of nurses in crisp, smart uniforms scurried along massive corridors with gleaming floors, rushing like ants on a mission to feed their queen. Doctors in scrubs or suits, hurried and harried, had little time for idle chitchat. I parked my car, now nine years old, closer to the few vehicles of like age.

An anachronism in the midst of plenty was the tiny physicians' lounge, with two chairs, one dirty sofa, an unclean refrigerator, and occasional insects. The lounge, without a TV or computer, seated four people. There was no other location where doctors could meet, consult, and develop friendships and professional connections. A larger lounge was built some years later to reflect the needs of over 1,500 physicians on staff.

The credentials of the doctors I met or heard about were phenomenal. The hospital had the capability to manage almost any critical illness, trauma, or surgery. I was truly impressed by the resources and facilities. We had the skills and finances to do everything that a large university medical center could do. There were scores of cardiologists and lung specialists, numerous heart surgeons and orthopedists. I had never understood why the place had eight neurosurgeons and so many trauma surgeons until I saw the volume of work. The staggering quantity of physicians was matched by their quality. They were, in general, very polite, humble, and highly competent. Most were kind and caring. Every now and then, I met a real jerk. Some were outright cruel and extremely obnoxious, making me question why they had become doctors.

The FMGs on the campus were generally one of three types: interns or residents who were hired during the years when American graduates did not apply in sufficient numbers; hospitalists, some terrible, some fantastic; or subspecialists who were almost invariably highly trained at American universities.

The office manager, Joanne Serio, and the nurse Denise Vance, were gifts from God to the practice. They looked after me, made sure the chart data I needed was available, brought me coffee when I was tired, and arranged my office schedule so I could spend 30 minutes with each patient rather than the standard 20 minutes. (New patients got 45 minutes.) My partners were okay with the arrangement, as long as the billing matched that of the others. My partners also left it up to me to decide whether to bill physicians and their families for consultations. I chose not to and never did. Perhaps thousands of dollars were "lost" as a result of this professional courtesy.

A couple of years passed as I got accustomed to this new lifestyle. The worst part was the sleep deprivation and the work on weekends, when one person covered for all the partners. The volume of old and new patients, the constant pages and calls, the long days without food or rest, and the pressure to complete the work in a timely manner made the days miserable. During on-call nights and on weekends, we often found 30–40 patients on the list, many unknown to us. The phone calls and pages never stopped. Here I was, working harder than newly minted interns. But the vast experience and learning from the work at this academic teaching center more than made up for the exhaustion.

There was a financial reward — and incentive — to work harder as well. The more patients you saw, the more notes you wrote, and the harder you competed for "business," the more money you earned. The practice, while very fair and generous, had a clause that stipulated a financial penalty if one's annual billing was below a certain threshold. There was no compensatory time off to rest and recover. This was the rat race I had been warned about.

I envied engineers, architects, professors, administrators, and others who worked fixed hours, never had weekend calls, slept well each night, and did not have to worry about making life-and-death decisions or facing lawsuits.

I was unwilling to do certain types of consultations. For example, I once refused a consultation to perform a history and physical for a newly admitted psychiatric patient who had been a patient in our practice at one time. I knew that the patient had no need for an internist or an infectious disease doctor; the psychiatrist was simply lazy. It reminded me of my days at Augustana Hospital in Chicago. I was a physician, whose job was to help others whenever I could, not to fleece them.

I never had my hand on the doorknob, a sure indication to a patient that the doctor was in a great hurry and trying to escape. Sometimes families said, "I have never had it explained so clearly before," and I would strut like a peacock for the rest of the day. Thank-you notes from families started coming in. Each had the same theme: a note of gratitude for compassion, patience, and support. Once, a very grateful daughter thanked me for recommending no further treatment and allowing her mother to die in peace. While I could have cured her mother's infection, I explained that the massive stroke would make her life a living hell. The daughter remembered my words, "It is time for her to go meet her ancestors."

The effort to maintain my "old-style" medicine was highly stressful, because I was always trying to catch up. My partners could not understand why I got home so late each night. One used the word *slug* to describe me and my work habits. He emphasized how "we have to keep things moving." But speeding up compromised my preferred way of practice and went against my principles. Medical students and residents loved the bedside rounds, the touching, the sharing of stories, and the challenge to learn, to be curious and humble.

Asha stayed awake late most nights to ensure I got at least one good meal. We were fortunate to be able to take time off and to afford travel throughout much of the world. We saw the ancient civilizations of Egypt, Greece, and China, the historic sites in Turkey, Israel, and the West Bank, the glory of Spain and Portugal, the castles and capitals of Eastern Europe, Schindler's Factory, and the concentration camps in Auschwitz. Here, where millions had been incinerated, their hair, shoes, and dolls in glass-encased displays, I recalled that the Nazis had misappropriated the holy symbol of Hindus, the swastika, and corrupted it. A symbol of good had been turned into evil by madmen.

We visited the magnificent Iguazu Falls in Brazil and Copacabana Beach, the pyramids in Chichen Itza and the ruins of Tulum in Mexico, the vast plains of Argentina, and the mountains and lakes in Patagonia. At Allende's palace, our American contingent was booed by Chileans gathered for some type of commemoration of his assassination. We took cruises to exotic islands in the Caribbean and sailed to Alaska and the Panama Canal, and across the Mediterranean Sea. We saw the graves of Vasco da Gama, Columbus, and Eva Peron, the Birla Gardens and the cremation site of Mahatma Gandhi, Qutub Minar and the Taj Mahal. We rode the waterways of Thailand and the hovercraft to Hong Kong. We visited the Forbidden City Palace in Peking and the terra cotta figures in Xian, where the farmer who had first discovered the buried treasure gave me his autograph. We had much to be grateful for.

Sandeep worked in sales at a variety of stores. I was not going to label his choice of a lifestyle a "failure." I did not have that right. My son was a decent human being with high virtue and values, and I was going to respect the choices he had made. We no longer quarreled. My love for him and my family was unconditional.

****

Very early in my work in the private sector, I realized that many physicians were contemptuous of the VA staff and its patients, in spite of the fact that many of them had received their training, at least in part, within the VA system. VA doctors, frequent targets of contempt and derision, rarely held leadership positions in local chapters of medical societies.

I never forgot one incident at the VA in 1981. A consultant from the private hospital who apparently did not think a physical examination was necessary was holding court with our fairly docile VA internists. I was scheduled to teach a class of students from 2:00–3:00 PM. After waiting for five minutes, I gently knocked on the conference door to inform the consultant—whom I did not know—that I had a lecture scheduled at 2:00 PM, and asked if he needed more time. He gave me an indignant look and turned away. He seemed deeply offended by my intrusion into his royal proceedings. I closed the door gently. The students and I waited. Another 10 minutes passed. I knocked again, this time a little louder.

The tall, thin bespectacled man got up abruptly, his chair almost knocked over, approached me, pointing his finger at my chest, and said something like, "If the VA wants us to take the time to provide expert consultations, we need to have uninterrupted access to conference rooms." He was angry and belligerent.

I politely said he could schedule longer sessions in the future and that I would have been happy to move to another room if he had requested that courtesy. He glared at me as if to indicate that I had tangled with the wrong person and walked away, brusquely shaking his head in disgust. I learned later that he was a senior leader at the private medical center with a great reputation as a teacher and scholar, but also known for imperial behavior. I discussed his behavior at a VA staff meeting. Soon after, we terminated his contract and hired a highly qualified specialist from Kansas. We also canceled the VA contracts for all the other local consultants.

In an ironic twist, after I joined the private hospital system, I won two prestigious awards named in honor of the man I had tangled with! One was for teaching from the residents and the other from the local chapter of the American College of Physicians for distinguished service.

Now, as a private doctor, I found myself defending the VA against generalizations. While we could not do many advanced procedures at the VA, I was convinced that the overall quality of our care was superior to that in the private sector, the error rates lower, and communication much better. I delighted in reminding all how primitive the non-VA medical record system was. It was, however, impossible to convince doctors, in spite of published literature, that the VA's record was equal to or superior to the private sector and its safety standards were very high. These studies, published in premier journals, had compared the care of veterans with similar Medicare populations in the private sector and found surprising parity. This was perhaps due to modern electronic medical records and 40 hours of mandatory training in Total Quality Management, the system practiced by Edward Deming. Thus the concept of safety and teamwork was known to us two decades before it was embraced by the private sector.

THE LAST SUPPER

Some people are never forgotten. Michael was one such individual. He had acute leukemia and was very angry. At age 18, he had undergone a marrow transplantation and had every imaginable symptom related to a graft-versus-host reaction. Constant fevers, bacterial infections, oral ulcers, fatigue, severe skin rashes that became blisters filled with yellow fluid, bloody diarrhea, achy muscles, and the inability to swallow without pain had resulted in anger, depression, and withdrawal from his family and caregivers. Hope had given way to despair and was now a raging fury. His eyes watered. There was a trickle of blood from one nostril and a pustule on one ear. His denuded scalp had just a few tufts of brittle, red hair. Before the diagnosis, he had been a feisty and handsome young man.

He wanted to be left alone, and rejected all advice. He wanted no touching, probing, or prodding. Occasionally, he resorted to foul language when a nurse or doctor tried to coax him into taking a test or a medication.

His mother sat by his side every day, sometimes touching his cold hand. He would push her away roughly, screaming so loudly that other patients in the unit became apprehensive. He told his girlfriend, who had shared his suffering for months, to leave him alone. She came daily anyway. His father, mostly silent and sullen, invariably found a chair in a distant dark corner of the room, as far away from the misery as physically possible. Occasionally, he exploded in rage when Michael's tantrum was particularly shrill.

Asked to see him for an infectious disease consultation, I knocked gently and entered with some trepidation. Chart notes suggested that I would receive a rude reception.

Weak and tired, through tears, he screamed with a squeaky voice, "Who are you? What do you want?"

Before I could explain, he asked me to leave. In fact, he wished everyone would just leave. He had seen his quota of fools for the day. His mother apologized and pleaded with Michael to allow an examination. Permission was not granted. I asked if I could do anything for him before I left.

"Get me out of this hellhole," he said.

"I do not have the authority to do that, and it is not a good idea."

"Then talk to someone who has the authority, and don't come back."

I placed some antibiotic orders and left. This same pattern continued for two more days. Michael felt slightly better, his fever had abated, and he tolerated small amounts of oral fluids. His behavior mellowed somewhat. On Good Friday, as I sat by his side, he asked if he could go home for Easter dinner with his family. I said I would ask his doctor.

I had just arrived from the VA system, where we had permitted carefully selected patients to leave on a "pass" for weddings, funerals, or birthdays, or simply to be with loved ones for a few hours. Although I did not share this idea with Michael, I thought it would be safe for him be home for 3–4 hours for the dinner. But I did not have the authority to make that call, so I asked the hematologist.

After a momentary pause, in an obvious dig at my VA background, he said, "We don't do things that way here. His insurance will not approve a pass for a few hours, and he is not quite ready to go home yet."

I had entered uncharted waters. But his comment about insurance coverage was correct. I should have known that those who sell such policies do not include a clause for compassion.

He added, "Michael and his family have been very difficult. They do not follow instructions and have given nothing but trouble to the staff."

I muttered something about him being just a kid. He in turn mumbled something under his breath and hung up. I got the feeling that he did not like me. We had tangled once before about the choice of an antibiotic for another patient, and he had chosen to criticize me in front of other physicians. I had fought back because I knew I had made the correct decision.

On Saturday morning, when the physician entered Michael's room to deny his request, Michael erupted in anger. "But Dr. Panwalker told me I could. Why can't I go? I am not a prisoner!"

Michael had either misunderstood or was trying to manipulate us against each other.

To my great surprise, when I returned on Monday, I was informed that the physician had discharged Michael that Saturday. The family was ecstatic. The Easter supper with 20 family members had been wonderful.

"He ate like a horse!" they said. Tears of misery had been replaced by tears of joy. They had laughed, joked, sang, and told stories late into the night. He returned to the hospital on Tuesday, in shock and on his death bed. Michael died peacefully that day.

For the next 10 years, during Easter and at Christmas time, his mother came to the office to leave food and gifts for me in gratitude for that last supper. No one had ever seen Michael so happy. His mom said that Michael had loved me for how I had cared for him and gone to battle to fulfill his last wish when no one else would.

In 2012, I ran into Michael's mother in the hospital. She had newly diagnosed lung cancer, had lost much weight, looked skeletal, and was dying.

"When I meet Michael in Heaven, I will tell him I gave you two hugs, one from me and one from you."

She turned her head away on the wet pillow and started weeping softly. I held her hand for a few moments and left quietly.

I wondered if my compassion had been misplaced. Had my intervention hastened his death? After all, he might have recovered from the fever, from the graft-versus-host reaction, and from his leukemia if he had stayed. At the end of the year, I received the Mark W. Maxwell award, given once each year, for compassion and humility. I believe Michael had something to do with that.

Then there was the woman who would become a dear family friend. She frequently encouraged me to write a book. She had been admitted after undergoing her second bone marrow transplant for leukemia. We had been called to manage a high fever. William Osler famously stated that there were three scourges of mankind: fever, famine, and war. She was fighting all three. A fever whose origin was unclear, an ongoing battle with leukemia, and severe malnourishment due to the ravages of her disease. Bedridden, she had sores in her mouth, aches and pains, no appetite, and profound weakness.

Her first bone marrow transplant had failed, and she had just had a second one. The family had lived in a mid-western state where she met her high-school sweetheart. They had moved to Delaware where she found a job as a schoolteacher. Their lives took an unexpected turn when leukemia was diagnosed, but she remained resilient and hopeful.

I introduced myself. Although barely able to whisper, she always found the strength to be polite, to stay awake, and to thank me for coming. On her bedside table was the inevitable emesis basin, morsels of food, and untouched bottles of Ensure or cans of soda. No flowers were allowed. Her children would visit but were very quiet. Her husband was at her bedside much of the time.

Near the beverage cans were cassette tapes that spoke of her devotion to Jesus. She never moaned, complained, or wallowed in self-pity. She had accepted her illness with dignity. Perhaps there had been quiet private moments of grief. During one of my daily visits, I noticed that she had a cassette of devotional songs in Hindi. She asked if I would like to listen to them. She had specially bought them for me.

The melodious tunes sung by Indian Christians praising Jesus were not entirely new to me. In college in Ludhiana, and once in a church in New Delhi, I had accompanied gospel singers on the tabla. The songs were sung with deep devotion, the melodies quite uplifting. I marveled at the predominantly Hindu nation whose secular democracy allowed all to worship without hindrance. The lovely voices soared to the ceilings above, without fear, and reverberated through the crowd, bringing tears to the eyes of the most devout.

She did not know this, but I had had a beef with God. I did not think a good God would be so heartless that He would let His subjects suffer so much. I had seen far too much misery and could never understand why the downtrodden were repeatedly beaten down, and not allowed to stand up without being hit again. Astonishingly, I had met people who felt that this was God's plan for them, and they would simply accept His will. They believed this was His way of testing their resolve and devotion. For Hindus, it was the price they paid for their misdeeds in a previous life, which they could not recall.

She sometimes said a prayer in my presence asking God to help me attain the knowledge and skills to heal her. She thanked the Lord for sending me her way. A devout Christian was asking her God to guide a Hindu, on the brink of atheism, to help. This was deeply touching yet troubling.

One time, she stated that she would have enjoyed having me as her friend rather than as her physician. I responded, "But we *are* friends!"

She recovered and thanked God for helping a Jewish oncologist and Hindu infectious disease specialist heal her. I wanted to give at least part of the credit to my professors, to my elders, and to my own attempts to master clinical skills.

This patient was having none of that. When things went well, it was God's grace. When things went south, it was God's will.

Her quiet husband said little and displayed no major emotion, but he was also convinced that faith in a kind and benevolent God would take care of things. And He did. The second transplant was successful. She left the hospital, and I thought I would never see them again.

Several months later, I received a note from both thanking me. They were on their way to an Islamic country in West Asia, to preach the word of Jesus in a time of great tumult. I thought that was insane.

They would be tarred, feathered, and killed. What a colossal waste of time, money, and resources! But they had heard the voice of God asking them to embark on this mission. So they went, lived in a two-bedroom apartment, and learned the local language, catching a bus daily to their place of work and trying their best not to proselytize too openly lest they be caught and punished. They wrote cryptic letters and sent emails, being careful to avoid any mention of God, Christianity, Jesus, or their precise location.

In 2013, and again in 2015, they contacted us and we met, first at our home, and the next time at the home of a neighbor and mutual friend. They prayed for Asha and me and our son, whom they had never met. We were touched by this affection and the plea to their God to keep us safe and happy.

She looked well. They were planning to return to an area where a fierce battle was raging, pitting Sunnis and Shias against each other. They were heading back to a region where allegiances, both political and pious, shifted like the desert sands. To a place where killing had become so routine that the daily tragedies failed to evoke sadness anymore. I was amazed by their grace, goodwill, and faith.

They did not change my views about God, but allowed me to understand how faith can sustain some people through the worst contingencies in their lives.

A devout Christian family was at peace in a place torn by chasms within Islam. And I, a non-practicing Hindu–Brahmin, watched in awe.

I just wished they would come home to the US before some lunatic chopped their heads off.

LEADERS, DOCTORS, AND ROBOTS

In 2007, the past president of the MD staff nominated me for the position of president-elect of the 1,500-strong medical and dental staff. Flattered, I said yes before fully understanding what I was getting into. He said the job entailed going to a "few" meetings and conveying physicians' concerns to the administration. As I reminded him later, he was not entirely truthful.

I fully expected to lose, but the idea of being a leader with little to do appealed to me greatly. It came as a surprise to many that I, the underdog, was elected by a slim margin. The president and CEO, Bob Laskowski, an intelligent physician with deep integrity and an impressive résumé, invited me to dinner at a club for the high and mighty. He answered my numerous questions, then I realized that I had finished my gourmet dinner but he had barely touched his. He took the meal home for his lucky dog.

The CEO liked to be known as a "servant leader." I had never thought of the word *servant* as a way to describe people in high places. But it seemed an appropriate way to describe a physician who must lead and also serve his patients. It is interesting how a word can have different meanings.

Soon I was hobnobbing with big shots on a first-name basis, amazed that there were so many. The number of meetings increased dramatically. The consensus among most doctors that administrators earned big salaries and worked fewer hours was true. Yet I felt their work had great importance.

I had not expected a stipend for "citizenship," but did not reject it. The added work made my clinical career quite difficult. I started using my personal vacation time for administrative tasks. I studied the rules, regulations, and bylaws. I took office at a lavish dinner for over 400 physicians and their families, and was introduced as Anand

"Skywalker" by the person I was succeeding. The applause was rather subdued.

Two years later, because of my election, I became a member and the vice chair of the board of directors of the hospital system and the executive committee. Here I met and learned much from eminent leaders in the community.

Meanwhile Asha, worried about my health, urged me to find a primary care physician. I had avoided getting annual physical examinations because of the conflicting literature about their value. When asked why I did not see doctors, my standard answer was, "I don't trust them. They find stuff even when you are feeling quite well." That evoked nervous laughter.

However, a severe heartburn led to a consultation with Scott Meyerson, a gastroenterologist and friend, who put a huge hosepipe down my gullet and diagnosed erosive esophagitis, an inflammation in the area just above the stomach. As part of the package, he coaxed me into signing up for my first colonoscopy at age 64.

"Would it not have been better to do both procedures together? A two-for-one thing?" I asked. He shrugged.

I told him, in jest, that I wanted to be treated as a VIP for the colonoscopy, whereupon he asked if we should have local television crews present for the procedure. I did not find that funny at all. The flimsy gown and the awkward state of near nakedness, with a female Indian anesthetist (an FMG to boot) and a burly technician watching were bad enough. They really did not need to remind me to take my underwear off. I was about to do that anyway once they stopped staring.

The team then stood in a row and sang, perfectly in tune, with obvious malice in their hearts:

"Happy colonoscopy to YOU, happy colonoscopy to yooouuu!"

It was not very dignified to treat a fellow physician this way. Then they knocked me out. When I came to, the gastroenterologist said the polyps he had found required monitoring every 5 years instead of the typical 10.

He added that they would not be singing every time.

That is what happens when you go see doctors: they always find something. Once trapped, you are forever a victim of the medical industrial complex.

I chose a fine internist, who was a friend as well, and told him that my "Welcome to Medicare" letter recommended an annual examination, which many professional organizations and countries think is worthless. Famous clinics make tons of money doing such examinations for kings, queens, and Arab sheikhs. They fly in on their personal jets and reserve the top suite of posh hotels for their entourage. Soon they will have their own airports and airstrips. Most of the tests they get are worthless. They return to their surly citizens—who often have no healthcare—assuring them that their leaders will not die anytime soon.

More annoying, public health officials keep changing the rules about when and if one should be tested routinely. Worse, there are competing organizations that say exactly the opposite of each other. One day, women are told to examine their breasts; the next year they are told not to bother.

Since I had no symptoms and was quite aware of the controversy about screening for prostate cancer, I put up a strong argument against it, whereupon the doctor reminded me that it was my decision. That is what doctors do. They force you to make the most important and difficult decisions so you will not sue them later.

In the end, I succumbed to curiosity. The results led to a biopsy, which identified the cancer. I learned there was a famous fellow named Gleason who decided whether I would live or die simply by looking at the biopsy samples.

Physicians often take a shortcut. They ask YOU whether you prefer open surgery, a robotic procedure, radiation, or an "expectant observation." How is a patient supposed to understand such jargon? Why can't they just say this is the best path forward? Wasn't that the purpose of their advanced training?

"Get it out," I begged the surgeon, a person called Fran, who turned out to be a man, in spite of his first name. To prove it, he showed me pictures of his wife and four children. I chose a little hospital away from the big one where I worked for privacy. I was aware that hospital gowns are poorly designed and strangers can see either your front or your back, or both, depending on how you tie the knot. I did not want everyone at my usual place of work to giggle behind my back.

My vital signs were perfectly normal before and after surgery. The Sikh anesthetist, another FMG in town, handsome and turbaned, told me his father had gone to Christian Medical College as well. Upon further inquiry, we determined that his dad had been my classmate!

Using my newly discovered Sikh connection, I expressed a desire to see the da Vinci surgical robot before the operation. The massive machine stood tall in a large room with high ceilings. It had huge arms. The surgeon, using a joystick, would command the monster to poke several big holes in my belly and pump air into them so I would be grotesquely bloated, to allow the organs to float and be seen clearly. The cutting would begin soon after. I did not like the fact that the surgeon was several feet away. Anxious, I asked them to knock me out. I heard a loud laugh as I drifted off.

I have sometimes wondered if that is what being dead feels like.

Asha waited anxiously in the waiting room with our friend Shaila Khaladkar. Friends who visited that evening looked much younger than they were, and the women more beautiful than usual. It must have been the anesthetic!

The next morning, my pal Husein took me home. The sun seemed to shine much brighter. I was exhausted. My partners brought food, fruit, and books. They had shared the burden of my work for four weeks and allowed me a lighter schedule for weeks thereafter. I was touched and very grateful.

Over time, I became a regular in emergency and operating rooms, requiring stents for blocked ureters and the removal of kidney stones. I had received outstanding care from my doctors. Too lazy to return for the removal of the stents within my plumbing system, I asked to remove them myself, at home.

Ouch!

When things go well, American medicine is the best in the world.

In 2012, I came to another fork in the road.

It was more difficult to maintain the hectic tempo. The "slug" was exhausted each day and the calls were brutal. My new administrative and leadership responsibilities did not diminish. It was going to be hard to keep going. However, I wanted to remain active, and we had no desire to move. From our travels to numerous states and countries, we had concluded that Delaware was truly a diamond.

Money, new homes, and cars did not interest me. Indeed, I was content with my now 20-year-old Camry, and we lived in a lower-middle-class neighborhood. A friend and vice chair of the department suggested that I speak to the chair of the Department of Medicine. She had trained at Johns Hopkins, was a senior member of the American College of Physicians, and was way ahead of her time in creating a culture of accountability. She was a true servant leader. She led the largest department at the institution, with responsibility for over 500 physicians.

I was flattered and excited when offered a part-time administrative and teaching position with the department beginning January 2012. I was to lead the team that managed errors within the system and questionable behavior by physicians. My partners graciously bought my shares in the practice and arranged a part-time schedule for me with no calls.

Months later, recognizing that I was working much longer than the contract stipulated, the chief medical officer, who would later become president and CEO, promoted me to Associate Vice President, Medical Affairs, as a full-time employee. She reminded me that she and her husband had been students of mine in the mid-1980s! Extremely bright, just, ambitious, and tough, she gave me a mandate to improve our peer review processes and the physician culture.

Physicians streamed to my office, on their own or at my request, to discuss events or patient situations. It became my task to enforce a culture of responsibility based on principles of justice. Others came to seek or give advice. I also became the support system for some stressed-out doctors. Some came to vent or chew me out.

I left my private practice and became a full-time administrator, and my clinical career was over. I would no longer see patients.

There is a deep divide between the doctors who work in the "trenches" and those "who live in gilded offices." There has always been a tension between the two, a mountain of distrust dividing them. Doctors in the rat race, working tirelessly day and night and most weekends, and taking care of so many while sacrificing their own pleasures and pastimes, resent the "cushy" life led by those who barely break a sweat. They do not think these well-paid executives appreciate their pain. They are suspicious of the motives behind every meeting and speech. Many think the new "value" initiatives are simply a way to exert more control over their lives, to reduce their clout (and income), and to make them subservient to the system. This suspicion boils over anytime major changes are contemplated or implemented.

Some of my clinical colleagues now said I had gone to the "dark side." Once again, something deeply disliked, feared, or loathsome was called dark or black.

THE DEPARTURE

My mother had lived alone in India until we brought her to the US in 1996. We had received word that she was frail, may have had a small stroke, and perhaps needed more care. I went to India to talk to her about it. As a frequent visitor to the US, she would likely adapt quickly and could always change her mind if she did not like it. Her initial hesitation was soon replaced by anticipation and enthusiasm.

Before leaving India, she funded the Prabhaker Moreshwar Panwalker Scholarship for students who got the highest scores in basic and advanced English. A former Chief Justice of India, Mr. Y. V. Chandrachud attended the ceremony at the Law College in Pune, Maharashtra, as my mother handed over a large check from her savings. Students continue to benefit from the award which honors my late father. We also sold her small apartment. Kumutai's husband graciously helped us negotiate the unwieldy Indian bank rules. Now my mother owned nothing in India.

I did not ask Asha how she felt about it, but I should have. The concept of duty toward our elders was deeply embedded in my being. An Indian son looks after his parents whenever the need arises. That was the only social security our elders had. It was expected that all the years of sacrifice and hard work would be repaid with love and caring under the same roof. Once my mother arrived, she adjusted quickly. Asha looked after all her needs, cooked meals to suit her taste, and also tried to get her involved in the community with introductions and suggestions for new connections.

Being gregarious, my mother fit in well, walked the neighborhood twice daily, and made more friends locally than Asha and I had in the 16 years we had lived in that area. She joined a group of elderly Indian immigrants, who met intermittently at community halls. The gathering reflected a miniature India (and one Pakistani couple) with a variety of medical ailments or other frailties. My mother was active, strong, enthusiastic, and multilingual and had little trouble mixing with everyone. She planned word games for other seniors. They went on picnics and ate at restaurants. There was never any negative discussion or comment about someone's language, religion, or caste. They giggled like schoolgirls when together. Asha and I became willing chauffeurs whenever they met. I offered to buy her a car, but she declined.

Neighbors and seniors came over for food and talk. My mom's chutney sandwich *bhajias* had been famous in Nairobi and now were in Delaware as well. All seemed well. We found her a wonderful doctor, Cynthia Heldt, who had been a student of mine. A wonderful orthopedic surgeon, Richard D'Alonzo, replaced both of her rickety, arthritic knees simultaneously, and she recovered in five days. She was tough, enthusiastic, and resilient.

Figure 25: My mother at the Outer Banks

When neighbors did not see her walking, they asked whether she was okay. She felt comfortable telling one neighbor to put his dog on a leash and another one to park his car properly!

But things changed in subtle ways over time. There was an argument in the senior center, a fight for leadership, and someone spoke harshly to my mother. Taking great umbrage at a younger person speaking to her in this manner, she announced that she did not wish to go to the center anymore. She became isolated. Instead of one or two crossword puzzles a day, she began to do more. She read books and continued walking in the neighborhood. We signed her up for Hindi programs and she watched movies on television.

Since she was so short, she had to stand on her toes and lean over the range to peer at a pot or stir the soup. One time, the edge of her sari started smoldering. Offended by advice to protect herself from this hazard, she simply stopped cooking. She believed that she had been prohibited from doing so. She also stopped inviting friends for *bhajia* parties.

On her 75th birthday, we reserved an entire Indian restaurant for a buffet dinner for all our friends in town. She was very happy that evening. Elderly people often do not get the attention they crave, and this was her day.

Vacations became more difficult for everyone since she could not keep up with us, and her vegetarian diet created difficulties. We were afraid to leave her at home alone. Asha, unable to satiate her wanderlust, which she had acquired traveling with her father in luxury, sometimes felt life was passing us by and we could not do fun things anymore. We had seen much of the world, except Russia, New Zealand, Australia, and Japan, but she had more places in mind.

Asha got her puzzle books and magazines from the library, took her on shopping trips, and made sure she always had what she needed. I did not ever hear them quarrel or disagree. But the unavoidable fact was that my mother was now dependent on us, felt guilty about imposing on us and became more vulnerable as she grew older and frailer.

Over time, my mother did not wish to travel at all, and urged us to go without her. But leaving her alone was not an option. Occasionally we asked relatives in London or Ottawa to look after her while we went on vacation. Relatives understandably became anxious about potential health issues. One time in Ottawa, she stared vacantly at the ceiling for several minutes and they thought she'd had a stroke. She acquired a noticeable limp shortly thereafter. Family members rightly suggested that we should not send her alone.

We took a disastrous cruise to the Bahamas to celebrate her 80th birthday in 2005. We had chosen a short cruise just in case she hated it. The idea was to give her a change of scenery. The cruise line cheated us by cramming all three of us into one tiny cabin when we had booked a larger one. They brought in a cot. When placed between the two bunks, there was zero walking space. Even the cabin boy could not believe it. I would have paid more if they had asked. It was too late to disembark. I complained, but they coldly said they could do nothing as they were fully booked. Somehow, we managed to squeeze in and out of the cabin.

Mom felt seasick and remained in the cabin the first day. Nausea medicine helped a bit. She ate nothing for a day, came to the deck briefly the next, but refused to go ashore to sightsee. When I urged her to come with us, she got extremely angry. On the last night, she agreed to come for the dinner, where the table members sang "Happy Birthday" and gave her a cake. She did not even smile. Upon our return, she went straight up to her room and did not thank us.

I wrote to the cruise company headquarters telling them how they had ruined our vacation even though we had been loyal customers for years.

Now little things caused my mother to be upset. One time, she complained she had no voice in making decisions. But she could not specify what she lacked or needed. I offered to take her to the store each week if she wanted to shop. She responded, "You are so tired and I am not going to bother you." She withdrew to her room after each meal. Our conversations became brief and strained. Resentment started building up in the home.

We thought she was pretending that her hearing was poor so she would not have to talk to visitors. She no longer called her brothers and sisters overseas. After an ENT evaluation and hearing tests, we got her a hearing aid, which cost a small fortune. She wore it for a day or so, but said it was too loud. Even the sound of chewing reverberated in her brain. We adjusted the aid. She said it was now excellent and gave me a grateful smile. I discovered soon after that she wore them only when I was present, so I would not be displeased, and removed them when I was at work. One day I caught her hearing aids dangling carelessly from her ear canal. She pretended they had just fallen out. I asked her if she really was using them, and she admitted that she did not want them and that I should return them. Her Hindi TV screen was now constantly on but muted, since she could hear nothing. She stared at the set day and night.

Hypertension, diabetes, and a mini-stroke required many medications. A tiny woman on many pills, she began to fall at regular intervals. One time she tumbled down the stairs, but miraculously suffered no immediate injury. Months later, a deformity of her spine was attributed to a fractured vertebral bone. Another time she fell headfirst on the ceramic tile floor in the kitchen. There was no blood or bruising, but there was a sickening thud, similar to the sound of cracking a coconut. She passed out for a few seconds. When she came to, she said she was fine and did not want to go to the hospital. I was worried about a clot on the brain.

Since she was now eating so little, we stopped all her blood pressure pills and even the diabetes meds. She blamed her inability to eat on painful loose teeth. In fact, an x-ray showed many cavities, and five teeth were extracted. She demanded her teeth back, saying, "They are mine!" The dentist, somewhat taken aback by the vehemence of her request, dutifully placed them in a small plastic container for her to take home. I'm still not sure what she did with them. Now she had hardly any teeth and could not chew most food. We planned on getting dentures for her. Her diet changed to semi-solids and liquids. Asha began to find it increasingly more difficult to prepare things that would be palatable to her.

My mother was never the same again. Everything tasted bland. All she wanted were sweet things, especially ice cream. We worried about her diabetes, but indulged her with a small scoop after each meal. Soon she wanted nothing but ice cream. When we frowned at this request, she sulked. We ate our meals together, but it became agonizing to watch her pick at little morsels.

She also started saying inappropriate things. A friend's son was to get married. She looked at the photographs and made an unkind comment. We then drove to the wedding reception. When asked if she enjoyed the dinner, she told the host and parents of the groom that she "did not like the food at all." But remarkably, she had eaten heartily that evening. She was getting cranky. Thankfully, the hosts were very gracious.

Her walks became infrequent and shorter. Occasionally, if a neighbor did not open the door as she stood outside, she got upset. She was sure they knew she was waiting outside.

Meanwhile, Asha fell and broke her left hip. The surgeon and the hospital provided exceptionally good care.

We installed a chairlift for Asha so she could get to the second floor. My mother initially refused to use the lift, telling others that I had bought it for Asha, not for her. Ultimately, she relented, but had to be supervised getting in and out.

Mom never said thanks to anyone except me, but it was Asha who did almost everything for her. Soon we were all scowling at each other. I just did not know how to manage this

She began to forget things. I asked her about Zanzibar to stimulate her memory. She wrote one bizarre paragraph that made no sense. She was now afraid to walk, and asked what to do at each step. Her balance became poor and she became very frail. It became hard for her to get into the bathroom. She refused an offer to have a higher commode installed. A huge scene followed. She could not get off the low commode by herself or get into the tub. We installed assistive devices and rails.

She became incontinent. And could not be left alone. Asha would call, crying and informing me of the latest calamity, and I would rush home to clean up. Tearfully, Asha pleaded, "I cannot do this anymore."

My supervisors allowed me to work from home for a week. We realized that a nursing aide was needed. I realized how hard nurses work in hospitals. Life is so difficult for the elderly and their caregivers at home. But the home care agency was inefficient and hard to reach. They canceled whenever they wanted. It became a nightmare. A new visiting nurse, a large, strong woman, was nice but this was her first day on the job. She had obviously not been trained. She did not know how to place a bath bench so my mom could slide into the tub. We had to show her how. Eventually, none of us could manage this now 89-year-old, 73-pound woman.

I felt guilty looking for nursing homes but understood that it was becoming necessary. I did not tell my mom that we were looking because I thought it would kill her. Ironically, I had always fought against the notion among many Indians that Americans dumped their elderly in nursing homes, because it was not true. Now I was in the position of having to make a tough decision.

I called her doctor and she, the angel that she is, came over on a Sunday afternoon, on her own time, to chat with my mom. I do not know what they spoke about, since I had been asked to leave the room so the "girls" could have a *tête-à-tête*. Cynthia Heldt came down and gently advised me to prepare for the end, which might be in weeks or months. The "dwindles," the failure to thrive, and the loss of joy were evident. A small dose of an antidepressant was given.

Mom felt no better. She began to grind her teeth. We could hear the gnashing all day all over the house. It was a sign of anxiety and depression, given the scientific name *bruxism*. There was really no remedy except reassurance and support. She knew she was grinding her teeth. It seemed to get louder when we were around. How was it possible for a tiny woman with so few teeth to create such a racket?

There were occasional shouts and screams at night. She was now not only depressed but also angry. The pressure began to build within our family. I had never imagined this type of end for my mother. It was far from peaceful.

One time, she admonished me in Marathi by asking, "Can't you do a little thing for your mother like placing a blanket on my feet?" She had stopped trying to do anything for herself and had become completely dependent on us for everything. In our effort to give her a semblance of self-sufficiency, we would ask her to do a few things herself. Her words hurt deeply, because our lives were now spent taking care of her night and day, but there was no kind word or appreciation for what we were going through. Guilt and exhaustion emptied us of all joy.

I began to envy families that were able to manage such events with much more grace. I felt unworthy that I could not do more for my own mother, even wished that she would die to spare her further agony. That thought made me feel even worse. A good death is supposed to be peaceful and dignified. We are told that those about to pass feel little pain, need little food, are at peace, and fear nothing. Outwardly brave, there was an inner turmoil in what remained of my mother's tiny body.

She once asked me about a pill to end it all. She had had enough. She wanted to die. Another time, she asked to me to put her in a "place for old folks." Perhaps she thought she might glean our intentions by suggesting it herself. Or she may have felt guilty for being "a burden."

When I saw her the evening of October 22, her speech sounded slurred. She said her mouth was dry, so she was having trouble speaking. This went on for several hours. She drank some juice, and I escorted her back to her room. She was not hungry.

The night was eerily quiet. I thought I heard a muffled scream around 3:00 AM. Exhausted and anxious, I tiptoed to her room, but it was quiet. By this time, she had lost all confidence to go to the bathroom by herself. So the next morning, as was my daily ritual, I went to her room to see if she needed to go to the bathroom and to change her diaper. But she was still. The blanket was off. Her eyes were shut. She did not respond to her name.

An unhappy life had ended badly. It was not a good death.

Dr. Heldt came home to pronounce her officially so she could be taken away to the funeral home. They wrapped a white sheet around her and placed her somewhat unceremoniously into the back of a hearse. Her body was to go to an ice-cold refrigerator while waiting for the cremation. Her passing had occurred on what would have been my father's 100th birthday. It seemed that she had planned it that way. Girija and Param had been with us when my father died in 1981, and were also here now when my mother left us, on October 23, 2014.

She had been a devout Hindu and had a created a little temple in her closet. The gods were now alone. We did not believe in rituals and were generally agnostic. She would have wanted a Hindu ceremony, although we had never spoken about it. A priest, who looked awfully young, was found. A scholar of Sanskrit, he had been hired by the local temple to perform the daily prayers. His ponytail was cute but traditional, and his iPhone was a concession to the modern era. He recited *shlokas* to bring peace to my mother's soul and help her journey onward.

Photographs mounted on a board commemorated her entire life story. The best picture was of her standing by a container full of ripe tomatoes from our garden. The pictures did not reflect the agony of her life or the turmoil in my family. I had tried hard to do the right thing for her. The thought that she had left unhappy, alone, and feeling unsupported made the death even harder to bear. Had we failed her?

People said wonderful things about how we had taken care of her for so many years. Why, then, did I feel so worthless? Her mortal remains, now reduced from 73 pounds to just 2 pounds of ashes and a few fragments of bones, were placed in a jar for immersion in the nearest river. When my father had been cremated in 1981, a whiskey-drinking Hindu priest from New York City had told us that "all bodies of water must meet somewhere one day." Recalling that, I assumed we did not need to fly to India to immerse the remains in the Ganges.

Asha, Sandeep, and I took the jar to the exact spot where we had immersed my father's ashes 31 years earlier. We did it discreetly, concerned that someone might object to us placing the remains of a departed loved one in the water where their children sometimes waded. No words were spoken and no tears were shed. We hoped that her ashes would find their way from Delaware to the water from the holiest river in India. The life of a strong and wonderful woman and a great teacher had ended in pain, suffering, and a desperate desire to end it all. She had been a great mother and was the reason for who I am today.

Time waits for no one. Regrets haunt the living, while the departed know not the deep heartache they have left behind. It was difficult to clear out her things. She had so little to show for a lifetime of labor. Her gods sat in a corner, the lamp unlit since the only believer had departed. The TV was now just a dark screen. The Hindi channel subscription was canceled. There was silence, no more moaning or grinding of teeth. Her place at the table was empty. There was no need to peek into her room, but I still did that occasionally out of habit.

To this day, none of us has had the heart to dismantle the board with the photographs or to touch the things in her room. The flowers sent by kind friends and neighbors dried up and were discarded.

A HAPPY ENDING

In April 2014, my heart sank when I received a letter stating that I was among several physicians and practices being sued for malpractice, for something that had happened two years earlier. I had never been sued before, but knew the litigation would drag on for years. I had jinxed myself by secretly celebrating the fact that I had escaped one of the greatest scourges of clinical practice, the lawsuit. I was proud of my record of teaching and patient care. This litigation demoralized me immensely, and I could find little joy in anything I did. Since arriving at this institution in 2003, I had received the Best Teacher award, the Mark Maxwell Award for Humility and Compassion, and four Clinical Pearls lectureships, and had been elected by 1,500 peers to lead them.

On June 5, 2014, I was invited to give the commencement address to graduating residents. Among other things, I had said, "Be honest. If you make a mistake, disclose the truth to the patient and their family. They may or may not forgive you, but you will sleep better. If you did nothing wrong, fight tooth and nail!"

I also quoted Churchill who, in a commencement speech at Harrow, had said:

> Never give in. Never, never, never, never – in nothing, great or small, large or petty – never give in, except to convictions of honour and good sense.

I had always taught that doctors should not fear their patients, who were very likely to forgive errors if the chemistry and communication was optimal.

Now I knew why they did not believe me, and how it really felt to be sued. I had not understood what a lawsuit does to a doctor. It brings everything to a halt. The joy of caring for patients and teaching residents and students vanishes. One is suddenly afraid of the people one is trying to heal.

Almost 50 years of caring for Americans, Kenyans, and Indians, giving them my respect and time, always holding their hands and being there for them suddenly did not count. True, I had behaved badly a couple of times in Kenya, once in Nyeri, and once in Nairobi, when managing extremely ill children who had been brought in too late. With those exceptions, my attention to patients and families had been sincere and meticulous throughout my career.

In this particular case, I was the one who had suggested the correct diagnosis and treatment the day I was consulted, had recommended a plan of action to the teaching team, and had spoken to the daughters every day. My three visits usually lasted an hour each. And the complications had occurred when I had been off for the weekend. I felt cheated and betrayed by this family and their lawyer.

There were depositions, discussions with the insurance company, and tons of correspondence. My desire to preserve the dignity of this patient, an alcoholic who had fallen off a ladder, hurt his back, and gone to another hospital first, collided with the need to preserve my reputation. I fought hard not to harbor unkind thoughts about the patient, his family, or the lawyer, who would get a large chunk of any settlement. I told my lawyer that I did not want the patient's alcoholism to become my defense strategy. There was no need to smear him in order to sway a jury.

In November 2015, at a glittering dinner for hundreds, I was awarded the Commendation for Excellence Award, which is given to one individual annually for qualities that one expects from a "model" doctor. Although deeply touched and honored, I still felt hollow, with the lawsuit hovering over me like an ominous cloud.

Two years passed. Expert witnesses were hired. Tons of time and money were spent. I had many sleepless nights, tossing and turning, trying to figure out what I could have done better for this man's care.

Then things started moving rapidly. Most of the affected doctors, their lawyers, and the hospital began to offer large cash settlements. They did not want to go through the hassle of a trial, which they could lose if the jury sympathized with the patient, especially if the patient arrived in a wheelchair and was coached to look sad and pathetic.

One of the doctors, a 40-year-old man, also settled, resigned from his practice, and joined an insurance company. He did not want to touch a patient ever again. They had all paid to buy peace of mind.

However, I did not feel I had done anything wrong, and expert witnesses from other universities supported my management. I was not going to accept an accusation of malpractice without a fight.

By November 2016, I was the only one left standing. It is a very lonely feeling. None of those who settled had the courtesy of discussing it with my lawyers or me. I refused to settle. I valued my reputation and my principles and thought I had a good chance of acquittal. My lawyers, the insurance agents, my partners, and I huddled. They all accepted my choice to fight on.

A month later, my lawyer received an email stating that the plaintiff was dropping the case against me. The trial, set for May 2017, would be unnecessary. Couched in legal terms, it essentially said that the patient was tired and wanted to get on with his life.

Sure, now that he was rich, he must have worried that he might lose, and why go through the hassle? What galled me was that he was said to be "paralyzed," but he was getting around without assistive devices and even driving on his own. What was the injury I had caused? The clot in his brain and the broken back were a result of his drinking. The infection was caused by another hospital, not ours. We had done the right tests and used the right antibiotics. The infection was controlled. I had done my job well.

But the dismissal did not lessen my angst or anger. For the first time in my career, I too was glad I would not have to touch another patient again. That thought was the very antitheses of who I am and why I entered the profession.

I had kept this information from my mother, son, family, and friends to save them from embarrassment and anxiety. Asha knew and remained firmly by my side, urging me to go to court. I felt this was yet another chance for God to reveal Himself to me, to lend me His benevolent hand. Had He just done that? Had He always been with me but perhaps was testing my devotion and resolve?

Most of the main characters in this story are gone. But they lived magnificent lives of toil, turmoil and triumph. Uprooted by upheavals, they kept going, strong and resilient. They broke the barriers posed by race, class, creed, color, and religious hatred. Our joint family, which once lived in two rooms in Nairobi, is now splintered and scattered across the globe. They live respectable lives in comfortable homes in free nations. Their humble roots and the struggles of their ancestors are largely forgotten. Younger members of the family no longer know each other. There are too many and they are too far apart, emotionally and geographically. Through individual effort, each one has embarked on an important career benefiting the nations that sheltered them.

Our Hindu–Brahmin family has assimilated into new societies in surprising ways. Many of the highly accomplished members of the family have married equally accomplished white men or women, acquired new identities, modified their cuisine, and sometimes even changed their religion. Most marriages have been happy. Children, good-looking, good-natured, and gifted, have sometimes struggled with their part-Indian identity and often carry western names. There is an interesting admixture of Christian, Hindu, Indian, and English names.

The children of these marriages have risen brilliantly to the top with degrees from famous universities all over the world. Although sometimes conflicted about who they truly are, they have inherited the best parts of two cultures and two religions. Such racial, social, cultural, and sexual interaction would have been impossible under the British system of apartheid in Kenya or in India.

Within a generation of living in open and free societies, the traditional mistrust and hatred that divided people has diminished considerably, but the complexion of one's skin continues to prevent a true integration of cultures. "Dark" and "black" are still used to describe undesirable people or things.

Recent political events and the rhetoric associated with elections have emboldened a few bigots who have been unable to camouflage their racism. On February 22, 2017, Srinivas Kuchibhotla, a 32-year-old Indian engineer, was shot and killed, and his friend Alok Madasani was shot and wounded, in an unprovoked attack by a white man who shouted, "Get out of my country!" Eerie echoes of "Go back to Bombay!" The grieving widow accompanied her husband's body to India for the cremation. But even within the story of this hate crime, there was a spark of hope. Ian Grillott, a 24-year-old white man, attempted to disarm the attacker and was shot as well. The local Indian community collected and gifted him $100,000 to thank him for his effort. Another white bar patron, Jeremy Luby, upset by the bigotry, paid the tab for the two men.

A few days later, a Sikh man was shot and told to leave the country and a Sikh woman was told to go back to Lebanon! Ironically, she was born in Lebanon, Indiana not the one in the Middle East, and does not cover her head. They were targeted because of the mistaken belief that they were either illegal immigrants or Muslims. People are now debating whether to continue wearing the hijab, the turban, or the dot on the forehead, all marks of their faith. Years ago, in New Jersey, a gang called the "Dot Busters" tore off the *bindi* from Hindu women's foreheads.

In early April 2017, several Nigerians and Kenyans were beaten up and molested in New Delhi, India. They were suspected to be drug peddlers, but were simply university students trying to get ahead in life with an education. Their crime: being black with curly hair.

Conflicts based on race, color, class, and religion will decrease as people begin to know each other and to understand that underneath the skin, we are all quite similar. Young people—open-minded, liberal, and secular—offer a solution to the chaos created by their elders. I continue to dream of a utopia where people will learn that Goodness is a great religion, and crusades in the name of a benevolent God will end. Of the day when all people will have food, shelter, and clothing. And when the hidden bigot within each one of us respects the intrinsic value every person brings to society.

Like most immigrants, we worked hard, struggled, and tried our best to be decent citizens.

In Kenya, we were told to "Go back to Bombay."

Britain had said we were not welcome and gave us a passport that allowed us to go anywhere in the world....but not in that country.

In Chicago, we were denied housing, asked to "Go back to Iran," could not get a haircut at a barber shop, and were advised not to sell our home to a black couple.

But in April 1971, at JFK airport in New York, an officer had spoken the unforgettable words, "Welcome home."

And I know that the number of decent, good people in our nation far outweighs the bigots.

We, the brown citizens of this great nation, have given our "blood, toil, tears and sweat...." and "we shall never surrender" to forces of evil and injustice.

I am still here.

I am not going anywhere.

No one is going to chase me out of my own country.

The Panwalker Family

My father, a decent and generous man, became a victim of his tobacco and alcohol abuse, developed throat cancer, and died of a heart attack on July 11, 1981, in our home in Delaware.

My mother, the epitome of resilience, courage, and integrity, died in Delaware in our home on October 23, 2014, after living with us for 20 years.

Asha, my wife, earned a degree in Nutrition from MS University in Baroda where she won the Gold Medal awarded to the top student. She also received postgraduate training at the prestigious All India Institute of Hygiene and Public Health before coming to the US, where she got another degree in Nutrition, with honors, from the University of Illinois. She served for some years at the Cook County Hospital in Chicago and then with the Women Infants and Children program in Delaware before retiring.

Sandeep, our son, worked in assorted sales positions in Delaware and loves cars, computers and cameras; strolls in the beautiful parks in Delaware and nearby.

Aji, my paternal grandmother, passed away after a protracted illness in Bombay, on December 9, 1982. Doctor Kaka visited her every fortnight.

Doctor Kaka was hit by a motorcyclist in Bombay in 1989 as he walked to a nearby club. He had cared for patients in Africa for over four decades.

Dinkar Kaka lived with his son, Pramod, in Pune, where he died on July 5, 2007 from a stroke.

Sunder Atya passed away on June 3, 1994 of old age. Her husband, Gurjar Kaka, died on July 11, 1966.

Prakash Panvalkar, the brother I never had, went to college and sold typewriters before computers took over. He gave selfless care to Aji. He lives with his family in Bombay. His happy marriage to Sheila produced two daughters, Swapna and Snehal, both of whom earned advanced college degrees.

Pratibha Panvalkar married a man born in Tanganyika with highly conservative views of women's role in the home and society. An outgoing woman with a college degree and diverse interests, her death at age 60 on August 20, 2010, occurred under suspicious circumstances. I was outraged when her husband expressed minimal sadness and complained about her "behavior" during the years they were unhappily married. He too died a few months later.

Pramila Panvalkar married a wonderful man and settled down in Indore, Madhya Pradesh. Her daughter Chitra is married to an engineer in Bombay. Arundhati Kirkire, the younger daughter, works for the Indian Railways. She became the wicketkeeper and batswoman for the Indian National women's team and played international matches against Australia, England, and New Zealand.

Pramod Panvalker became a banker in Pune and retired recently. His daughter graduated from college with distinction.

Surekha Panvalkar, my childhood friend and cousin from Nairobi, earned degrees in mathematics, statistics and political science in India and further training in the UK. She married Anand Badve, an engineer from Dar es Salaam trained at the Imperial College in London and together they built businesses in Bombay and Hyderabad employing hundreds of Indians. Anand was an Indian Navy commander during India's assault on Portuguese forces in Goa.

The Bhagwat Family

Gopalrao Bhagwat (Dada) died in Nairobi on May 28, 1962, while I was sailing toward Bombay. He served Kenya as a teacher for 24 years. Author, patriot, teacher, he was the best grandfather ever.

Shantatai Bhagwat (Mai) passed away peacefully on April Fool's Day in 1993 in Baroda, India, with her son, Subhash, by her side. She was the gentlest and sweetest person I would ever know.

Prabhaker (Bhau), my mentor and frequent savior, worked as a senior lecturer at the London Polytechnic. He was a scholar, co-author

THE PLACE OF COLD WATER

of a book titled *Number 13* about superstitions associated with that number. A photograph was taken one minute before his unexpected death, while visiting his son, Prakash, in Doha. A bench in New Milton, UK, commemorates his contributions to the Lions Club. He received the highest award possible from Lions International. Nalutai lives in New Milton. Prakash Bhagwat, who as a two-year-old had made wedding rounds with me, is now an IT consultant in London. Asha Peppiatt and her husband, both teachers, live in New Zealand but are currently teaching in Singapore. Varsha Rae lived in the Middle East, France, and UK with her husband, who is a lawyer.

Sharad Bhagwat gave up his dreams of Bollywood and became a prominent lawyer in Chelmsford, UK, where he lives with his wife, Sudha, who received a kidney transplant from a Scottish man. Their daughter, Smita Edwards, is a top-rated lawyer in London. Nina Bhagwat Warren, a director with BBC Channel 4, also lives in England.

Sudha Kanhere settled down in Ottawa and worked for a government agency. Her husband, Shreebhau, a research chemist, worked for the University of Ottawa and now runs a yoga school. He was honored by the Canadian prime minister for his volunteer work. All their children were born in Kenya. Medha married Steve Russell and both are nationally ranked shooting champions who represented Canada in international tournaments. Chitra and Sanjay work for the Canadian government.

Anil Bhagwat, a retired Xerox engineer, holds patents for several inventions and is now the director of a music school in London. He had his own music band, which performed on BBC television each week. He has accompanied some of India's leading musicians on a variety of instruments. In 1966, he cut a record with George Harrison and the Beatles (Love you To in the album Revolver). He married Kundan, who is the director of a culinary department. Their son, Ameet married Clare Ashhurst and is an IT expert. Daughter Aneesha is a radiology technician in UK.

Mira Jejurikar lives in Chicago. She was the principal of a school for the disabled in St. Paul, MN, before retiring. Her husband, Subhash, earned a PhD and was head of the forensic toxicology department for the State of Minnesota. Their son Sandeep, an MD from Ann Arbor, Michigan, is a plastic surgeon in Chicago and got his training at the famed University of Louisville program in Kentucky and the University of Chicago. Samir, also a plastic surgeon, practices in Texas.

Subhash Bhagwat became a chartered accountant and the only sibling to settle down in India. He opened a fully computerized office in Baroda almost four decades ago, and trained numerous students and accountants. He married a sweet and gentle woman named Aruna, who passed away from a brain tumor. I accompanied her on one of her radiation treatment visits in Baroda. Subhash is an avid bird watcher, computer genius, and philanthropist. His daughter, Mona Patel, lives in England and Satyajit is in Hyderabad, India.

The Sathe Family

Vishvanath Sathe, my father-in-law, became one of the highest-ranking engineers serving on the Railway Board of India. A thorough gentleman, he passed away in Pune on March 5, 1995 after a stroke.

Indutai Sathe, my mother-in-law, a gentle voice of reason, an artiste who made beautiful dolls, passed away from a stroke in Pune.

Kumutai Kulkarni, my sister-in-law, one of the nicest people I have known, lives in Pune with her husband, Sudhakar. Their three sons, Nitin, Sushil, and Jayant, are senior executives and engineers in the US.

Suresh, my brother-in-law, died alone in a small village in Maharashtra, on August 1, 2014.

Vijay, my brother-in-law, received MS, MBA, and PhD degrees in the US before teaching at Georgia Tech and the Harvard Business School, then left to work with Peter Drucker, the world-famous management guru. Vijay holds the Davidson Chair in Management at Claremont College in California and is the author of several scholarly books about organizational culture.

Famous Kenyans of Indian Origin

Dr. Rosendo Ribeiro, the first physician in Kenya, the first to tame a zebra and ride it to work, scientist, epidemiologist, and philanthropist, made huge contributions to Kenya. The names of the schools and institutions and roads named after him were changed after independence. He was buried in Nairobi.

Olaf, the grandson of Rosendo Ribeiro, became a world-famous plant pathologist. He left Kenya, even though he was a citizen, because he felt unwelcome. Years later, they called him for consultations about forestry and agriculture. He saves ancient trees and now lives on Bainbridge Island. When he visited the burial site of his father and grandfather in Nairobi, he found it overgrown with brush and weeds. The area was so dangerous that during a visit to Kenya in 2015, Olaf had to hire armed guards to accompany him to see the place the graves.

Pio Gama Pinto- a journalist, freedom fighter, and confidant of Jomo Kenyatta- was assassinated for political reasons in Kenya while his 18-month-old daughter was in the car with him. His widow, Emma, lives in Ottawa.

Giridharilal Vidyarthi and Makhan Singh were the first to demand freedom for Kenya.

Sharad Rao became a lawyer, judge, and leading legal authority in Kenya, and served at the International Court in Hague for several years. He still lives in Nairobi and speaks and writes eloquently about the contributions of Asians in Kenya. His brother, Babu Rao, entered the oil business and lives in London with his wife, Hema, the daughter of our family physician, Dr. Patwardhan.

Innumerable other Indians, from a variety of professions, gave distinguished service to Kenya. These unsung heroes gave their lives to build the nations and its infrastructure.

Friends Who Left East Africa (in alphabetical order)

Mahmood Ahmed: His family owned Ahmed Brothers, outfitters for Hollywood actors who came to shoot movies in Kenya. The movie *Born Free* had a connection with their upscale shop. He went on to get a degree from the London School of Economics before settling down in Calgary, Canada.

Harinder Bharij: He won the Kenya Open Scholarship, obtained his medical degree from Glasgow University and became an obstetrician. He died prematurely at the age of 44, of a presumed heart attack in Guelph, Canada. I attended his funeral and remembered how we stole loquats together, the thrashing we got for diving into the well in Eastleigh, and how his mother had saved my mother from an assault.

Avinash Chitnis: He too won the Kenya Open Scholarship, studied engineering at the Imperial College in London and was a research scientist with a British telecommunications system before moving to Canada to work for Bell. He then relocated to California. Neeta, his wife, attended college in Baroda. Their daughter, Tanuja, is a neurology professor doing research on multiple sclerosis at the Harvard Medical School. Their son, Anup, is the MD director of an emergency department in New York.

Ashok Jamenis: My friend from Dar es Salaam became a senior executive with the industrial giant Kirloskar in Pune, India. One of his daughters, Sharvari, is an actress in Marathi and Bollywood movies. His brother, Baiju, is a dentist.

Kaustubh Kolhatkar: He introduced me to the generous Pakistani couple on the SS *Amra* in 1962, joined the aviation industry, and lived for years in Denver. He now lives in California with his wife, Madhuri. His daughter Gauri, got her medical degree from Stanford University and was a Robert Woods Johnson Foundation Scholar at UCLA.

Vinod Patel: My classmate from Nairobi and co-intern in Chicago, is a nephrologist who lives in Florida with his wife, Harshveena. One of his sons, Sandeep, is a dentist and the other, Danny, is a nephrologist.

Shiraz Rabady: My classmate, who helped me climb Kilimanjaro, went to Vienna to learn violin from the masters. He learned German, entered medical school, and spent some time in the Golan Heights between Syria and Israel as part of the UN Austrian peace team. He recently retired from a medical practice in Vienna. His wife, Renate Welsh-Rabady, is a well-known author in the German speaking world. I found him after 55 years, as I sought his permission to write about our friendship in Nairobi. We spent unforgettable moments together on top of Mount Kilimanjaro in April 1961.

Ashok Shah: He earned his MD from Glasgow University and moved to New York, where he worked as a nephrologist until his recent retirement. He married my classmate from high school, Nila Patel, a psychiatrist, who went to medical school in Ireland. Their daughter is a lawyer and their son is a PhD researcher.

Shashikant Shah: He went to Sheffield University for his medical degree and practiced near Harrow. His family continued their sawmill business in Kenya. His death from oral cancer was slow and painful, but he continued to play golf, his passion, until the end. We spoke often as he was dying, fully prepared for what was to come. Sushi stood by his side through the ordeal. A daughter, Nishma, lived with them. I fondly remember watching the musical *Lion King* with him in London, and our healthy academic competition and deep friendship as schoolchildren and in the Rhodes Avenue Clinic in Nairobi.

Vinod Shah: He was my classmate with whom I stayed in Baroda in 1962. He worked for Lufthansa Airlines in Nairobi. I suspect he helped some Indians in dire straits board planes to enter Britain during the crisis in 1968. He now owns a travel agency in the UK.

Mohan Sood: A self-made man, and one of my best friends, he became an insurance executive. Karuna, his wife, runs her own embroidery shop and school in Houston. A son, Amar, is a top lawyer and avid motor-racing enthusiast. A daughter, Suloni, is on the faculty of arts at the University of Texas in Austin. Mohan's sister, Pramila, was the head of the microbiology lab at the MD Anderson Cancer Institute.

Friends from Ludhiana

Younus Masih, a lung specialist, lives with his wife, Nalini, a pathologist, in Connecticut. Their son Rohit is a major in the US Marines, and Arun is a financial advisor in Boston.

Raj Bala Bansal is a pathologist in Allentown. She married Chad Carver, and their son, Christopher, is a lawyer in State College, PA.

Hospitals

Augustana Hospital in Chicago was demolished to make way for luxury town homes.

The Wilmington VA Hospital was downsized and lost its affiliation with Jefferson University in 2016.

The hospital system I work for, The Christiana Care Health System in Delaware, has a reputation for clinical excellence and is highly regarded for its educational activities and innovation.

The Steam Ship Amra

This ship took me from Mombasa to Seychelles, Karachi and Bombay in 1962. It made its last voyage in 1965.

The Lunatic Express

Over 2400 Indian laborers died building the original rail line. In 2017, the Chinese modernized the rail system, reducing the travel time from Mombasa to Nairobi to 4.5 hours instead of the previous 12.

Nairobi

A city of 300,000 people is now a metropolis with 4 million people. Many of them live in slums no better than the "housing" the British had forced upon them.

City Names

Bombay is now called Mumbai, Poona is Pune, Calcutta is Kolkata, Baroda is Vadodara, Simla is Shimla.

BIBLIOGRAPHY

Belsare, R.D. Maharashtrians in East Africa and Nyasaland. W. Boyd and Co. LTD, 1946.

Bhagwat, Gopalrao. Majhi Janmathep: A biography of Veer Savarkar translated from Gujarati to Marathi. RR Seth and Sons, 2014 (first edition in 1932)

Butler, L. and S. Stockwell (eds). The Wind of Change: Harold Macmillan and British Decolonization. Palgrave McMillan. Basingstoke, 2013.

Close, William. Ebola: A novel of the first outbreak by a doctor who was there. New York: Ballantine, 1991.

Churchill, Winston. "I have nothing to offer but blood, toil, tears and sweat." This was Churchill's first speech to the British Parliament in May 1940. www.winstonchurchill.org/resources/speeches.

Churchill, Winston: "We shall never surrender..." Speech in Parliament on June 4, 1940

Collins, Larry and Dominique Lapierre. Freedom at Midnight. New York: Avon Books, 1976.

Dalrymple, William. The Great Divide, the New Yorker magazine, June 29, 2015

www.newyorker.com/magazine/2015/06/29/the-great-divide-books-dalrymple

Desai, Ketan. Germs of War. London: Minerva Press, 1999.

Deshpande, Pandurang Ganesh. Gujarati to English Dictionary. Ahmedabad: University Book Production Board, 1974.

Deshpande, P. G. Universal English to Gujarati Dictionary, 24th Edition, Oxford University Press, 1987.

Easton, Valerie: Reviving the Ancients. Seattle Times Magazine, January 14, 2007 (Olaf Ribeiro story)

Fernandes, Cyprian and Pereira Benegal: The Pio Gama Pinto story described in an interview in Canada with Pinto's widow Emma Pinto. Daily Nation magazine, February 14, 2015

Friedman, Thomas L. The Earth is Flat: A Brief History of the Twenty-First Century (1st Edition). New York: Farrar, Straus, and Giroux, 2005 (the fable of lions and gazelles is cited here)

Gupta G. R., Panwalker A. P., Olouch M. A. East African Medical Journal. 48:6. June 1971. PubMed ID 5136921

Hajari, Nisid. Midnight's Furies: The Deadly Legacy of India's Partition Illustrated. Houghton, Mifflin, Harcourt. 2015

Humphrey, Hubert. Remarks at the dedication of the Hubert H. Humphrey Building. Congressional Record, vol. 123. 1977.

Kennedy, John F. Profiles in Courage. New York: Harper and Row, 1956.

Kenyatta, Jomo. Facing Mt. Kenya. Vintage Books Edition, 1965 (first published in London 1938)

Macmillan, Harold. Pointing the Way 1959-61. London: Macmillan, 1972.

Miller, Charles. The Lunatic Express: An Entertainment in Imperialism. The Macmillan Company, 1971.

Montano, Don. "The Other Dimension: Technology and the City of London: A survey, 'Lions or Gazelles?'" London: Economist Newspaper Ltd 1985.

Pinsky, William W: the Importance of International Medical Graduates in the United States. Annals of Internal Medicine Vol 166; No.11 June 6, 2017.

Powell, Enoch: 'Rivers of Blood' speech in Birmingham on April 20, 1968.

http://www.enochpowell.net/fr-79.html

Rao, Sharad: Lecture in the House of Lords on March 7, 2017 (Personal Communication)

Rao, Sharad: Lecture in Kenya for the Gandhi Memorial Trust April 15, 2016 (Personal Communication)

www.gandhimemorialtrust.org/index.php/.../197-public-lecture-by-mr-sharad-rao

Author unknown: Rosendo Ribeiro story: Nairobian magazine. March 24, 2016 www.sde.co.ke/thenairobian/article 2000195960.

Smart, James. A Jubilee History of Nairobi, 1950 (publisher unknown)

Tharoor, Shashi. Inglorious Empire: What the British did to India. London: Hurst Publishers, 2017.

Verghese, Abraham. My Own Country: A doctor's story of a town and its people in the age of AIDS. New York: Simon and Schuster, 1994.

Wolpert, Stanley. A Tryst with Destiny. Oxford University Press, 1996.

ACKNOWLEDGEMENTS

This book could not have been written without the help of all members of the Bhagwat family — my grandparents, uncles, and aunts — who gave my mother and me shelter and unconditional love during critical periods in our lives. Many rallied to find old photographs, to share their recollections of our lives together and to fill in the blanks. Sudha Kanhere provided me with a copy of the book *Maharashtrians in East Africa and Nyasaland* and introduced me to Emma Gama Pinto. In addition to sending me old photographs and helping me to edit them, Subhash Bhagwat sent me a copy of Dada's translation of Veer Savarkar's biography. Anil Bhagwat provided details of his musical journey in London and his collaboration with George Harrison of Beatles fame.

The Panvalkar family in Bombay gave me unconditional love and became beloved parts of my extended family.

Dr. Mahadev Panvalkar, by placing *Gray's Anatomy* in my lap and letting me carry his black bag in Dar es Salam, sowed the seed of public service in my mind.

Christian Medical College in Ludhiana gave me a sound education, a fact I appreciated only after my arrival in the US. The western teachers who had left their homeland to come teach us continued to do their work diligently despite the abuse we had hurled at them in when we went on a strike in 1963. I have deep regrets about our conduct during that turbulent time.

My mentors in Chicago, George Jackson, Morton Bogdonoff and Clifford Pilz, saw something in me and shared their knowledge and wisdom with me. The University Of Illinois Medical Center and its teaching staff made me a better doctor.

The power of faith in healing was brought to light by the bone marrow transplant recipient. I cherish her friendship and respect her request for anonymity.

Kellie McQueen, from the Christiana Care Patient Relations Department in Newark, Delaware, suggested that I write a book to share my stories with others.

Numerous friends -of all colors, religions and races- made our lives in America an exciting journey. You know who you are.

James Lee, author of the book *Resilience and the Future of Everyday Life* helped me navigate the publishing landscape, for which I am very grateful.

Lois Hoffman, author of *The Self-Publishing Roadmap* and other books patiently guided me through the complex process of converting words into a book.

Julia Willson, my editor, was instrumental in shaping my manuscript into a readable form. Her careful attention to grammar and punctuation ensured that I would not blight the memory of my English teachers!

David Cohen, Alfred Bacon, John Piper, and Stephanie Lee, my partners at Infectious Disease Associates, were great colleagues and remain good friends. Stephanie introduced me to her husband, James Lee, the author mentioned earlier. David shared my manuscript with his brother, Richard Cohen, the President of the Southern Poverty Law Center. I am grateful for their interest.

I am very grateful to Denise and Jeff Vance and Joanne and Frank Serio for their friendship.

My sincere thanks to Bob Laskowski, Janice Nevin, Neil Jasani, Ken Silverstein, Ginger Collier, and Rob Dressler- all from the Christiana Care Health System- who forgave my transgressions and guided me skillfully through a new administrative career, a difficult transition from the "trenches" (a term which active clinicians use for their work) to the "dark side!"

Sharad Rao, the author of the book *Indian Dukawallas; Their Contribution to the Political and Economic Development of Kenya published in 2016*, graciously shared the lectures he delivered at the Gandhi Memorial Trust meeting in 2016 and the House of Lords in London on March 7, 2017 (see bibliography).

Dr. Olaf Ribeiro shared anecdotes of his life in Kenya and gave me permission to include the iconic photograph of his grandfather, Dr. Rosendo Ribeiro, making medical rounds on a zebra in 1906 in Nairobi.

Emma Gama Pinto graciously allowed me to write about her husband, Pio, a Kenyan freedom fighter and patriot of Indian origin. I am grateful to Sudha Kanhere (my aunt) for the introduction to Emma, who currently lives in Ottawa. The Pinto and Ribeiro families knew each other in Nairobi.

Ms. Heidi Postlewait, on behalf of the Secretary of the United Nations Publication Board, gave me permission to reproduce the maps of East Africa and India. I am most grateful.

My deepest gratitude to my distinguished friends Bennett Lorber, George Jackson, Joseph DeSimone, Omar Khan and Joan Delfattore who read my stories before publication and gave extremely valuable suggestions.

Dr. Dennis Witmer, Vice Chair of Surgery at Christiana Care, shared his excitement and joy to have reached the summit of Mount Kilimanjaro, and kindly provided color photographs for unrestricted use.

My parents, Kusum and Prabhaker Panwalker, sacrificed much so I would not want. They are not responsible for the flaws within me.

My son, Sandeep, helped me understand the mysteries of cyberspace in a Herculean effort to make me computer literate. My wife, Asha, proof read parts of the book and made it much better. Both thought this book would be either a bust or a best seller and strongly advised me to postpone buying a tuxedo to accept a Nobel Prize for Literature. My life would be empty and incomplete without them.

ABOUT THE AUTHOR

The author, born in British Kenya to Indian immigrants, got his medical education in India and is a Clinical Professor of Medicine at the Sidney Kimmel School of Medicine in Philadelphia and the Associate Vice President for Medical Affairs in the Christiana Care Health System in Delaware. He is a Fellow of the American College of Physicians and the Infectious Diseases Society of America as well as a member of Alpha Omega Alpha (AOA). The recipient of numerous awards for teaching, clinical excellence and leadership, he enjoys Indian music and gardening and lives with his wife Asha in Newark, Delaware.